S0-BQX-544

THREATENED CHILDREN

THREATENED CHILDREN

Rhetoric and Concern about Child-Victims

JOEL BEST

The University of Chicago Press
Chicago and London

JOEL BEST is professor in the Department of
Sociology at California State University, Fresno.

The University of Chicago Press, Chicago 60637
The University of Chicago Press, Ltd., London
© 1990 by The University of Chicago
All rights reserved. Published 1990
Printed in the United States of America
99 98 97 96 95 94 93 92 91 90   5 4 3 2 1

Library of Congress Cataloging-in-Publication Data

Best, Joel.
    Threatened children : rhetoric and concern about child-victims /
Joel Best.
        p.   cm.
    Includes bibliographical references.
    ISBN 0-226-04425-4 (alk. paper)
    1. Child abuse—United States.   2. Missing children—United
States.   3. Mass media—Social aspects—United States.   I. Title.
HV6626.5.B47   1990
362.7'6'0973—dc20   89-48508
                                                         CIP

For Eric and Ryan
whose father worries anyway

CONTENTS

TABLES AND FIGURES

TABLES

FIGURES

ACKNOWLEDGMENTS

Authors accumulate many debts. In my case, I owe special thanks to Michael Schudson for his advice and encouragement. In addition, I benefited from the suggestions and assistance of Gail Abbott, Eleen A. Baumann, Joan Best, Loy Bilderback, Richard Cheung, Jack Colldeweih, Camilla A. Collins, Jeanine Congalton, Roy Dalrymple, Gary Alan Fine, Cynthia Gentry, Daniel C. Hallin, Beth Hartung, Paul Hoag, Gerald T. Horiuchi, Joseph F. Jones, Donileen R. Loseke, David F. Luckenbill, Diane Luckenbill, Colleen A. Mitchell, Edward E. Nelson, James A. Scrabeck, Cynthia J. Spear, J. K. Sweeney, John N. Tinker, Ronald J. Troyer, and Diane R. Ybarra.

Support for some of this research came from the National Endowment for the Humanities' Summer Stipend and Summer Seminar programs and from several small grants of money and time for research from California State University, Fresno. In addition, Dean Peter J. Klassen came through on two occasions when I needed extra funds.

The cooperation of the CSU Social Science Research and Instructional Council and the Field Institute (particularly Mark DiCamillo) let me help design the California Poll questions analyzed in chapter 8. In addition, the Federal Bureau of Investigation and the California Bureau of Criminal Statistics made data available for analysis.

Earlier versions of some chapters appeared elsewhere: chapter 2— "Rhetoric in Claims-Making: Constructing the Missing Children Problem," *Social Problems* 34 (1987): 101–21; chapter 3—"Missing Children, Misleading Statistics," *The Public Interest* 92 (1988): 84–92, and "Dark Figures and Child Victims: Statistical Claims about Missing Children," in Joel Best, ed., *Images of Issues: Typify-*

xi

ing Contemporary Social Problems (New York: Adline de Gruyter, 1989), 21–37; chapter 5—"Secondary Claims-Making: Claims about Threats to Children on the Network News," in James A. Holstein and Gale Miller, eds., *Perspectives on Social Problems,* vol. 1 (Greenwich, CT: JAI, 1989), 259–82; and chapter 7—"The Razor Blade in the Apple: The Social Construction of Urban Legends," *Social Problems* 32 (1985): 488–99 (written with Gerald T. Horiuchi).

1
The Rise of the Child-Victim

Here in Derry children disappear unexplained and unfound at the rate of forty to sixty a year. Most are teenagers. They are assumed to be runaways. I suppose some of them even are.

—Stephen King, *It* (1986, 151)

Stephen King's *It* topped the best-seller lists as soon as it appeared in September 1986. A main selection of the Book of the Month Club, the huge, eleven-hundred-page horror novel sold 1,200,000 copies during 1986 (becoming that year's best-selling hardcover work of fiction) and remained at or near the top of the best-seller lists well into 1987. *It*'s success was predictable. Stephen King had a long string of consecutive best sellers, and Viking, his publisher, mounted an elaborate promotion campaign. Still, *It* sold especially well in hardcover—far better than any of King's other books. Perhaps this exceptional success reflected public interest in the book's theme— threats to children.

It is set in Derry, Maine, a medium-sized city inhabited by the title character, a monster that preys on children. The monster can take any form, and the book contains more than a dozen graphic scenes of children being menaced by vampires, werewolves, mummies, and other horrible creatures. Derry's townspeople recover some of the victims' bodies, but many children simply disappear. Others avoid the monster, only to suffer neglect or physical abuse from their parents. In Derry, children are victims.

The novel's theme suited the nation's mood. During the 1980s, threats to children came under intense scrutiny; there was widespread concern about child abuse, child pornography, incest, child

1

molestation, harmful rock lyrics, missing children, and related dangers. Consider some events from mid-September 1986 to mid-February 1987—the period *It* remained near the top of the best-seller charts:

- A poll of California adults found that 67 percent considered missing children a "very serious" problem; another 29 percent considered the problem "somewhat serious."
- A national survey of youth aged eight to seventeen found that the kidnapping of children and teenagers ranked highest on a set of national concerns (76 percent of the respondents said they personally felt "very concerned"). The possibility of nuclear war and the spread of AIDS tied for second place (each with 65 percent "very concerned").
- Popular magazines published an average of one story about child abuse, child molestation, or missing children each week. Titles included "How to Protect Your Children from People They Trust" (*Ebony*), "Our Daughter Was Sexually Abused" (*Parents*), and "The Mind of a Molester" (*Psychology Today*).
- The prestige press and the network news covered several hard news stories about threats to children: a former prosecutor in the McMartin Preschool child molestation case criticized the way his former colleagues had investigated the charges against the defendants; Minnesota authorities indicted a woman for murdering her adopted three-year-old son twenty-one years earlier; and Florida authorities arrested two members of the Finders (which initial press reports described as a Satanic cult involved in abducting children).
- Both the Child Abuse Victims' Rights Act of 1986 and the Child Sexual Abuse and Pornography Act of 1986 became federal law.
- Eddie Murphy, a leading box-office attraction, starred in *The Golden Child*. Murphy played a specialist in finding missing children who rescues a mystical boy from the demonic forces that hold him captive. The movie was the biggest hit of the 1986 holiday season.
- Within a two-week period, NBC broadcast two made-for-television movies: "Adam: His Song Continues" and "When the Bough Breaks." The former, a docudrama sequel to 1983's "Adam," con-

tinued the story of John Walsh's role in the missing-children movement. The latter was a thriller about a child psychologist who uncovers a conspiracy of child molesters.

• Public service messages featured the new antidrug slogan "Just Say No." One popular commercial showed a youngster running from older boys who presumably were enticing him to use drugs. Rumors about LSD being peddled to preschoolers spread nationwide.

These examples suggest that *It*'s theme fit the contemporary mood. The Derry monster did not seem that far removed from everyday reality. Threats to children were the focus for widespread concern during the fall and winter of 1986–87—just as they had been throughout the early 1980s.

CHILD SAVERS AND THEIR IMAGES OF CHILDREN

Of course, concern for children is not new. Children replenish society's population, and adults must insure that enough children survive and that they learn the ways of their people. In this sense, protecting children is central to social life.

Most historians agree that modernization has increased adults' concern for children's well-being (deMause 1974; Shorter 1977). As a society's economy industrializes, its cities grow; health care improves, and birth rates fall. While preindustrial parents raised large families, knowing that many infants would not reach adulthood, modern parents have fewer children and expect that each will survive. With fewer children, parents have more at stake with each child, the emotional ties between parent and child become closer, and children receive better treatment.

In particular, the nineteenth century saw important changes in American attitudes toward children. There was a "surge of sentiment" (Shorter 1977), a "sacralization" of childhood (Zelizer 1985). Children came to be seen as redeemers of adult failures; after 1870 "the sentimental notion that somehow it is better to be a child than an adult, that the best standards of life are those of naive and innocent children becomes an increasingly powerful theme in American culture" (Wishy 1968, 85). People became more likely to view chil-

3

dren as priceless, lovable, vulnerable innocents to be cherished for their own sakes.

By the second half of the nineteenth century, discussions of childhood no longer began with the assumption that children were innately depraved, but adults recognized that children still needed help and guidance. While middle-class families might be able to meet most of their children's needs, many other children required the help of outside experts, specialists in child shaping (Rodgers 1980) and child saving. American social reformers devoted much of their attention to children's problems. Their efforts to improve child welfare created dozens of programs we now take for granted: public schools, juvenile courts, scout troops, Sunday schools, foster homes, inoculation programs—the list goes on and on (Cohen 1985; Cravens 1985).

In devising these programs, the child savers were guided by their images of childhood, children's needs, and children's problems. People addressing a social problem inevitably typify it, characterizing it as a problem of a particular sort (Best 1989). Although usually taken for granted, these typifications are not as obvious as they seem. Any social problem can be typified in various ways: troublesome drinking can be—and has been—viewed as sinful, criminal, or symptomatic of illness; runaway children can be characterized as adventurous, delinquent, or vulnerable to exploitation. Typifications change, often in response to changes in the larger society. Changing typifications are important because different images emphasize different features of a problem and suggest different solutions. They may recommend protecting the innocent or punishing the guilty, fine-tuning what already works or making revolutionary changes in what doesn't. To understand responses to social problems, we must appreciate how those problems are typified.

Several different images of children have played important roles in the history of American child saving. Perhaps the most common image is *the rebellious child*. Rebellious children reject the adult world's expectations; they run away from home, have sex, break the law, and adopt disturbing tastes in music or dress. In short, rebellious children make troublesome choices, and reformers usually respond to rebellion by trying to control the choices children make. Often the

4

new reforms invoke legal authority (e.g., the juvenile justice system) to compel children to make the right choices.

Another very common image is *the deprived child*. Deprived children face poverty, disability, family problems, or other constraints on their lives. These are matters of circumstance, not choice. Even with circumstances for which adults are held responsible (e.g., poverty), blame rarely extends to children. Reformers seek to overcome these deprivations, to make childhood more complete. Here their goal is to compensate for what is missing, to minimize the damage to the child. If rebellion often leads to legal solutions, the solutions to deprivation usually involve social welfare institutions.

A third image has grown increasingly important with the twentieth century's advances in medical science. *The sick child* has a medical problem. Where once little could be done, the modern presumption is that medical problems can be solved. Now reformers hope to care for—and cure—sick children. The near eradication of polio, whooping cough, smallpox, and other childhood diseases has encouraged reformers to mount new campaigns against other medical problems, such as sudden infant death syndrome (SIDS) and muscular dystrophy.

The child-victim is a fourth image. Menaced by deviants, child-victims are vulnerable to harms intentionally inflicted by others. Like deprived and sick children, child-victims are not held responsible for their plight. Reformers seek to protect child-victims, both by helping children protect themselves and by cracking down on those who would harm them.

A concern for child-victims runs through the history of American social reform. The Society for the Prevention of Cruelty to Children was founded in 1876 to protect children from abuse by employers and parents (J. Johnson 1985; Pfohl 1977). The Progressives conducted active campaigns against white slavery (Connelly 1980) and child labor. Concern about sexual psychopaths (a term that encompassed child molesting as well as other sexual offenses) emerged during the 1930s and again in the 1950s (Freedman 1987). Still, the image of the child-victim has played a relatively modest role; most reformers have concerned themselves with rebellious, deprived, or sick children.

5

However, during the 1970s and 1980s, child-victims began receiving a larger share of public attention. This recent wave of concern for child-victims is the subject of this book. I use the term *threats to children* to refer to the kidnappers, child molesters, child pornographers, drug pushers, pimps, Satanists, Halloween sadists, and other deviants who victimize children. Obviously, we sometimes describe other phenomena—pesticides and preservatives in food, diseases, televised violence and television commercials, nuclear extinction, and so on—as threatening children. However, I will restrict my attention to those threats involving deviant adults thought to exploit children deliberately.

The image of the child menaced by deviants has shaped public reactions to a surprisingly wide range of social problems. Although pro-choice activists preferred to speak about a woman's right to control her body, their pro-life opponents attacked abortion in terms of millions of murdered babies. Mothers Against Drunk Driving (MADD) typified that issue by describing killer drunks and their child-victims. Even the AIDS epidemic seemed to hold little interest for Middle America—until parents began demonstrating to keep children with AIDS from bringing the disease into local schools. Some of these characterizations were controversial; many would not agree that abortionists, drunk drivers, and people with AIDS should be seen as threatening deviants. Still, child-victims were important symbols in these campaigns, and concern for protecting children from menacing deviants became a central, visible theme in debates about social problems. People continued to address problems involving rebellious, deprived, or sick children, but missing children, abused children, sexually exploited children, and other child-victims became the subjects of intense concern.

THE NEW CHILD SAVERS

The new interest in child-victims has come from several quarters. Physicians and other professionals played key roles in promoting some causes. For instance, the 1962 publication of a research report, "The Battered-Child Syndrome," in the *Journal of the American Medical Association* marked the beginning of contemporary concern about child abuse (Kempe et al. 1962). This article drew the attention of other professionals, as well as the popular press and legislators. In an age that grants medical authorities considerable prestige, announcing in the leading medical journal that physicians had identified a new "syndrome" gave the cause instant legitimacy. Similarly, professionals brought other problems to public attention: during the 1970s, psychologists and social workers campaigned to have child sexual abuse recognized as a family problem (Weisberg 1984); and lawyer-psychiatrist Judianne Densen-Gerber led the attack on child pornography in 1977 (U.S. House 1977).

Other problems became visible through the efforts of social activists, whose concern for child-victims emerged from broader social agendas. Thus the women's movement provided an "umbrella constituency" for a wide range of causes; feminists argued that women were at the center of family life and child rearing, so that children's issues were women's issues (Schur 1980, 204–7). In particular, as feminists drew attention to domestic violence and sexual exploitation as social problems, concern about child abuse, incest, and child pornography became part of the larger feminist agenda (Rush 1980; Russell 1986). In much the same way, the New Right's social agenda emphasized the reaffirmation of traditional family values, particularly the need to shelter children from the corruption of the larger society. The pro-life movement provided a central focus for New Right energies, while related campaigns sought to promote chastity and restrict young people's access to contraceptive services. But the movement also saw threats in the messages in the mass media (particularly "porn rock"), child molestation (Mawyer 1987), and even the growing authority of protective service workers to interfere in family life (Pride 1986).

Still other threats to children became visible thanks to grass-roots organizations—particularly those formed by parents of child-victims. MADD's campaign against drunk driving offers the most familiar example because MADD became a well-publicized, national organization (Reinarman 1988). Other problems fostered dozens of local, regional, and national grass-roots organizations. For instance, various child-search organizations drew attention to child snatching (i.e., abductions by noncustodial parents) and, later, missing children. Other grass-roots organizations were self-help groups (often

7

modeled on Alcoholics Anonymous) and treatment programs for adults who had harmed children, such as Parents Anonymous (child abuse), Parents United (incest), or Together We Can (pedophilia).

Finally, as new laws assigned responsibility for dealing with threats to children to various agencies, officials in those agencies took an increasingly active part in shaping public perceptions of those issues. For instance, the federally funded National Center for Missing and Exploited Children instantly became a major player in several policy debates (U.S. House 1986b). Some officials found that identifying new threats to children could help justify their calls for expanded authority and increased resources.

In short, professionals, activists, grass-roots organizations, and officials all had a hand in promoting recent interest in threats to children. The new child-saving movement had a broad base. But why did this widespread concern with child-victims appear when it did?

EXPLAINING THE RECENT CONCERN: FOLK WISDOM AND OBJECTIVIST SOCIOLOGY

Folk wisdom offers two apparently contradictory explanations for contemporary interest in child-victims. The first refers to social decline. Civilization, it warns, is collapsing: children no longer obey their parents; citizens no longer respect the laws; the social bond no longer holds. In this cowardly new world, basic decency cannot be taken for granted. Monsters prey upon society's children, its most vulnerable members. We are experiencing a wave of child abuse, an epidemic of missing children. Things are getting worse, and their deterioration explains our growing concern. We now worry more about child-victims because we have more of them.

It is hard to evaluate this argument. Social collapse is easy to assert but difficult to prove. There are no reliable records of child victimization that go back more than a few years, so we have no way of measuring the changing incidence of, say, child abuse, no way of learning whether it is increasing or decreasing. In fact, instead of increasing abuse causing growing concern, it may be the reverse. What looks like a recent wave of new offenses may reflect nothing more than improved record keeping. Growing concern about a problem may lead officials to keep better track of the cases that come to their

8

attention—or even to seek out additional cases—thereby producing records that seem to show things getting worse. In short, there is no clear, compelling evidence that the recent concern for child-victims reflects a real increase in children's victimization.

The second folk explanation emphasizes progress, not decline. It argues that we have become more sophisticated; we now realize that threats to children exist, we appreciate their seriousness, and we can recognize and do something about them. Once naive, we have become knowledgeable. It is not clear whether the incidence of threats to children is increasing, decreasing, or remaining constant, but neither is it important. What matters is that we now understand the problem. Thus our new concern for threats to children reflects our recent enlightenment.

This argument also assumes a great deal. In particular, it takes for granted the correctness of our current interpretations of social problems. No doubt people in every era make the same assumption, that they correctly understand the nature of their societies' problems. Salem's congregations believed they had discovered demonic forces at work, and the Progressives congratulated one another for recognizing the threat posed by white slavers. Yet when historians look back on witch crazes, red scares, and white slavery conspiracies, they regularly conclude that there was less deviance than met the contemporary eye. Certainly Americans have recently become quick to spot threats to children. Whether that readiness reveals a better understanding of those phenomena is an empirical question—not something we should assume at the start.

In other words, both folk explanations assume that the contemporary concern with child-victims reflects our recognition of real dangers that children face. While these folk explanations are vulnerable to criticism, they are not very different from the standard sociological explanations for social problems. It seems commonsensical to define social problems as harmful social conditions, to assume that anything that harms people or interferes with society's smooth operation is a social problem. Similarly, sociologists' discussions of social problems usually equate social problems with troublesome social conditions. For instance, a sociologist interested in child abuse might ask what causes abuse or how the larger culture promotes

9

abuse. Such questions focus on child abuse as a social condition; they take the designation of child abuse as a social problem for granted.

This is sometimes called the *objectivist* approach to social problems because it defines social problems in terms of objective social conditions (Hazelrigg 1987; J. Schneider 1985). The principal difficulty with objectivism is that it takes our interest in these social conditions—our declarations that certain conditions are social problems—for granted. Let's return to our example of child abuse. According to one historian:

> The history of childhood is a nightmare from which we have only recently begun to awaken. The further back in history one goes, the lower the level of child care, and the more likely children are to be killed, abandoned, beaten, terrorized, and sexually abused. (deMause 1974, 1)

This suggests that the social condition—the way children are treated—has, if anything, improved. But interest in child abuse as a social problem is relatively recent. Why has concern about child abuse emerged at a time when children seem relatively well treated? Because they take child abuse's status as a social problem for granted, objectivists can only respond with some version of the folk explanation that we are now more sophisticated. The reasoning is circular: we have come to fear threats to children because we now recognize that these are frightening problems.

We return, then, to the question I posed earlier: what accounts for our current concern with threats to children? By viewing threats to children as conditions, objectivist sociology begs this question.

THE CONSTRUCTIONIST APPROACH

Some sociologists argue that social problems should be understood as concerns, rather than conditions. That is, instead of trying to study the causes and consequences of the social condition of child abuse, we should examine the causes and consequences of the concern about child abuse. From this perspective, the question of how and why concern about threats to children emerged when it did becomes central.

Sociologists refer to this as the subjectivist or, more often, the *constructionist* approach to social problems. Constructionists argue that conditions must be brought to people's notice in order to become social problems. The standard statement of the constructionist perspective defines social problems as "the activities of individuals or groups making assertions of grievances and claims with respect to some putative conditions" (Spector and Kitsuse 1977, 75). In this view, social problems are socially constructed; people make claims arguing that particular conditions are social problems, and others respond to those claims. It is this process of claims-making that turns conditions—which previously may have gone unnoticed or been taken for granted—into objects of concern—social problems (J. Schneider 1985).

Most constructionist research emphasizes the social organization of claims-making. That is, case studies tend to concentrate on identifying the players and explaining how and why they got into the game. Three concepts guide this research—interests, resources, and ownership.

Constructionist studies often identify the claims-makers' *interests* in promoting a social problem; identifying these interests explains why particular social problems emerged. Claimants often stand to profit if their claims are successful: officials may be able to protect or even expand their agencies' turf; professionals may acquire more influence, control, or prestige; activists may gain clout and even official standing. Even when successful claims do not lead directly to greater wealth, power, or prestige, there may be indirect, symbolic benefits: successful claims can reaffirm the correctness of the claims-makers' values, ideology, or life-style. For example, Pfohl (1977) argues that, by identifying the battered-child syndrome, pediatric radiologists played a key role in early claims-making about child abuse. He suggests that, while family doctors were reluctant to risk accusing parents of beating their children, most pediatric radiologists were researchers and hospital staff physicians who did not have to worry about damaging their practices. Moreover, by associating their specialty with the identification of a life-threatening disorder, the radiologists stood to gain prestige within the medical profession.

If interests supply the motive in constructionist analyses of claims-

11

making, *resources* provide the means. Claimants must assemble the resources needed to make their campaigns successful; they may need to recruit members to the cause, raise funds, attract press coverage, gain legitimacy, and so on. Claims-makers may try one tactic after another, never sure which ones will work, although this sense of uncertainty is sometimes lost in case studies, which typically describe the process of resource mobilization that led to a particular campaign's success.

Winning combinations of resources depend upon the issue and the arena within which the campaign is fought. For instance, Nelson (1984) details how U.S. Senator Walter Mondale led the struggle for what would become the Child Abuse Prevention and Treatment Act of 1974. As chair of the Subcommittee on Children and Youth, Mondale designed his bill to be noncontroversial, fostered supportive press coverage by holding dramatic public hearings, and otherwise used his knowledge of and stature within the Senate to gain passage.

Perhaps the ultimate success for claimants is to achieve *ownership* of a problem. Ownership involves "the ability to create and influence the public definition of a problem" (Gusfield 1981, 10). This occurs when your construction of a problem gains acceptance, when you become the authority to whom people turn, when you assume effective control over social policy. Social problems construction tends to be a continuing process, with one claim following—and building upon—another.

Once claims-makers own a problem, they have a far better chance of controlling how the issue will evolve. John Johnson (1985) suggests that, while child abuse emerged as a medical problem, it soon fell into the hands of the "child maltreatment movement," which viewed it as a social welfare problem. The problem's new owners shaped federal and state legislation (e.g., laws requiring that suspected abuse be reported to child protection agencies) that, in turn, reaffirmed their control over child abuse.

These concepts—interests, resources, and ownership—are central to most studies of social problems construction. A typical case study asks how a particular problem came to be constructed, then answers that the claimants had vested interests that led them to mobilize enough resources to gain ownership of the problem. Such explanations emphasize the social organization of claims-making—the claims-makers' interactions with one another, their opponents, and policymakers.

INSIDERS, OUTSIDERS, AND THE SOCIAL PROBLEMS MARKETPLACE

Claims-makers want change; they want others to do something. Getting others to respond to claims can be difficult, especially when a social problem is not well established. When claimants first draw attention to a problem, they must get people to acknowledge that a particular condition exists and to see that condition as a social problem. In contrast, well-established social problems already have wide recognition; their status as social problems—conditions about which something ought to be done—is acknowledged generally by the public, journalists, legislators, and even sociologists who write social problems textbooks.

Most well-established social problems are owned by well-established claims-makers. They are insiders to the policymaking process—forming what political sociologists call pressure groups. Pressure groups "are ordinarily part of the polity, the set of groups that can routinely influence government decisions and can ensure that their interests are normally recognized in the decision-making process" (Useem and Zald 1982, 144). Most pressure groups began as constituencies mobilized during earlier claims-making; these claimants became insiders as their social problems became well established and they achieved ownership of the issues.

In contemporary America, there are three principal kinds of insider claims-makers. Most obviously, there are lobbying organizations, such as the National Rifle Association and the Sierra Club, employing paid staffs to represent the interests of their clients and/or dues-paying members. Second, there are professionals, the specialists charged with handling the problem, who have responsibility for and expertise about what should be done. Finally, official agencies can be claimants, struggling with rival agencies to extend or protect their bureaucratic turf. All three forms usually have direct access to—and influence over—policymakers.

13

Claims-making by insiders tends to concern new wrinkles in the familiar fabric of established social problems. Thus the National Rifle Association finds itself making pronouncements on Teflon-coated bullets and plastic guns, while the National Institute on Alcohol Abuse and Alcoholism warns about teenage drinking. In contrast, claims that seek recognition for new social problems often come from those outside the polity. These claims-makers can be individuals—cranks, lone crusaders, moral entrepreneurs. Or the claims can be made by social movements, seeking to gain recognition both for their social problem and for themselves as the problem's owners. Compared to insiders, these outsiders have limited access to and little influence with policymakers. They find it much harder to change policy.

Outsiders also find it harder to reach nonpolicymakers. While pressure groups have membership lists and know that their members share a concern about their cause, outsiders must locate potentially concerned individuals, gain their attention and sympathy, and mobilize them. Often outsiders try to take their message to the general public, hoping to gain widespread recognition and acceptance for their claims and, in the process, enlist members in the cause.

This means that the mass media are especially important to claims-making by outsiders. Claimants can attract the news media's attention by generating either hard news (e.g., by conducting demonstrations or holding press conferences) or soft news (e.g., by appearing on talk shows or giving interviews for feature stories). Both sorts of coverage can help outsiders' claims-making. Media coverage attracts public attention to the cause. In turn, this may bolster a social movement's membership, both because people learn about the movement via the media and decide to join, and because media coverage gives the movement more credibility, generating enthusiasm among potential members. Coverage also pressures policymakers, who may feel that they have to respond to media coverage, or who may begin to be pressed by the movement's members or the general public.

Figure 1.1 compares the claims-making processes for insiders and outsiders. For insiders' pressure groups, the principal channel of influence flows directly from claims-maker to policymaker. This pro-

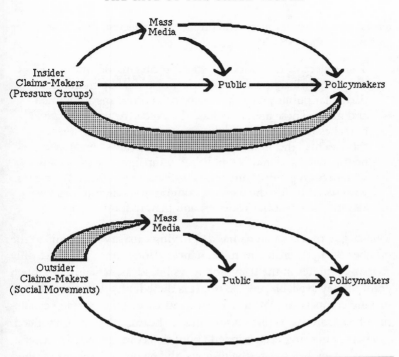

Figure 1.1. Claims-Making by Insiders and Outsiders

cess can be quite discreet, with claimants exploiting their access to policymakers to lobby for policy changes without attracting the notice of either the public or the press. Of course, pressure groups may have tactical reasons for choosing to conduct public campaigns, as when the NRA mobilizes its members in a letter-writing campaign designed to remind Congress of its clout. But insiders have a choice; they can decide to use a discreet approach for one campaign while seeking maximum publicity for the next. In contrast, social movements by outsiders typically depend upon reaching the media, because media coverage seems to offer the best route to public sympathy, a larger membership, and access to policymakers.

Claims-makers must compete in a *social problems marketplace*. At any given time, there are many different claims-makers—both insiders and outsiders—trying to get the attention of the media, po-

15

tential constituents, the general public, and policymakers. Hilgartner and Bosk (1988, 58–59) suggest:

> The collective definition of social problems occurs not in some vague location such as society or public opinion but in particular public arenas in which social problems are framed and grow. These arenas include the executive and legislative branches of government, the courts, made-for-TV movies, the cinema, the news media (television news, magazines, newspapers and radio), political campaign organizations, social action groups, direct mail solicitations, books dealing with social issues, the research community, religious organizations, professional societies, and private foundations.

They argue that each arena has a "carrying capacity"—a limit to the number of social problems it can handle at one time. There are only so many minutes in the television news broadcast schedule, so much grant money available, and so on. It is these limits that make claims-making competitive. Would-be claimants exceed the carrying capacities of most arenas. While some claims are heard, others go unnoticed.

There is nothing even-handed about this competition. In general, the advantage belongs to the insiders, the owners of well-established social problems, with ready access to policymakers and the media. Outsiders are at a disadvantage. Their chances are particularly remote in some arenas; legislátures are far more likely to respond to the concerns of lobbyists and other insiders than to claims from outsiders. In comparison, the media, with their constant need for fresh material ("news"), are more receptive to outsiders' claims. But because the media offer the best hope for many outsider claims-makers, the competition for media attention can be fierce.

CULTURE AND CONSTRUCTIONISM: ACCOUNTING FOR THE RISE OF THE CHILD-VICTIM

Those calling attention to child abuse, missing children, and other threats to children have had a good deal of recent success in the social problems marketplace. The current interest in threats to children began in the early 1960s with claims about the battered-child syndrome. Other problems followed, including runaways and Halloween sadism in the late 1960s, sexual abuse, child pornography, and child snatching in the 1970s, and missing children and ritual abuse in the 1980s. For the most part, these were not well-established problems, and the claims-makers could not trade on their status as insiders. Most claims about threats to children have come from outsiders seeking to bring neglected topics to public attention.

Why were these claims successful? The standard constructionist answer would focus on the organization of the claims-making campaigns—the claimants' interests, their resources, and the like. I propose to emphasize a rather different set of issues in trying to answer these questions.[1]

We can approach claims-making in terms of its culture, as well as its organization. All claims emerge within a cultural context. In seventeenth-century New England, claims were routinely couched in religious language. Three centuries later, religion rarely plays a significant role in policymaking, and claims-makers are more likely to use terms from medicine or science.

The language adopted by claims-makers is meant to be persuasive. Claimants want to convince others that their concerns about particular social conditions deserve attention, that their assessments of those conditions are correct, and that their proposals offer solutions that should be adopted as social policy. Their emphasis on the social organization of claims-making often leads constructionists to gloss over the style and content of claims. This is a mistake. Not all claims will work. Given the realities of the social problems marketplace, many claims will fail. Claims-makers need to convince the media that their concerns merit coverage, potential members that the cause is worth joining, the public that the issue deserves attention, and policymakers that action should be taken. Interests, resources, even ownership are not enough; claims need to be compelling if they are to be successful.

Once they become competitors in the social problems marketplace, claimants discover the importance of making persuasive arguments. We can apply the standards of rhetoric—the study of persuasion—to analyze the content of claims (Gusfield 1981). Chapter 2 explores the rhetoric of claims-making, using the construction of the missing-children problem as a case study. Claims-making about missing children offers a particularly interesting example because it was highly successful; within just a couple of years, the problem gained considerable publicity, widespread public concern, and willing cooperation from a broad range of policymakers and officials. Yet, while the content of missing-children claims packed a powerful rhetorical punch, these claims adopted a form used in claims about many other social problems.

Although the missing-children movement began with a good deal of success, controversy followed. Critics charged that the claims-makers had used questionable statistics to exaggerate the problem's extent, and, in turn, the critics' counterclaims came under attack. Chapter 3 examines this debate and the larger questions it raises. Statistics are a standard element in modern claims-making rhetoric. What sets claims about missing children apart is not their use of statistics, but the way those statistics became central to the ongoing debate.

Chapter 4 continues the focus on claimants' rhetoric, examining how definitions of social problems can evolve. Here my substantive focus shifts to child abuse, and I trace how that problem's scope, or domain, has expanded. Initially confined to severe physical abuse of very young children (the battered-child syndrome), the definition of child abuse extended to encompass neglect, sexual abuse, and a wide range of other harms. These new, expanded definitions of child abuse have been promoted by a diverse set of claimants who have found it easier to advance their claims by building upon others' successful claims-making. Taken together, the three chapters on claims-makers' rhetoric reveal the importance of what is said initially about social problems.

The mass media play central roles in contemporary claims-making. Claimants who hope to attract wide notice—and this is especially important for outsider claims-makers—usually turn to the media. Their tactics include demonstrations, press releases, press conferences, and other deliberate efforts to draw coverage. We can call this *primary claims-making*. Often claims-makers hope that the media will serve as a channel through which they can transmit their message to a larger audience. But the media have their own concerns and conventions that shape whatever messages are sent. The media do not just transmit messages, they translate and transform them for the media audience. Thus the media's coverage might be called *secondary claims-making*. To the degree that claimants depend upon the media to spread their message, secondary claims-making is important. While policymakers may have direct contact with claims-makers, the public's sense of social problems is more likely to come from secondary, rather than primary, claims.

The most obvious forum for secondary claims is the news. Chapter 5 considers press treatment of threats to children, focusing on coverage on the television networks' evening news broadcasts and asking what forms these secondary claims took. This chapter examines network news coverage of both hard news stories (i.e., reports on the day's developments in investigating the Atlanta child murders), and so-called soft news (i.e., feature stories on teenage runaways). While most discussions of the media's influence implicitly equate the press or the mass media with coverage of hard news, feature stories, talk shows, and other forms of soft news have become increasingly important forums in the social problems marketplace.

If soft news stands outside what most analysts mean by "the media," chapter 6 extends the discussion even further afield. It considers how successful claims-making about threats to children was adopted and adapted as a subject for fiction, films, and other forms of popular culture. A best-selling novel such as *It* may not shape public attitudes toward social problems in precisely the same way that news coverage does, but it shapes them all the same. Just as the news media transform claims, so do the demands of various popular culture genres affect their treatment of social problems. During the 1980s, popular culture frequently depicted threats to children, but it portrayed these problems in ways that fit existing entertainment formulas.

Successful claims are not merely repeated, they come to be accepted. Successful claims change the everyday actions of ordinary people: individuals stop smoking, save glass for recycling, install dead-bolt locks, and contribute money to causes. In societies with elaborate mass media, people are bombarded with secondary claims. Some are taken to heart, while others are forgotten. What accounts for these successes and failures?

The public clearly took many claims about threats to children to heart during the 1970s and 1980s. Evidence for this comes from two very different sources—folklore and public opinion polls. Chapter 7 explores contemporary folklore (especially urban legends) concerning threatened children. Because folklore is disseminated orally—people have to consider it worth remembering and repeating—it reveals deep-seated concerns. Thus I argue that the popularity of urban legends about Halloween sadism, shopping mall abductions, and Blue Star Acid is one response to claims-making about threats to children.

Folklore is an indirect means of assessing the public's reaction to claims-making; public opinion polls offer a more straightforward reading of the public's understanding of social problems. Just as the media transform primary claims into secondary claims, the public constructs its own interpretation of the media's messages. Chapter 8 examines the responses to sample surveys about threats to children conducted during the mid-1980s. It is no surprise that these surveys found widespread concern about threats to children. However, some of the patterns in the responses are unexpected; they suggest that vulnerable portions of the public used concern with threats to children as a means of coping with anxieties about their own lives.

The organization of this book, then, parallels the process by which successful claims emerge. Chapters 2, 3, and 4 concern primary claims-making, the ways outsider claims-makers frame issues in order to attract attention in the social problems marketplace. Chapters 5 and 6 explore how the mass media adapt primary claims to their own purposes. And chapters 7 and 8 consider how the public, in turn, responds to the media's secondary claims. Content and meaning evolve as claims move through these stages.

Finally, chapter 9 attempts to locate claims-making about threats to children within its larger context. I argue that there are reasons why the new child-saving movement took hold in the 1970s and 1980s rather than, say, the 1950s. The campaigns against threats to children benefited from an ongoing wave of social reform, institutional developments conducive to claims-making, and the meanings ascribed to childhood in the late twentieth century.

In short, this book treats the recent crusades about missing children and other threats to children as a case study of the processes of contemporary claims-making. Instead of emphasizing the organization of the new child-saving movements, it focuses on the meanings of threats to children as those meanings are constructed by claims-makers, the media, and the public.

2

Rhetoric in Claims about Missing Children

Now, Gentlemen, I am going to indulge in one of the favorite techniques used in the past to generate a reaction on the part of legislators. I am going to tell you a story from real life, imply that it represents the tip of an iceberg and infer that only you can offer redress, justice or correction. It worked before, why not again?
—Charles A. Sutherland (U.S. House 1986c, 92)

By the mid-1980s, the missing-children problem had achieved extraordinary visibility. Americans saw photographs of missing children on milk cartons and grocery bags, billboards and televised public service messages. Toy stores and fast-food restaurants distributed abduction-prevention tips for both parents and children. Parents could have their children fingerprinted or videotaped to make identification easier; some dentists even proposed attaching identification disks to children's teeth. Commercial child identification kits were available, and at least one catalog offered a transmitter that could be attached to a child's clothing: "Guardian Angel surrounds your child with an invisible circle of protection—in or around the house, in shopping areas, amusement parks, on picnics or outings. The bright yellow finish warns off would-be abductors" (Sharper Image 1986, 33). In short, ordinary citizens may have encountered explicit reminders of missing children more often than reminders of any other social problem.

This problem achieved prominence quickly; the term "missing children" seems to have been coined in 1981.[1] The term encompassed three familiar phenomena: runaways (children—most often adolescents—who chose to leave home and usually returned within a

22

few days); child snatchings (noncustodial parents who illegally took their own children without the custodial parent's permission); and abductions by strangers (who might keep, sell, ransom, molest, or kill the child).[2]

Between 1979 and 1981, several cases in which children presumably were abducted by strangers received national publicity. These included the 1979 revelations that John Wayne Gacy had murdered thirty-three youths, the 1979–81 series of twenty-eight murders of Atlanta youths, the 1981 murder of Adam Walsh (age six, who disappeared from a shopping mall and whose severed head was later recovered), the 1979 disappearance of Etan Patz (age six, who left for school one morning and was not seen again), and the 1980 return of Steven Stayner (age fourteen, who had lived with his kidnapper for seven years).

Assisting in some of these cases were existing child-search organizations, such as Child Find, which had been established primarily to help locate children taken during custody disputes. By 1981, child snatching had received a good deal of attention, but the response of the press, law enforcement, and the general public was ambiguous. Magazine articles and television programs sometimes portrayed the kidnapping parent favorably (see Anonymous 1979; Jares 1981). Federal legislation—the 1980 Parental Kidnapping Prevention Act— had little effect, because the Justice Department refused to pursue cases without evidence that the child was in danger of abuse or neglect (Spangler 1982). Moreover, public opinion remained split; only 64 percent of the respondents to a 1981 CBS/*New York Times* poll fully agreed that federal kidnapping laws should apply to child snatching.

Organizations like Child Find clearly found it advantageous to link their cause to the widespread sympathy for parents whose children were abducted by strangers.[3] The label "missing children" made this link possible. The U.S. Senate held its first hearing on missing children in October 1981.[4] Magazine and newspaper articles began to appear. On October 10, 1983, NBC broadcast "Adam," a docudrama about Adam Walsh that ended with a roll call of fifty-five missing children.[5] The National Center for Missing and Exploited Children—funded by a federal grant—opened in 1984. By the year's end, pictures of missing children were being printed on milk cartons, shopping bags, and other paper products. The concept of missing children had become common currency.

RHETORIC AND CLAIMS-MAKING

Because constructionist interpretations usually emphasize the importance of social organization, most researchers pay far more attention to the process of claims-making and the people who make claims than to the claims themselves. This is intentional. Spector and Kitsuse (1977) acknowledge that claims may be grounded in values, but they warn against trying to explain claims-making by simply specifying claimants' values and motives. Instead, they argue that "values are one of the resources members use in their efforts to define conditions as social problems" (96). However, they do not explore systematically how values become incorporated into claims. Similarly, most constructionist case studies seem to treat claims as a given.

Claims have received some critical examination (Aronson 1984; Gusfield 1981). In particular, Gusfield insists that scientific evidence used to support claims about the drinking-driving problem must not be viewed simply as objective evidence but should be seen in terms of rhetoric—part of the claims-makers' efforts to persuade. This chapter extends Gusfield's argument; it applies rhetorical analysis to claims made in the construction of the missing-children problem, then attempts to assess the broader role of rhetoric in social problems construction.

Claims-makers inevitably hope to persuade. Typically, they want to convince others that X is a problem, that Y offers a solution to that problem, or that a policy of Z should be adopted to bring that solution to bear. While the success of claims-making may well depend in part on the constellation of interests and resources held by various constituencies in the process, the way claims are articulated also affects whether they persuade and move the audiences to which they are addressed. Claims-making, then, is a rhetorical activity. Rhetoric—the study of persuasion—can be used to analyze claims.

In *The Uses of Argument,* Stephen Toulmin (1958) examined the structure of arguments. He began by drawing a distinction "between

24

the *claim* or conclusion whose merits we are seeking to establish (C) and the facts we appeal to as a foundation for the claim—what I shall refer to as our *data* (D)" (Toulmin 1958, 97—emphasis in original). The link between D and C can only be established by reference to a third kind of proposition—what he called warrants (W), "which can act as bridges, and authorise the sort of step to which our particular argument commits us" (Toulmin 1958, 98). Thus Toulmin suggested that every argument has a basic structure:

Toulmin wrote *The Uses of Argument* as a contribution to logical theory, and he applied these concepts to the analysis of simple three-sentence micro-arguments. But rhetoric and argumentation scholars have found Toulmin's scheme useful in analyzing larger, more complex arguments (Willard 1982, 1983; Ziegelmueller and Rhodes 1981). Toulmin's analysis has been expanded and modified (Toulmin et al. 1979). Recent versions incorporate additional, minor types of statements and substitute the term "grounds" for "data."[6] Toulmin's principal categories of statements—grounds, warrants, and conclusions—can be used to analyze the rhetoric of the missing-children campaign.[7] While these claims refer specifically to the missing-children problem, their rhetorical structure parallels claims-making for many social problems.

GROUNDS

In any argument, statements about grounds provide the basic facts that serve as the foundation for the discussion that follows. Obviously, facts are themselves socially constructed knowledge. Claims-makers and their audiences may agree to accept grounds statements without question, or one or both parties may have reservations about the statements' truth, their relevance, the methods used to establish them, and so on.[8] Although the specific facts at issue depend upon the particular claims being made, some types of grounds statements recur in many claims-making campaigns.[9] Three types of

25

grounds statements consistently appeared in claims-making about missing children: definitions, typifying examples, and numeric estimates.

Definitions

Perhaps the most fundamental form of claims-making is to define a problem, to give it a name. Identifying the topic under discussion limits what can be said; a definition makes some issues relevant, while relegating others out of bounds (Gusfield 1981; Lake 1986). Definitions can both establish a topic's domain and offer an orientation toward that topic.

Domain Statements. A definition identifies a phenomenon, setting its boundaries or domain. Someone who understands a definition can examine phenomena and determine which do and which do not fall within the defined category's domain.

Domain statements are particularly important when claimants hope to call attention to a previously unacknowledged social problem. Following Pfohl (1977), we might speak of discovery movements—claims-makers who announce that they have discovered a new problem. They may argue that the problem is in fact new (e.g., modern technology is destroying the ozone layer), or they may describe the problem as something that presumably has existed for some time but has only now been recognized for what it is (e.g., child abuse). In either case, such domain statements have the power of novelty; they attract interest because they claim to identify a new phenomenon.

Claims-making about missing children involved the creation of a new domain. In this case, there were few efforts to offer precise, technical definitions; claims-makers usually did not specify the age at which one stops being a child, or the length of time a child must be gone to be considered missing. The term was intended to be broad, inclusive, to encompass several misadventures that might befall children. Thus, in the initial U.S. Senate hearings on missing children, Kristin Cole Brown of Child Find argued:

> It is absolutely critical that we establish a policy which guarantees that the various criteria used to determine whether or

26

not a child is to be considered a missing child be subject to the most generous interpretation. We must not begin by discriminating against *kinds* of missing children (U.S. Senate 1981, 75—emphasis in original).

Most claims-makers preferred an inclusive definition of missing children. Some child-search organizations distributed photos of missing individuals who were in their twenties. Other crusaders argued that children who returned home after even a brief disappearance should be considered missing children. As John Walsh put the case: "If it was your daughter, Mr. McCloskey, and you were waiting for her and she didn't come home for 4 hours and after that time she came home with bloody underpants and she had been raped, was she a missing child? Damn well she was" (U.S. House 1985b, 18).

Orientation Statements. Typically, claims-makers' definitions give an orientation to the problem. That is, in addition to specifying a problem's domain, there is some assessment of the sort of problem it is. The literature on medicalization offers a standard example; in the twentieth century, medical authorities have frequently argued that specific problems should be recognized as diseases (Conrad and Schneider 1980). Even when a domain is not in question, orientation can be at issue. We can contrast discovery movements with reorientation movements—claimants who cast familiar problems in the fresh light of a new perspective. Thus, by arguing that rape should be viewed as a violent crime, not a sex crime, feminists offered a different perspective on the topic (Rose 1977). Definitions, then, guide the way we interpret the problem, suggesting appropriate avenues for response.

Claims-making about missing children emphasized that "missing" meant endangered, that even runaways and children taken in child snatchings faced terrible risks:

Once they are on the street they are fair game for child molestation, prostitution, and other exploitation. To label them "runaways" and disregard their safety is to suggest our own lack of compassion and real understanding for this difficult problem (Senator Hawkins in U.S. Senate 1981, 2).

27

Parental child abuse is a fact. Parents hurt, and kill, their children every day. . . . We must assume that a parent who breaks civil laws [by child snatching] will break the laws of responsible parenting (Kristin C. Brown in U.S. Senate 1981, 76).

This theme of potential violence and exploitation received support by coupling definitions to horrific examples of missing children.

Typifying Examples

Although definition might seem to be the logical first step in claims-making, it frequently follows an introductory example. Newspaper and magazine articles that called attention to the missing-children problem routinely began with one or more atrocity tales.[10] Similarly, the initial U.S. Senate (1981) hearings on the problem began with the parents of Etan Patz, Adam Walsh, and Yusuf Bell (age nine, one of the murdered Atlanta schoolchildren) describing their children's disappearance.[11]

Opening with an emotionally riveting "grabber" is a standard journalistic technique (J. Johnson 1989). By focusing on events in the lives of specific individuals, these stories make it easier to identify with the people affected by the problem. Horrific examples give a sense of the problem's frightening, harmful dimensions.

In addition to these obvious effects, atrocity tales perform another, less visible function. The atrocity—usually selected for its extreme nature—typifies the issue; it becomes the referent for discussions of the problem in general. Crusaders routinely used stranger-abductions—which they acknowledged to be the least common cause of missing children—as referents. Between 1981 and 1985, congressional hearings featured testimony by parents of eleven missing children; eight of these children had been abducted by strangers. John Walsh became especially prominent, testifying before several congressional committees as well as many state legislatures, while Etan Patz's mother, Julie, was the only parent of a missing child on the U.S. Attorney General's Advisory Board on Missing Children. As visible reminders of the horrors of stranger-abduction, these parents implicitly helped define the problem. More overtly, sociologist

28

Michael Agopian, director of the Child Stealing Research Center, testified: "We are all aware of the Adam Walsh case, but please recognize that there are tens of thousands of additional Adams that are not so prominently reported by the media" (U.S. House 1984, 102), and "behavioral consultant" Frank Osanka distributed flyers advertising his readiness to lecture on "The Other Adams: Facts About Child Abductions in America." Similarly, John Walsh warned, "This country is littered with mutilated, decapitated, raped, strangled children" (U.S. Senate 1983a, 33). Atrocity tales do not merely attract attention; as typifications, they also shape perceptions of the problem.

Estimating the Problem's Extent

Once examples establish a problem's human dimensions, claims-makers often try to assess its magnitude. The bigger the problem, the more attention it can be said to merit, so most claimants emphasize a problem's size. For missing-children crusaders, these estimates took three forms.

Incidence Estimates. Perhaps the most straightforward way to establish a social problem's dimensions is to estimate the number of cases, incidents, or people affected. Claims-makers argue that a widespread problem demands attention. Thus claims-making about the missing-children problem relied heavily on estimates of the number of children affected. These were necessarily inexact. Missing children need not come to official attention. Moreover, the various official agencies that might learn about missing children had no standard set of criteria for defining cases. Some police departments, for instance, required that twenty-four or seventy-two hours pass before a child could be deemed missing. And even if local agencies kept records, there was no national clearinghouse to compile statistics.

One commonly cited figure was 1.8 million cases per year—a total that included runaways (which claims-makers acknowledged constituted the vast majority of all cases), abductions by noncustodial parents (frequently estimated at one hundred thousand annually), and abductions by strangers. The latter category received most of the attention, although estimates generally declined over time:

29

The most conservative estimate is that 50,000 young people disappear each year, because of "stranger kidnappings." That is the most conservative estimate you will get anywhere (Representative Simon in U.S. House 1981b, 10).

20,000 to 50,000 are snatched by strangers—most never to be seen again (Thornton 1983, 63).

Somewhere between 4,000 and 20,000 children each year are abducted by non-family members. (Cerra 1986, 14).

Frequently these estimates were buttressed by claims about the number of missing children found murdered: "There are about 4,000– 8,000 of these children each year who are found dead and probably a majority have experienced some type of sexual exploitation" (Representative Simon in U.S. House 1981b, 11).

Although the initial claims-making about the missing-children problem did distinguish among runaways, custodial kidnappings, and stranger-kidnappings, those who repeated the claims often lost sight of these distinctions. Thus a pamphlet, "To Save a Child," distributed by a Chicago television station, began: "Nearly 2,000,000 children in this country disappear from their homes each year. Many end up raped, forced into prostitution and pornography. Many are never heard from again." By including runaways to estimate the number of missing children and then focusing attention on atrocity tales about stranger-abduction, claims-makers led many people to infer that the most serious cases were commonplace. Public opinion surveys found that many people assumed stranger-abductions were common, accounting for a large share of missing children (Field Institute 1987; Fritz and Altheide 1987; Miller 1985).[12]

During 1985, the larger estimates of the number of missing children came under attack. Led by the *Denver Post* (which earned a Pulitzer Prize for its coverage of the issue), the press used FBI and other criminal justice statistics to challenge the estimates' accuracy (Abrahms 1985; Griego and Kilzer 1985; Karlen 1985). The articles emphasized that stranger-kidnappings accounted for a very small proportion of missing children.[13] These counterclaims were newsworthy, in part, because the originally acknowledged distinction among types of missing children had become lost in later claims-making.

Growth Estimates. A second claim that may be made about a social problem's dimensions is that things are getting worse—the problem is growing and, unless action is taken, there will be further deterioration. "Everyone close to the missing-child problem agrees that it is a large one—and growing" (Turbak 1982, 61). Claimants often describe problems as epidemic—a metaphor that suggests more people will be affected as the problem spreads (see U.S. Senate 1983a, 74).

Range Claims. The epidemic metaphor also suggests that people may be indiscriminately affected, that the problem extends throughout the social structure. Often, this claim is explicit: "[Missing] children come from small towns in rural America, and from our largest cities. They are from all races and ethnic backgrounds. They grow up in upper class neighborhoods, in the suburbs, and in the inner cities" (Senator Howard Metzenbaum in U.S. House 1985b, 9).

Claims that a social problem's range extends throughout society serve an important rhetorical function. By arguing that anyone might be affected by a problem, a claims-maker can make everyone in the audience feel that he or she has a vested interest in the problem's solution. Thus recommendations that all parents maintain files with current pictures and fingerprints that could be used to identify their children cast every child as a potential victim.[14] Like other grounds statements, these claims presented missing children as a problem that could not be ignored.

WARRANTS

Warrants have a special place in Toulmin's scheme; they are statements that justify drawing conclusions from the grounds. Disputes about grounds (e.g., whether stranger-abductions annually number in the hundreds or the tens of thousands) need not damage conclusions. A claims-maker might argue, for instance, that even a single child abducted by a stranger is one too many, and that, therefore, something must be done. But concluding that something must be

31

done demands that one accept some warrant that the problem deserves attention:

> Unless, in any particular field of argument, we are prepared to work with warrants of *some* kind, it will become impossible in that field to subject arguments to rational assessment. The data we cite if a claim is challenged depend on the warrants we are prepared to operate with in that field, and the warrants to which we commit ourselves are implicit in the particular steps from data to claims we are prepared to take and to admit (Toulmin 1958, 100—emphasis in original)

This passage refers to two important issues. First, it notes that there are fields of argument. Toulmin (1958, 14) originally defined fields in terms of types of arguments: geometric proofs, legal reasoning, and so on. More recent analyses (Willard 1982, 1983; Ziegelmueller and Rhodes 1981) suggest that fields must be understood sociologically; within specific social units (e.g., a dyad, an academic discipline), members hold particular lines of reasoning to be valid. Thus, for an argument to be persuasive, the individual to be persuaded must ordinarily belong to a field that deems the warrant valid.[15]

The second point to which Toulmin alludes is that warrants often are implicit. Although an argument may advance in a thoroughly public fashion, with each step available for inspection, there are good reasons to gloss over warrants. It is in the warrant that values most often come into play.[16] While it is relatively easy to debate the merits of grounds statements, it is more difficult to defend a warrant that one's audience refuses to validate. An implicit warrant may circumvent the discovery that the audience belongs to a different argument field.

Because references to warrants may be oblique or implicit, any list is necessarily selective. The following discussion considers six warrants that figured prominently in claims-making about missing children. While each warrant was tailored to some degree for discussions of missing children, each also represents a more general type of justification found in claims-making about various social problems.

32

The Value of Children

Zelizer (1985) argues that children have become defined as economically worthless but sentimentally priceless. Missing-children claimsmakers often referred to the extraordinarily high sentimental value of children. Kenneth Wooden charged that priceless children

> are being treated like garbage. Raped and killed, their young bodies are discarded in plastic bags, on trash trucks, and left on dumps. . . . Like litter, they are thrown into lakes, rivers, and streams—the tender drift wood of life. Some are found on roadsides like empty soda and beer cans, . . . or cast aside like broken furniture in dirty, empty houses or stripped, abandoned cars in wooded or swamp areas. . . . Poor little wilted flowers, plucked from the vases of home and safety of parents, are, in large part, left unburied and alone in the openness of fields—and now the closed minds of our thoughts (U.S. House 1984, 55).[17]

Claimants argued that children were "our most valuable resource" (U.S. House 1985b, 1), "the leading endangered species of today" (U.S. Senate 1985b, 31), deserving "the highest of all priorities" (U.S. House 1981b, 124): "One missing child is certainly too many. And one missing child should be the concern of the Government" (U.S. House 1985a, 8).[18]

Claims-makers contrasted law enforcement's reluctance to respond when priceless children were reported missing with its reaction to reports of stolen property. Senator Hawkins pointed to the FBI's refusal to investigate reports of children abducted by strangers, then suggested:

> The kind of investigation we are seeking did occur when Fanfreluche, 10, disappeared from her home in Kentucky. The FBI became immediately involved in the case. . . . She was found, still in the State of Kentucky, and was returned to her home. Fanfreluche was a racehorse (U.S. Senate 1983a, 10).

Because children were deemed priceless, the terrible uncertainty felt by parents of missing children became a prominent warrant. Parents' first-person testimony, as well as many journalistic accounts, focused on the parents' extraordinary sense of loss. The readiness with which crusaders referred to the value of children indicates that this warrant was uncontroversial—literally a motherhood issue.

Blameless Victims

In addition to emphasizing the devastation felt by parents, claimants focused on the horrors experienced by missing children. John Walsh testified: "Right now at this very moment there are little children out there in the hands of whatever, crying, pleading and are begging that mommy and daddy or Mr. Policeman or some one [*sic*] come to their aid or look for them to save them" (U.S. Senate 1981, 30). The understanding that children are powerless innocents, coupled with a definition of all missing children as facing terrible risks, presented a strong warrant.

Claims-makers described children as blameless, as well as priceless. Even runaways, who might be considered responsible for their situation, were not to be blamed: "Many are running from abuse, both physical and sexual, or from intolerable home lives" (Senator Hawkins in U.S. Senate 1981, 2). Similarly, references to so-called throwaways—children who had been expelled from their homes—dealt only with the failings of the caretakers who rejected the children, never with the children's behavior.

Blameless victims offer rhetorical advantages to claims-makers. Public opinion and official policy often distinguish between "innocent" victims and those who are thought to share some complicity for their fate. Christie (1986) argues that the "ideal victim"—the one most likely to elicit sympathy—is weak, engaged in a respectable activity, and overcome by a more powerful stranger. Victims who do not fit this pattern may be stigmatized, rather than supported (Kitzinger 1988). Certainly, presenting victims as blameless makes it more likely that claims will be ratified.

Associated Evils

Claims-makers argued that missing children often were stolen by or later became prey to child abusers, sex offenders, pimps, pornographers, drug dealers, organized criminals, and Satanists. Occasionally crusaders also referred to the damaging effects of popular culture;

the U.S. Attorney General's Advisory Board on Missing Children (1986, 30) called for research

> to probe the relationship between the exploitation and victimization of children and violent and sexually explicit facets of the popular culture such as art, rock music, lyrics, and video games. . . . Would children be less vulnerable to running away, to sexual exploitation, to sex rings, and destructive cults if they were more sheltered from lurid, everyday depictions of perversion?

Charges implicating deviants or popular culture in the missing-children problem suggest possible alliances between the claims-makers and those concerned with other problems. But the choice of associated evils was selective. Claims-makers devoted remarkably little attention to exploring the causes of the missing-children problem. And when causes were mentioned, they usually involved individual pathology: runaways sought to escape abusive parents; child snatchers were motivated by hatred. Crusaders made little effort to locate causes in complex social conditions, preferring to assign responsibility to criminal or perverted individuals.[19]

Deficient Policies

Claims-makers insisted that existing policies and resources could not handle the missing-children problem. Assuming that most missing children were runaways who would return on their own, many local police departments delayed investigating until a child had been missing a day or more. But claims-makers warned that waiting even a few hours made it more difficult to locate a missing child who did not return, especially in cases of abduction. Similarly, the FBI sometimes refused to investigate missing children—even reports of stranger-abduction—without ransom demands, proof of interstate flight, or other compelling evidence that the case fell within federal jurisdiction. John Walsh and other parent/claimants denounced the FBI's failure to enter their cases (see U.S. Senate 1983a).

Typically, claims-makers explained that local and federal law enforcement agencies delayed entering missing-children cases because most children returned without official intervention.[20] But atrocity tales demonstrated that some reports involved serious crimes. The crusaders, then, sought to change official priorities, to have law enforcement respond to every missing-child report.

Claims-makers also attacked current policies toward runaways. They criticized the "self-proclaimed 'child advocates'" who had fought for the 1974 Juvenile Justice and Delinquency Prevention Act which "labeled runaway children . . . as 'status offenders,' and required them to be 'deinstitutionalized,' and not controlled, treated, or protected" (U.S. Attorney General 1986, 2). Because police no longer held runaways, parents might not be informed when their children were located. Claims-makers argued that the JJDP Act needed modification, so that officials could take runaways into custody.[21] Insisting that current policies and resources could not locate all missing children, claimants presented a warrant for change.

Historical Continuity

Claims-makers often expressed surprise at the FBI's failure to pursue reports of stranger-abductions. The bureau, they argued "was primarily created to assist in the war on kidnaping" (John Walsh in U.S. Senate 1981, 56). Greater federal involvement in missing-children investigations, then, would be consistent with the history of federal law enforcement. Similarly, passing one federal law related to missing children provided a warrant for advocates of additional bills; relying solely on the original "Missing Children's Act would be like treating major surgery with Band-Aids" (U.S. Senate 1984, 98).

Using historical continuity to justify future actions is usually a conservative warrant. Emphasizing consistency with past policies—or with founders' intent—may be especially useful when claimants address bureaucracies or institutions. Other crusaders adopt a very different approach, arguing that a problem calls for a revolutionary break from the past. Such a claim seems most likely to persuade those with little invested in past policies.

Rights and Freedoms

In the United States, claims-making about government policy commonly involves warrants about rights and freedoms. Debates about abortion and illicit drugs feature detailed analyses of constitutional issues. In contrast, references to rights and freedoms served as little more than a touchstone for missing-children claims-makers; when they did raise the issue, it was to endorse the rights of victims. John Walsh testified: "A country that can launch a space shuttle . . . but does not have a centralized reporting system or a nationwide search system for missing children, certainly need [*sic*] to reaffirm the very principles that this country was founded on, namely, *personal freedoms*" (U.S. Senate 1981, 25—emphasis in original). In later testimony, Walsh responded to concerns that centralized records systems threatened personal freedoms:

> Well, believe me, the women who are murdered by these people and the children, their privacy is invaded to the maximum. I think people have had it, I think that personal freedom now relates to the possibility and the ability to have personal freedom from crime and to be not afraid to go shopping or a woman to leave an office to go to her car in a parking lot (U.S. Senate 1983b, 28).

Similarly, the Dee Scofield Awareness Program argued: "Once it is determined that the slightest possibility of foul play exists, a child's constitutional rights are violated if that child is not considered a victim until it can be proven otherwise" (U.S. Senate 1981, 196). In short, missing-children claims-makers spoke of freedom from abduction and exploitation, of rights to protection by the authorities.

CONCLUSIONS

Like other forms of argument, claims-making presents conclusions—typically calls for action to alleviate or eradicate the social problem. Claims-makers may have an agenda with several goals. In the case of the missing-children problem, claims-makers hoped to affect the general public—in particular, parents—as well as official policy.

Awareness

Initially, missing-children crusaders sought to bring the problem to public attention. Their goal was not merely greater public awareness; they hoped to enlist the public in searching for children. Originally these efforts reached relatively few people. Reporters who covered the story were urged to accompany their articles with photos of missing children, while Child Find and other child-search organizations distributed directories filled with pictures of missing children. With the 1983 broadcast of "Adam," the problem became well established; commercial and government agencies began printing billions of images on milk cartons, utility bills, and so on. These efforts had some success; the advertising campaigns were credited with locating some children, and polls showed considerable public awareness of the missing-children problem (Field Institute 1987; Miller 1985).[22]

Prevention

Claims-makers also emphasized the importance of prevention. They urged parents to assemble files of recent photographs, fingerprints, and other material that could be used by investigators if a child disappeared. Pamphlets gave lists of safety tips—ways to protect children from abduction—and parents could choose among many new books and videotapes designed to teach children to protect themselves.

Typifying the problem with atrocity tales about stranger-abductions shaped the construction of these preventive measures. Typically, both the safety tips and the materials intended for children focused on warnings about strangers. Prevention campaigns had such titles as "Too Smart for Strangers" and "Strangers and Dangers," while one standard tip warned that having a child's name on clothing might let a stranger approach and call the child by name. However useful such advice might be in preventing stranger-abductions, it had limited relevance for child snatchings and runaways.

Social Control Policies

Dissatisfied with official efforts to locate missing children, claimants demanded new social control policies. The 1982 federal Missing Children's Act insured that parents could list a missing child with the National Crime Information Center's computers; if a local police department refused to enter the child's name, federal agents were required to do so. Claims-makers also campaigned for state laws to require police to begin searching immediately upon receiving a report of a missing child and to list all reported children with NCIC (see Elliott and Pendleton 1986). Other recommended policies included requiring schools to notify parents whenever children were absent and to transfer school records and birth certificates whenever children changed school districts, modifying FBI practices so that all reported stranger-abductions would lead to federal investigations, and giving police greater authority to apprehend and hold runaways.

Two themes united these recommendations. First, believing that the thousands of local law enforcement agencies made it harder to coordinate searches, claims-makers sought to centralize police power. John Walsh described the states as "50 little feudal kingdoms" (U.S. Senate 1982, 46), and the Dee Scofield Awareness Program argued:

> We maintain that every missing child deserves the protection of specially trained investigators who are authorized to transcend every local, county and state boundary. . . . In our opinion, every missing child under 18 should have the benefit of FBI jurisdiction, whether or not voluntary flight was involved (U.S. Senate 1981, 196).

Second, crusaders argued that children and adolescents should be subject to greater social control. The U.S. Attorney General's Advisory Board on Missing Children blamed the 1974 JJDP Act for limiting police powers to hold runaways and rejecting "the historic notion that children have a right to be in the custody of their parents or legal guardians" (1986, 2). The Board recommended amending the act. Similarly, the President's Child Safety Partnership urged that law enforcement agencies make full use of their powers under the act "temporarily to detain runaways while various alternatives are considered" (1987, 123).

Other Objectives

In addition to advancing ways to prevent abductions and recover missing children, claims-makers promoted several other causes. Because everyone agreed that statistics on the number of missing children were little more than guesses, claims-makers sought a federal study to count missing children. Other objectives wandered further afield. Senator McConnell noted, "When you are talking about the exploitation of children, the missing children issue has been a good peg to focus attention on . . . sexual assaults against children by non-strangers" (U.S. Senate 1985b, 2). In fact, crusaders used missing children as a peg in attacking a wide range of evils. The U.S. Attorney General's Advisory Board on Missing Children's (1986, 22–30) recommendations included prosecuting the "adult offender who abuses children, leads them into prostitution, victimizes them by pedophilic conduct or pornography, or pushes them into street crime"; extending the statute of limitations for "child sexual abuse crimes"; "careful screening of people who work with children"; and studying the relationship between popular culture and child exploitation. In these cases, "missing children" apparently served as a rubric for addressing a range of other threats to children.

RHETORIC IN SOCIAL PROBLEMS CONSTRUCTION

The example of the missing-children problem suggests that rhetoric plays a central role in claims-making about social problems. Atrocity tales typified the missing children problem; case histories of stranger-abduction, coupled with estimates that there were two million missing children per year, convinced many people that the problem could not be ignored. People responded empathically to the horrors experienced by parents and children. The claimants' warrants—the emphasis on the priceless, blameless nature of children, the association of missing children with other evils (especially exploitative sexual deviance), and the assertion that existing policies and resources could not cope with the problem—drew much of their power from the examples of atrocities. The campaign's conclusions about the need for increased public awareness, prevention, and social control also followed from the perception that atrocities were in some sense representative. Kidnapping, mutilation, and murder had few defenders; presented this way, the missing-children problem was uncontroversial.

Nor is the missing-children problem atypical. Claims-makers routinely use examples or case histories to typify social problems: where the Federal Bureau of Narcotics once personified marijuana smokers as homicidal drug fiends, advocates of decriminalization describe users as well-adjusted, otherwise law-abiding citizens; where pro-choice advocates insist that abortions must be available for victims of rape and incest, pro-life crusaders portray women who abort as callous, concerned only with their own convenience; and where welfare advocates focus on the deserving poor, their opponents speak of welfare Cadillacs. Such images become a convenient shorthand for describing complex social conditions. By characterizing a problem in terms of an individual's experiences, the claims-maker helps the audience imagine how they might respond under the same circumstances. The portrait may invite sympathy and understanding, or it may encourage the audience to feel that they would never succumb to the same pressures or temptations; in either case, the problem becomes less abstract, the claims easier to comprehend.

If grounding claims in examples is commonplace, finding convincing warrants is essential. Warrants bridge the gap between grounds and conclusions. An audience might accept a claimant's version of a problem without adopting the recommended policies. Warrants, through references to values and interests, justify solutions. Viable claims (J. Schneider 1985) have compelling warrants.

Rhetoric is central, not peripheral, to claims-making. Claims-makers intend to persuade, and they try to make their claims as persuasive as possible. Claims-making inevitably involves selecting from available arguments, placing the arguments chosen in some sequence, and giving some arguments particular emphasis. These are rhetorical decisions. Moreover, as claims-makers assess the response to their claims, or as they address new audiences, claims may be revised and reconstructed in hopes of making them more effective. In such cases, even the most ingenuous claims-maker must become conscious of doing rhetorical work.

TOWARD A SOCIOLOGY OF RHETORICAL WORK

Obviously, the choices made by those doing rhetorical work will depend upon the nature of the claim, who makes it, and who is being addressed. While every claim has its own unique features, some patterns of rhetoric are likely to emerge.

Spector and Kitsuse (1977, 83) state, "A claim is a demand that one party makes upon another." Their discussion concentrates on demands for action, for new policies or additional resources. But the initial demands—particularly when made by outsider claims-makers—often call for interpretive change. The claims-makers want their audience to acknowledge a problem's existence, or to adopt a new orientation toward it: X is a problem, and it is a problem of this sort. Unless the audience first ratifies these interpretive or conceptual claims, it is unlikely to concede to demands for action (see Aronson 1984). Those with the power to act may choose to do so once they adopt the claimants' interpretation, or in more sensitive cases, policymakers may delay action until there is evidence that the claims-makers have successfully shifted public opinion on the issue, making it safe to change policy.

Claims-makers can generally be expected to act in ways consistent with their own values and interests. But as claimants gain experience, their presentations may become more sophisticated, even cynical. Claims-makers learn ways to mobilize and maintain public support; they learn how to get press coverage by constructing claims that are newsworthy; and they learn to identify key policymakers and recognize the levers that can move policy. These lessons may come through personal experience, or through watching the successes and failures of other claims-makers promoting other issues, but the result is increasingly polished claims.

Claims-makers' behavior also depends on their perception of their audience—perceptions that can be more or less accurate. On the one hand, claimants may have occasion to address the converted—individuals belonging to or allied with their movement.[23] At the other extreme, some audiences are resolutely hostile; a claims-maker may assume that they cannot be moved, regardless of how they are addressed. In between are the audiences deemed persuadable, those who might respond to the right appeal. Of course, most claims have multiple audiences; a claims-maker may simultaneously address members of the movement, the press, the general public, and policymakers—audiences with very different concerns.

Claimants often take special care when addressing the press. The news media serve as a gatekeeper for would-be claims-makers; simply receiving coverage helps validate a claim as worthy of consideration in the social problems marketplace. Case studies of the media's treatment of the antiwar (Gitlin 1980), environmental (Molotch and

Lester 1975; Schoenfeld et al. 1979), and women's movements (Tuchman 1978) describe claims-makers' struggles to have their claims reported. Rhetoric is central to this process; claims must fit the media's criteria for what Gans (1979) calls "story suitability." Journalists are more likely to grant respectful coverage to claims featuring what they take to be relevant, appropriate grounds and warrants. Obviously, claims prepared with the media's practices in mind are more likely to get coverage.

These considerations—the natures of the demand, the claims-maker, and the audience—affect rhetorical work. Perhaps the most straightforward claims emphasize rectitude, arguing that values or morality require that a problem receive attention. The rhetoric of morality (Spector and Kitsuse 1977, 95) or rectitude is most likely to appear under specific conditions. It tends to be adopted by relatively inexperienced outsider claims-makers during the early stages of social problems construction. Although experienced activists may shift their attention to a new social problem, newly constructed problems often feature outsiders who are propelled into the public arena by their outrage, claiming that something should and must be done. The rhetoric of rectitude is more likely to be directed either toward the already converted—who share the crusaders' values—or toward those who are openly hostile. The former group can be counted on to respond favorably when values are invoked, while the latter's negative reaction can help dramatize the conflict as one of principle. Finally, the rhetoric of rectitude is more likely to be associated with demands for reinterpretation, because moral considera-

TABLE 2.1 PATTERNS IN RHETORICAL WORK

	Central Rhetorical Theme	
Characteristic of Claims-making	Rhetoric of Rectitude	Rhetoric of Rationality
Stage in Claims-Making Movement	Early	Later
Claims-makers' Experience	Outsiders—Less Experienced	Insiders—More Experienced
Primary Demand	Interpretation	Action
Perception of Audience	Converted or Hostile	Persuadable

tions can justify viewing a problem in a different way. Moreover, the conventions of news coverage give preference to stories featuring conflict, outrage, and novelty, making the rhetoric of rectitude ideal for bringing new problems to public attention (see J. Schneider 1985).

In contrast, other claims feature a rhetoric of rationality; the audience is told that it will somehow benefit by ratifying the claims. Claims-makers may offer an exchange; in return for ratifying the claim, the audience stands to gain gratitude, loyalty, favors, or material rewards. Or the promised benefit may be more abstract; e.g., analysis reveals that X is the most cost-effective way to respond to problem Y. Experienced insider claims-makers, representing pressure groups' positions on well-established social problems, usually favor the rhetoric of rationality. These claimants often can maneuver from a beachhead of accepted principles established during earlier campaigns demanding reinterpretation. Their later campaigns tend to feature more detailed agendas for policy changes, as well as a clearer sense of which items—whether out of principle or pragmatism—deserve priority. The audience is likely to be seen as persuadable, so that a rhetoric of rationality lets the claims-maker negotiate successful advances. Here the demands tend to be for action; a rhetoric of rationality is more likely to be invoked to shape policy.

Obviously, the patterns outlined in table 2.1 oversimplify the reality of claims-making. Most claims incorporate both rectitude and rationality. Rhetorical work involves choosing to emphasize some elements in order to make the most persuasive case. Similarly, dichotomies cannot do full justice to the complex character of claims-makers, demands, and audiences. A thorough analysis of rhetorical work would require a detailed comparative analysis of claims-making campaigns.

Sociologists of social problems and social movements cannot afford to ignore rhetoric's role in claims-making. How claimants portray a problem affects how others come to understand that problem, and those understandings may endure long after the claims-making campaign ends. In the case of the missing-children movement, the images created by coupling examples of stranger-abductions with large statistical estimates returned to haunt the claims-makers.

3

The Numbers Game: Statistics as Claims

Senator HAWKINS. Mr. Walsh, do you have any comments?
Mr. WALSH. Well, we were told not to come here without some statistics.
—U.S. Senate Hearings (1981, 54)

Novice claims-makers soon discover that statistics are an important, almost essential element in their rhetoric. Congressional subcommittees, like the press and the public, expect claims-makers to offer statistics. Numbers, rates, and percentages help describe a problem's dimensions; they gave a sense of the claim's urgency. Moreover, figures strengthen a claimant's argument because they can be offered (and are usually accepted) as facts, as correct, indisputable, more than the claims-maker's mere opinion.

Of course, all statistics are the products of social processes. Someone has to decide what to count and how to go about counting. Even the census totals and crime rates calculated by official agencies are imperfect measures that reflect those organizations' practices and priorities (Kitsuse and Cicourel 1963). However, the press, policymakers, and the public usually ignore (or are unaware of) the processes which produce statistics. Numbers tend to be treated as facts, regardless of how they came into being (Friedrich 1964; Gusfield 1981; Tuchman 1978).

When claims-makers promote a new, previously neglected social problem, they often seem to know more about that problem than anyone else. One feature of past neglect is the absence of official statistics—no agency has been charged with keeping track of the phenomenon. Claimants inevitably present themselves as knowing enough about the phenomenon to bring it to our attention. In the absence of official statistics, this putative knowledge seems to give the crusaders' estimates the weight of authority. Their extrapolations, even their educated guesses and ballpark estimates, may be the best information available, and others, less knowledgeable about the problem, may be reluctant to challenge these statistics. Once the press begins repeating a figure, the number takes on a life of its own. Soon most people accept the statistic as accurate, although they no longer recall its source. It becomes part of the public's image of the problem and may help justify new public policies.

However, sometimes this process is disrupted and the claims-makers' statistics come under attack. The claims and counterclaims about the missing-children problem illustrate the politics of claims-making statistics.

CLAIMS-MAKERS' ESTIMATES FOR MISSING CHILDREN

Missing-children crusaders routinely presented statistics. The most frequently repeated figure placed the total number of missing children at 1.8 million per year. The claims-makers agreed that the great majority of these were runaways, but they estimated that 100,000 cases involved child snatchings and that another 50,000 were stranger-abductions.

The latter statistic attracted the lion's share of the attention, if only because claims-makers relied on examples of stranger-abduction to typify the larger problem. U.S. Representative Paul Simon said that fifty thousand stranger-abductions was "the most conservative estimate you will get anywhere" (U.S. House 1981b, 10). Child Find estimated that only 10 percent of abducted children returned to their parents, another 10 percent were found dead, and the remaining forty thousand cases per year remained missing (*New York Times* 1982, 77). The American Bar Association's president stated that Americans buried five thousand unidentified children each year, "and that is a figure I think we can agree on" (U.S. House 1985a, 76).

The origins of these numbers are unclear. Some early claims-makers alluded to "Department of Health and Human Services estimates" (see U.S. Senate 1981, 3), but once the initial claims had been made,

46

claimants began citing one another (e.g., "general agreement among professionals") (U.S. House 1984, 85).[1] Many of the early estimates came from legislators and representatives of the missing-children movement. In contrast, most law enforcement officials who testified at the same congressional hearings did not offer national estimates; one even referred to "organizations that cite inflated figures about the number of children that are missing" (U.S. House, 1984, 118–19; U.S. Senate 1984, 89–96). An Office of Juvenile Justice and Delinquency Prevention (1985, 1) memo warned: "A significant problem in using available statistics . . . is that none of the confirmed estimates was derived from studies designed or intended in any way to provide a comprehensive, verifiable assessment of the missing child phenomenon."

Still, the crusaders' statistics gained wide circulation. The press repeated the figures, and other claims-makers soon began to adapt missing-children statistics for their own purposes. Reverend Donald Wildmon, an antipornography crusader, argued: "Each year 50,000 missing children are victims of pornography. Most are kidnaped, raped, abused, filmed for porno magazines and movies and finally, more often than not, murdered" (quoted in *Playboy* 1986, 41). An ex-Satanist, speaking on a television talk show, noted: "Over two million children are missing in this nation right now, and a number of them have been murdered, maimed or are in Satanic cults practicing Satanism today" (Investigative News Group 1988, 5–6). One child-safety guidebook put the number of stranger-abductions at four hundred thousand annually (Arena and Settle 1987, 128).

Outsider claims-makers who want to draw attention to a social problem can use statistics to emphasize its magnitude and importance. They have nothing to lose by offering big numbers, particularly if there are no authoritative official statistics. In fact, claimants can use the limitations of existing official statistics to their advantage. Thus missing-children crusaders emphasized that their figures were rough estimates, "haphazardly gathered statistics" (U.S. House 1984, 50): "We simply do not know how many children disappear from their families each year" (U.S. Senate 1981, 1). This reflected the failure of existing policies—police departments did not take reports of missing children seriously, and there were no state or federal

47

clearinghouses compiling local records. Whatever the official figures, they were surely too low, just the tip of the iceberg.

In a sense, the claims-makers' critique was sociologically sophisticated.[2] They understood that official statistics were products of agencies' organizational practices:

> Police do not record children who were first reported as missing, and later discovered as rape or homicide victims as missing children. They are catalogued according to their final classification. This further obscures obtaining an accurate account (U.S. Senate 1981, 70).

In short, the claims-makers argued that, until officials began taking missing children seriously, official statistics were useless. As a substitute, they offered their own large estimates that drew press coverage and captured the public's imagination.

COUNTERCLAIMS AND BACKLASH

By 1985, the movement was well-established. There was a federally funded National Center for Missing and Exploited Children (NCMEC), and pictures of missing children had achieved wide circulation. At the same time, the crusaders' claims came under closer, more critical inspection. In a Pulitzer Prize–winning series, the *Denver Post* suggested that the risk of stranger-abductions had been blown out of proportion. The *Post* exposed a "numbers gap," contrasting the well-publicized figure of fifty thousand with the sixty-seven FBI investigations of children abducted by strangers in 1984 (Griego and Kilzer 1985). A *Post* editorial suggested that the actual number of stranger-abductions was "fewer than the number of preschoolers who choke to death on food each year" (*Denver Post* 1985, 6H).

The *Post's* numbers gap became the centerpiece for counterclaims. One child-safety pamphlet cited sociologist Richard Gelles: "The odds of a child's being abducted by a stranger are about the same as his chances of being struck by lightning" (*Parenting Adviser* 1988). Arguing that the risks of stranger-abduction had been exaggerated, journalists redefined concern about missing children as "a faddish hysteria" (Kraybill 1986, 81), "an unwitting or witless conspiracy

48

BLOOM COUNTY   **by Berke Breathed**

Figure 3.1. By the mid-1980s, there were widespread charges that missing-children crusaders had exaggerated the stranger-abduction menace. ("Bloom County"—21 November 1987. © 1987, Washington Post Writers Group. Reprinted with permission.)

by people in the missing children business" (von Hoffman 1985, 11), or "a national myth" (P. Schneider 1987, 50) (see fig. 3.1). Abduction-prevention training, campaigns to fingerprint children, and the distribution of missing children's photographs came under a backlash of criticism. Critics, including pediatricians and child psychologists, charged that these programs were unnecessarily frightening, that fears of abduction might harm more children than kidnapping (Andrews 1986; Kantrowitz and Leslie 1986; Kraybill 1986; Vobejda 1985).[3]

This backlash distorted what the missing-children crusaders had actually said. Several critics seemed surprised that "most missing children are missing because they've run away from home or been carted off by parents in custody fights" (Kraybill 1986, 81), yet missing-children claims-makers had always argued that stranger-abductions accounted for a small proportion of missing children. Nicholas von Hoffman (1985, 10) ridiculed claims that there were 1.5 million cases per year: "In a decade, that means that 15 million people have gone through the doughnut hole into the anti-world." But the missing-children crusaders knew that relatively few children remained missing; most cases involved runaways who returned home within a short time. In short, the critics equated missing children with stranger-abductions; they were responding less to the problem described by the missing-children movement than to the movement's typification of that problem.

49

Similarly, the critics emphasized the gap between the crusaders' figure of fifty thousand stranger-abductions and the sixty-seven cases investigated by the FBI in 1984. But by 1985, representatives of the missing-children movement were offering substantially lower estimates of stranger-abductions. The critics adopted the FBI's statistics with the same uncritical enthusiasm with which the press had accepted the crusaders' estimates four years earlier. Of course, the official statistics had an advantage. The press seeks authoritative sources, and the FBI, which had served as the principal source of crime statistics for decades, had great authority. In promoting new social problems, official statistics count more—are more likely to be treated as facts—than unofficial statistics.

Yet the FBI figures were vulnerable to criticism. The missing-children movement regularly criticized the FBI's reluctance to enter stranger-abduction cases. Several congressional hearings featured testimony from parents of children abducted by strangers—most notably John Walsh—who had found the FBI unwilling to investigate; one 1983 hearing had been devoted to this problem (U.S. Senate 1983a). If the crusaders' estimates now seemed too high, the FBI figures repeated by the movement's critics were certainly too low.

Still, the movement had to respond to its critics. The missing-children problem had been typified by stranger-abductions, and with that typification under attack, the entire movement was vulnerable. Asked about the *Post*'s charges, NCMEC president Ellis E. Meredith responded:

> I don't think anything has surprised me more than this preoccupation with numbers, and the . . . "only 67 or only 68 or only 69." . . . These are little helpless citizens of this country being held hostage, scared to death, totally unable to take care of themselves, being held hostage by terrorists. What is it with the "only," sir? (U.S. House 1986b, 39)

Having once given great weight to statistics, Meredith and other crusaders now argued that numbers were irrelevant, that "one missing child is too many." At the same time, NCMEC officials began redefining the threat of stranger-abduction.

50

REDEFINING STRANGER-ABDUCTION

In theory, the missing-children movement might have responded to its critics by retypifying the issue, perhaps focusing attention on the plight of runaways. But stranger-abductions had been an effective typification, and the crusaders chose to retain that focus while expanding the definition of stranger-abduction to include offenses very different from those described in the movement's early stages.

In 1986, the NCMEC released a study of 1,299 recent cases of stranger-abduction. Included were 709 cases from 1984—the same year for which the critics cited the figure of 67 FBI investigations—and the NCMEC stated that this was "the very minimum number of cases," implying that, given the study's methodology, the actual number was far greater (National Center 1986a, 26). In fact, most of the data were collected haphazardly, making it impossible to generalize from the findings.[4] However, the study did include an analysis of police records of every reported crime involving a kidnapping or attempted kidnapping of a child by a non-family member in Jacksonville, Florida, and Houston, Texas, during 1984.[5] There were 269 such cases. Since these two cities held 0.9 percent of the U.S. population (and a slightly larger proportion of the nation's children), we can extrapolate that there were roughly 29,889 stranger-abductions nationwide during 1984—a figure that many might consider in the same ballpark as 50,000. However, this extrapolation is easy to challenge, because both cities had unusually high rates of serious violent crimes (Federal Bureau of Investigation 1985). In 1984, the national rate for murder and nonnegligent manslaughter was 7.9 per 100,000; Jacksonville's murder rate was 17.7, and Houston's was 26.2. Similarly, the rates for forcible rape were 35.7 nationwide, 100.8 in Jacksonville, and 70.3 in Houston. Since the two cities had two to three times the national incidence of serious violent crimes, we probably should halve the extrapolated number of kidnappings to something like 15,000.

Moreover, it is important to understand what sorts of offenses fall within this study's definition of stranger-abduction. The center's researchers included both attempted and completed kidnappings; over one-fifth of the cases involved an unsuccessful attempt. The Jacksonville and Houston cases reveal a clear pattern: 88 percent of the victims were female, 97 percent were missing less than 24 hours, and the police recorded 61 percent of the cases as sex offenses. In short, most were cases of molestation, albeit technically involving kidnapping (moving the victim to a different place).[6] The victim might have been missing for no more than a few minutes. Without discounting the seriousness of these experiences for the victims, these crimes do not fit the missing-children crusaders' earlier claims that most stranger-abductions end in murder or permanent disappearances.

The Jacksonville/Houston data did include some very serious cases; six children were murdered, at least four were gone more than twenty-four hours. Unfortunately, the center's report does not reveal whether these two categories overlapped. Assuming that the two cities had ten very serious incidents, we can extrapolate a nationwide figure of 1,111 stranger-abductions involving either murder or a child missing for more than one day. Or, considering the two cities' high rate of violent crime, we might reasonably halve the estimate to roughly 560 very serious cases.

OTHER OFFICIAL STATISTICS ON STRANGER-ABDUCTIONS

By defining stranger-abduction very broadly, the NCMEC study offered a basis for high (fifteen thousand to thirty thousand) estimates for the annual number of stranger-abductions. We can compare these estimates to others derived from official statistics. While there is no single, authoritative figure for stranger-abductions, several official agencies collect relevant data. Although seeming to yield very different estimates, these data can be reconciled. Taken together, the data demonstrate that the number of stranger-abductions depends on one's definition of the crime more than on anything else.

National Crime Information Center Records

The 1982 Missing Children's Act established that the FBI's National Crime Information Center (NCIC) would serve as a national clearinghouse for missing-children investigations. The law gave parents the right to check whether a missing child had been listed with the NCIC and the right to request a listing if local authorities had failed

52

to list the child. Missing-children advocates also supported state legislation requiring local law enforcement agencies to report all missing children to the NCIC. By the beginning of 1986, most states had such laws (National Center 1986b).

The NCIC includes reports of stranger-abductions within the larger category of *involuntary missing:* "a person of any age who is missing under circumstances indicating that the disappearance was not voluntary, i.e., abduction or kidnapping" (U.S. Senate 1984, 92). During 1985, the NCIC entered 14,816 cases in its involuntary missing files. Most of these people were located; the NCIC cancelled 13,763 cases during 1985, leaving 4,245 active cases.[7]

At first glance, the 14,816 cases reported to the NCIC seem to correspond to our earlier estimate of 15,000 stranger-abductions derived from the NCMEC's study. This impression is mistaken for at least two reasons. First, the NCIC figures include missing adults; although the NCIC does not specify the proportion of adults in the file, it is probably substantial. Nearly two-thirds of federal kidnapping investigations involve adult victims (see table 3.1). Second, it seems likely that the involuntary missing category includes a large proportion of child snatchings and other misadventures. Many states have made child snatching a felony, and such cases presumably account for another substantial share of the involuntarily missing. Certainly it is unlikely that most of 1985's 14,816 new cases involved stranger-abductions. During that year, the FBI received only 867 requests to investigate kidnappings, and it is inconceivable that only 1 case in 17 comes to the bureau's attention.[8] In sum, children abducted by strangers represent an unknown but probably modest share of the cases recorded by the NCIC.

State and Local Police Records

Most of the cases in the NCIC records come from local police departments. Typically, the local police receive the initial reports of missing children, and record-keeping practices vary a good deal among police forces, even within the same state (Joe 1988). As a practical matter, police know that most reported missing children are runaways, most of whom return home within a few days. Therefore, police may discount the seriousness of missing-children reports—

53

particularly those involving teenagers—and give their investigation low priority. The vigor of the police response depends, in part, on the nature of the community, the state's laws regarding juveniles, and the way the police department assigns responsibility for investigating missing-children reports (Maxson, Little, and Klein 1988).

The missing-children movement complained that police statistics undercounted missing children, and they sought new federal and state laws to insure that missing-children reports would be taken seriously. While record keeping has become more thorough, it remains uneven. For instance, a summary of the cases entered into New York State's Missing Children Register during 1988 includes 21,795 runaways, 246 familial abductions, 30 acquaintance abductions, 5 stranger-abductions, and 3,118 cases of unknown circumstances (New York State Division 1989, 17). But how should we interpret these figures? Should we treat stranger-abductions as a class by themselves, or should we add acquaintance-abductions to form a category of nonfamilial abductions? And what should we make of the unknown category—one-fifth of all reported cases?[9] Similarly, a review of all 1984 missing-persons reports in an eastern city classified 2.3 percent of the 541 missing juveniles as "Taken by Third Party/in Danger," a classification that might include child snatchings, or even a juvenile female accompanying her adult boyfriend, as well as stranger-abductions (Hirschel and Lab 1988). Or take the data from Illinois—a leader in developing statewide missing-children records. Illinois agencies can classify cases in eight categories, but record-keeping practices clearly vary among agencies. In 1986, Chicago's records (with 41 percent of the statewide cases) did not list any cases in four of the categories (including those for runaways, endangered, and foul play certain) (Illinois State Police 1987). While the missing-children movement's efforts may have made police records more complete, the resulting data are not yet in a form that readily lends itself to assessing the incidence of stranger-abductions.

FBI Kidnapping Investigations

Many people assume that local records are unimportant, that the FBI has jurisdiction in all kidnapping cases, but this is not true. Before entering a case, the bureau demands evidence that the offense some-

54

TABLE 3.1 KIDNAPPINGS KNOWN TO THE FBI, 1981–86

Year	(A) Opened Cases	(B) All Investigations	(C) Child-Victim Investigations	(D) % of Opened Cases Investigated	(E) % of Investigations with Child-Victim
1981	853	120	35	14	29
1982	641	141	49	22	35
1983	946	170	70	18	41
1984	1035	169	69	16	41
1985	867	156	53	18	34
1986	664	149	57	22	38

(A) Total number of kidnapping cases opened by the FBI.
(B) Number of cases determined to be a violation of the Federal Kidnapping Statute for which an investigation was conducted.
(C) Number of investigated kidnappings in which it was clearly established that a child was abducted.
(D) Percentage of opened cases which led to investigations (B/A).
(E) Percentage of investigations involving child-victims (C/B).
Sources: Nemecek 1986; U.S. Senate 1984, 94.

how violates federal statutes (e.g., use of the mail to deliver a ransom note, or transporting a hostage across state lines). Only a fraction of the kidnappings "opened"—brought to the bureau's attention—are found to involve violations of the Federal Kidnapping Statute (U.S. Senate 1984, 89–96). In 1985, the FBI decided to investigate 156 of 867 opened cases (see table 3.1). Most investigations involve adult hostages; the FBI investigated only 53 cases of abducted children in 1985.

These figures are hardly authoritative. David F. Nemecek (1986), chief of NCIC, acknowledged that "state and local agencies also investigate other matters which are not included in these statistics." A 1983 U.S. Senate Subcommittee on Juvenile Justice heard three parents who had been unable to get the FBI to investigate when their children were kidnapped by strangers. At the hearing's end, Senator Arlen Specter questioned FBI Assistant Director Oliver B. Revell:

SENATOR SPECTER. How can we help you, either by statutory changes or otherwise, to do a better job in directing your efforts on the kinds of cases which we have heard about here today?

MR. REVELL. Well, I believe that the Justice Department and the Bureau have to do a better job in screening and determining those cases that we should enter on our own. (U.S. Senate 1983a, 81)

This exchange apparently had some effect; table 3.1 shows that investigations of child abductions rose in 1983. Still, even under congressional pressure, the bureau never found more than seventy cases to investigate in a single year.

The National Child Safety Council Listings

What of the long-term missing, the children whose faces appear on milk cartons? In 1984, the National Child Safety Council (1986) began publishing the *Abducted Children Directory,* a "comprehensive listing of involuntary abducted/kidnapped children." The NCSC distributes copies of the directory to schools and law enforcement agencies in hopes of locating these children. As of 1 March 1986 this directory listed 132 children, including 15 children taken during the 1970s and 1 taken in 1965. It takes some time to get a child listed (the 1986 directory did not include anyone kidnapped after November 1985), and children missing a long time may not be listed because their parents have given up hope.

For these reasons, it makes sense to focus on the figures for 1984. Parents of children taken in 1984 would have had at least fifteen months to list their children. Not surprisingly, 1984 was the peak year for abductions of the children in the directory; 30 of the children disappeared during 1984 (the directory listed 22 cases from 1983 and 18 from 1985). Obviously, not every case will be listed, but we might imagine that most parents would choose to take advantage of the NCSC listing. This suggests that the annual number of long-term victims of stranger-kidnappings is in the range of thirty to fifty.

Homicide Data

Of course, not all victims of stranger-abductions stay missing. Some return home, while others are killed. Although most crimes go unreported, murders normally come to official attention, and detailed case records—such as the Supplementary Homicide Reports (SHR) assembled by federal and state agencies—are available for analysis.

California's SHR records for 1984 reveal that the state had 223 homicide victims under age eighteen: 53 were killed by family members; 51 (almost all teenagers) died in juvenile-gang-related killings; and 75 were killed by others known to the victim. There were only 44 homicides in which the killer either was a stranger or remained unidentified; 24 of these involved teenaged victims. The SHR also give a precipitating event for each offense. If we exclude homicides by family members, and if we also exclude homicides linked to arson, narcotics offenses, robberies, burglaries, and larcenies, there remain 28 felony-related homicides involving rape (14), other sex offenses (1), other felonies (2), or suspected felonies (11). (There were no cases in which the precipitating event was listed as kidnapping.) This would seem to be the upper limit for homicides related to stranger-abductions; these 28 cases undoubtedly include some incidents in which abduction did not occur. Assuming that California has 10 percent of the population, we can extrapolate that abductors probably killed fewer than three hundred juvenile victims nationwide.

In fact, the national data suggest that this estimate is far too high. Analysis of the FBI's SHR for 1984 reveals that California accounted for 16.5 percent of the nation's 1,337 homicide victims under age eighteen. The national total for felony-related homicides (excluding those linked to theft, arson, or narcotics) committed by non–family members was only 112.[10]

Unidentified Remains

But what about those thousands of unidentified children's bodies recovered each year? Couldn't some of them be victims of kidnappers? There are no national data on unidentified bodies. However, the figures from California are most revealing. County coroners in California send records of all John and Jane Does (unidentified bodies) to the state's Missing/Unidentified Deceased Program. In 1986, the program reviewed all outstanding cases from 1980 through 1984 to learn what proportion involved juveniles. When the age was in doubt (e.g., estimated as seventeen to twenty-one), the body was considered a juvenile. Under this most generous of definitions, the five-year period yielded only fifty-six unidentified bodies of juveniles—about eleven per year (M. Kelly 1986). California has roughly 10 percent of the U.S. population, but there is reason to suspect that it has more than its share of unidentified bodies. The state has a large number of illegal migrants, whose bodies are especially difficult to identify, and it has long been a mecca for runaway youths. It is, then, very unlikely that there are many more than one hundred bodies of unidentified youths discovered each year.[11]

THE RHETORICAL ADVANTAGES OF BROAD DEFINITIONS

Taken together, these data—summarized in table 3.2—suggest the dimensions of the stranger-abduction problem. Obviously, the figures are derived from different sources, and they need to be read with care. Official statistics inevitably reflect the organizational prac-

TABLE 3.2 ESTIMATES OF CHILDREN ABDUCTED BY STRANGERS

Crimes involving kidnapping or attempted kidnapping of children by nonfamily members (includes brief incidents in which the victim was physically moved), 1984 (National Center for Missing and Exploited Children)	15,000
Serious crimes involving kidnapping (leading to death or a child missing more than 24 hours), 1984 (National Center for Missing and Exploited Children)	560
Involuntarily missing individuals (includes adults and probably some child snatchings and other sorts of cases), 1985 (National Crime Information Center)	14,816
FBI investigations of federal kidnapping violations involving child-victims, 1984 (FBI)	69
Children who were involuntarily abducted in 1984 and still missing in 1986 (National Child Safety Council)	30
Felony-related homicides of juveniles by nonfamily members (excludes homicides related to robbery, burglary, arson, and narcotics offenses), 1985 (California Supplementary Homicide Reports)	210
Unidentified juveniles buried per year, 1980–84 (California Missing/Unidentified Deceased Program)	110

58

tices of the agencies that compile them. Still, the figures in table 3.2 are not inconsistent; rather, they reinforce one another.

First, it is apparent that the missing-children crusaders' initial claims greatly exaggerated the extent of the problem. There is simply no evidence to support claims of fifty thousand stranger-abductions annually, of forty thousand permanently missing victims, five thousand abduction-related homicides, or five thousand unidentified juvenile corpses.

Second, the scope of the problem depends upon one's definition of stranger-abduction. Criminologists know that, in general, the more serious the offense, the less commonly it occurs. If we focus on the most serious cases—those involving murder or a child's prolonged absence—there are relatively few cases, numbering perhaps two hundred to six hundred per year. However, if we adopt a much broader definition—including even brief incidents—the number of cases known to the authorities rises to perhaps fifteen thousand.

The missing-children movement favored a broad definition. The Kevin Collins Foundation for Missing Children (an organization specializing in the problem of stranger-abductions) criticized criminal justice record-keeping practices for misclassifying stranger-abductions:

> Current police statistics (including the FBI statistics) fail to show that STRANGER ABDUCTION of children is a significant problem requiring National attention to correct it. . . .
>
> There is a reason why the current crime statistics fail to reflect a true picture on the *numbers* of STRANGER ABDUCTIONS. That reason is that whenever a previous or subsequent crime occurs in conjunction with STRANGER ABDUCTION . . . the crime of abduction (kidnapping) most often ceases to be shown.
>
> [Stranger abduction] would be a recognized problem if statistics were kept!
>
> When statistics make the problem graphic, police/public attention will be directed to the problem and it will be diminished (Kevin Collins Foundation 1987, emphasis in original).

Thus the foundation estimated that strangers annually abducted one thousand California children: "The vast majority are kept against their will for a short time, then released" (Kell 1989, A2).

Official agencies also began adopting the NCMEC's broad definition. A review of missing-children reports in New York State found that 85 percent of all cases involved teenagers, that half of all cases were cancelled (i.e., the child was reported found) within four days, and that 99 percent of the cases reported in 1985 had been cancelled by May 1986. In 1985, New York's records did not classify types of missing children, but these findings seem consistent with a high proportion of runaways. However, citing the NCMEC's claim that many stranger-abductions are short-term crimes, the report warned that "there is no evidence that would justify defining New York State's missing children as essentially a 'runaway' problem" (New York State Division 1986, 29).[12]

Moreover, while advocating a broad definition of stranger-abduction, claims-makers continued to use frightening language and horror stories to typify the problem. Thus NCMEC president Meredith spoke of little children "held hostage by terrorists," and Jay Howell, NCMEC's executive director, testified:

> Unfortunately, a lot of the children, whether it is Adam Walsh, Vicki Lynn, a lot of the kids that are well known in this country were killed in a very short period of time, so you typically have a scenario where one person kidnaps a child, takes them to a second location, usually somewhere in that geographic area, sexually assaults them and releases them hours later, and sometimes they are murdered. (U.S. House 1986b, 38)

The combination of big numbers, broad definitions, and horrible examples made these claims compelling.

The debate over the numbers of missing children led the federal government to sponsor the National Studies of the Incidence of Missing Children (Office of Juvenile Justice 1987). Politicians and journalists assumed that this large-scale research project would provide an accurate, authoritative measure of the problem's extent. But, of course, the study's findings would depend upon whether the researchers chose a broad or a narrow definition of stranger-abduction—and the importance of that choice was likely to remain hidden. As the project began, there were indications that a broad definition would be adopted. One of the pilot surveys sponsored by OJJDP used a broad definition in phrasing a key question: "Since the first of this year, was there any time when _____ [NAME] was missing from your household and you were worried about where (he)(she) was . . . even if it was only for a few hours?" In addition to surveys, the proposed research design included "a separate study of law enforcement records," in which researchers would select a representative sample of law enforcement agencies, from which "records concerning all nonfamily abduction situations will be identified." While this says nothing about the definition of stranger-abduction, the methodology described recalls the NCMEC study.[13]

Typically, the combined efforts of researchers, the press, and claimants reduce the results of applied social research projects such as the National Studies of the Incidence of Missing Children to a few key facts. Few ever read the reports of major research projects. More often, a report running several hundred pages is condensed into a brief press release which summarizes key findings, e.g., by giving a single number for stranger-abductions. The media report the number in the press release while ignoring the choices that produced that number rather than some other figure. Claims-makers then appropriate the number for their own rhetorical purposes. In this process, everyone is likely to forget that a different definition of stranger-abduction might have produced very different results.

THE POLITICS OF
SOCIAL PROBLEMS STATISTICS

The history of the missing-children problem reveals three rules of thumb for claims-makers' statistics. First, because they are more dramatic, *big numbers are better than little numbers*. The public could not ignore claims that strangers kidnapped fifty thousand children each year. Second, *official numbers are better than unofficial numbers*. When the *Denver Post* contrasted the missing-children crusaders' estimates with far lower figures from the FBI, most commentators assumed that the FBI's figures were accurate, if only because the FBI had been the authoritative source for criminal justice statistics for fifty years. The third principle can be derived from the first two: *big, official numbers are best of all.* By advocating a broad definition of stranger-abduction for the National Studies of the Incidence of Missing Children, the NCMEC sought to construct official proof that the problem was widespread.

The dispute over missing-children statistics is not unique. Claims-makers' figures often cannot bear close inspection. Some estimates are little more than guesses plucked from thin air, others are extrapolations from minimal data. For instance, claimants promoting the problem of "elder abuse" (mistreatment of the elderly) based their claim that one million elderly Americans were abused on a survey of 433 elderly residents of Washington, D.C.; only 73 of those people responded to the survey, and only 3 of those reported being abused (Crystal 1987). Other claims-makers selectively focus on part of the data. Thus those who note that there are 1.5 million reports of child abuse annually often fail to mention that two-thirds of those reports are designated "unfounded" upon investigation (Besharov 1986).

Because big estimates play a central role in claims-making, claims-makers are quick to denounce rival numbers, even when they are the result of careful research. Thus advocates for the homeless attacked researchers who found that the number of homeless people in Chicago was far lower than claims-makers had estimated (Rossi 1987). Similarly, when a national survey conducted by leading sociologists in the field found that the incidence of family violence declined from 1975 to 1985, the study came under fire from activists, who apparently feared that statistics on declining incidence would be used to justify decreased funding for child-abuse programs (Gelles and Straus 1988, 108–15).

While these examples suggest that claimants have little trouble getting their statistics accepted, not all debates over social problems fit this pattern. In fact, Gillespie and Leffler argue that claims-makers' figures typically face resistance: "Social problems claims-makers must present irrefutable evidence that the condition is widespread in the general population" (1987, 492); "the burden of proof lies with those who challenge the status quo" (1987, 491). They suggest that most claims about a problem's extent are dismissed for insufficient evidence, and, since claims-makers rarely have the resources to conduct sophisticated social research, it becomes nearly impossible to get new claims taken seriously. But Gillespie and Leffler drew their conclusions after studying the construction of sexual harassment as a social problem. This is significant because, under the law, sexual harassment is a form of sex discrimination. Corporations challenged claims and opposed federal funding for research that might establish that sexual harassment was a widespread, institutionalized problem; such findings might help employees win large-scale judgments against their employers. This example suggests that crusaders' statistics will meet opposition when their claims threaten established interests. Where there are no such interests—no one, after all, spoke in favor of stranger-abductions—claims-makers' statistics are more likely to gain acceptance.

Statistics, then, help shape definitions of social problems. The numbers that eventually gain acceptance can affect social policy.[14] Thus the missing-children movement offered large estimates and a broad definition of stranger-abductions while using atrocity tales about raped or murdered children to typify the problem. They defined missing children as a serious problem that required new policies, including both education/prevention and expanding the social control apparatus. If most of the commercial products designed to educate children about the dangers of abduction were reasonably priced, it remains difficult to calculate the social costs of encouraging both parents and children to believe that terrifying crimes are common. Similarly, the crusaders called for greater social control: schools should require detailed identification records from every student; police should have the power to hold runaways; federal police powers should be expanded; courts should accept testimony from very young children; and so on. The unspeakable threat posed by the stranger-abduction epidemic justified these changes; the new policies' potential costs and dangers received little attention.

Former U.S. Senator Paula Hawkins (1986, 51) asks: "But when you think about it, does it really matter whether the number [of stranger-abductions] is 4,000, 20,000, or 50,000? . . . No abstract statistics should distract us from the plight of even one innocent child who is in danger of any kind of exploitation." In fact, such statistics shape our sense of a problem's urgency, which in turn affects policy. Claims-makers use statistics to persuade; their numbers need to be understood for what they are—part of the rhetoric of claims-making. Statistics are products of social processes, and they can have social consequences. When trying to understand social problems, we need figures we can count on, but we especially need to know what it is we are counting.

4

Definition, Typification, and Domain Expansion

DEAR READERS: Have you ever abused your child? Perhaps without realizing it, you have. Words can hit as hard as a fist. For example: "You disgust me. Just shut up!"
—Abigail "Dear Abby" van Buren (1987)

There is nothing unusual about the missing-children movement's efforts to promote a broader definition of stranger-abduction. Social problems claims-making is rarely static; claims evolve over a problem's history. Initial claims-making must persuade people that a problem exists. Once these early claims gain acceptance and the problem becomes well established, with its own place on the social policy agenda, claimants may begin reconstructing the problem. Reconstructing a social problem requires revising the claims-makers' rhetoric. In particular, claims-makers are likely to offer a new definition, extending the problem's domain or boundaries, and find new examples to typify just what is at issue.

The realities of the social problems marketplace give claims-makers several reasons for reconstructing problems. First, claims-makers usually adopt a rhetoric of rectitude to present their initial claims; this helps evoke widespread sympathy and consensus. Claimants delay making more controversial demands until they have a foot in the door. Second, as a problem becomes established and familiar, media coverage tends to decline (Downs 1972). New claims not only expose additional facets of a problem, they help keep the issue fresh and newsworthy, thereby holding the attention of the media and the public. Third, as an acknowledged subject for concern, a well-established social problem becomes a resource, a foundation upon

65

which other claims may be built. Rather than struggling to bring recognition to a new problem, claimants may find it easier to expand an existing problem's domain. These new claims take the form: [new problem] X is really a type of [established problem] Y.

The recent history of the child-abuse problem illustrates these processes. For nearly thirty years, child abuse has been defined and redefined. Once child abuse acquired widespread legitimacy as a social problem, successive waves of claims-makers sought to expand the problem's domain to incorporate their concerns. The missing-children movement was just one campaign in the larger evolution of the child-abuse problem. This chapter sketches the evolving definitions and typifications for child abuse, then examines some more general questions about definition and domain expansion in social problems construction.

THE BATTERED-CHILD SYNDROME

Child abuse achieved public recognition as a social problem in 1962, when the *Journal of the American Medical Association* published the research report "The Battered-Child Syndrome" (Kempe et al. 1962).[1] This article defined the syndrome as "a clinical condition in young children who have received serious physical abuse" and went on to state that "in general, the affected children are younger than 3 years" (17). The researchers presented two typifying examples—both young patients (aged three months and thirteen months) with serious fractures.

The researchers' article (and the accompanying *JAMA* editorial) attracted the notice of journalists, who in turn brought battered children to public attention. These newspaper and magazine articles often began by typifying the problem. For instance, the first long, popular magazine article on the topic led with descriptions of a four-year-old girl with a fractured skull and an eight-month-old girl with severe burns, then introduced the term "battered-child syndrome" (Flato 1962). Photographs—typically featuring a bruised, emaciated infant or toddler wearing only a diaper—accompanied these articles and helped typify battering.

In short, early reports in both the medical literature and the press portrayed the problem as one of extreme physical violence against very young children. Early definitions of child abuse focused on these elements, and, equally important, the examples used to illustrate the problem had these features.[2] This image remained central to discussions of child abuse. For instance, a 1976 network news feature story on child abuse began with nine slides of bruised infants and toddlers lying in hospital beds wearing only diapers and bandages, while the correspondent spoke: "What you are seeing now are the actual results of severe child abuse" (ABC, 12 December 1976). The people viewing this story could easily assume that battering remained the issue.[3]

ABUSE, MALTREATMENT, AND NEGLECT

In fact, by 1976, the issue encompassed a much broader array of conditions threatening children. The more general term "child abuse" had replaced the earlier, narrower concept of the "battered child," and the even broader expression "child abuse and neglect" had gained currency among professionals.

The question of how broadly child abuse ought to be defined was not new. The U.S. Children's Bureau had begun calling child abuse to the attention of professionals during the 1950s. The bureau soon found that "two different versions of the problem had emerged": child-welfare professionals defined abuse and neglect broadly, to include a wide range of social welfare problems, while physicians tended to focus narrowly on physical abuse (Nelson 1984, 43). But the broader definition also found favor among some medical professionals. At the same time that people began speaking of battered children, physician Vincent J. Fontana promoted the label "maltreatment syndrome in children":

> A maltreated child often presents no obvious signs of being "battered" but has multiple minor physical evidences of emotional and at times nutritional deprivation, neglect and abuse. In these cases the most acute diagnostic acumen of the physician can prevent the more severe injuries of in-

flicted trauma that are a significant cause of childhood death. . . . Awareness by the physician of the signs and symptoms of this preventable disease can be lifesaving (Fontana, Donovan, and Wong 1963).

Like "child battering," Fontana's concept of the "maltreated child" emphasized how physicians' expertise could save lives. This claim had appeal both for physicians—who gain professional prestige from their ability to make life-and-death decisions—and for legislators—who could define diagnosis as a noncontroversial, medical matter (Nelson 1984; Pfohl 1977).

The term "maltreatment" never took hold; "child abuse" became the accepted usage. But both terms included considerably more than physical brutality; professionals now viewed battering as only a particularly severe form of abuse. Still, claimants continued to use battering to typify child abuse, even as they promoted a broader definition. Consider the 1973 hearings on the Child Abuse Prevention Act, organized by Senator Walter Mondale. Mondale began his opening remarks by typifying the problem:

> Only 10 days ago the stepmother of 9-year old Donna Stern of Cedar Grove, Md. was found guilty of the premeditated murder and torture of the child. The child had been beaten, burned, and whipped by the stepmother.
>
> Ugly as it sounds, this is not an isolated case. Each year some 60,000 children in this country are reported to have been abused (U.S. Senate 1973, 1).

Yet Mondale's first two witnesses offered much broader definitions. According to Professor David Gil, "Any act of commission or omission by individuals, institutions or society as a whole, and any conditions resulting from such acts or inaction, which deprive children of equal rights and liberties, and/or interfere with their optimal development, constitute, by definition, abusive or neglectful acts or conditions" (U.S. Senate 1973, 14). And Jolly K., a leader of Parents Anonymous (a self-help group for child abusers), warned that "verbal abuse can destroy, almost kill" (U.S. Senate 1973, 50).

This was controversial territory. (Gil found himself arguing with

Senator Jennings Randolph over whether parental spankings or corporal punishment in the schools constituted abuse. At one point, Randolph charged: "You present . . . a namby-pamby, wishy-washy attitude which is absolutely not realistic as we think in terms of the learning process and the growing process of children" [U.S. Senate 1973, 46].) There were clear advantages to emphasizing atrocity tales of physical abuse while skipping over precise definitions. Mondale warned Gil:

> I think if we pursue your course, I doubt that we are going to succeed. In the meantime, children are being poisoned, mangled, slaughtered, abused, chain-whipped. . . . Don't you think it is worthy of our efforts to try and ameliorate that problem until better times come along? (U.S. Senate 1973, 47)

Battering had few defenders; it offered a basis for consensus. So crusaders continued to typify the problem in terms of battering, even as they lobbied legislators to amend child-abuse laws to encompass other sorts of mistreatment.

Gradually, the broader definition made its way into the public's consciousness. For instance, a 1976 public-service pamphlet asked:

> What is "CHILD ABUSE"? . . . It's REPEATED MISTREATMENT or NEGLECT of a child by parent(s) or other guardian resulting in INJURY or HARM. Child abuse may be: PHYSICAL—shaking, beating, burning; failure to provide the necessities of life (e.g., adequate food); EMOTIONAL—failure to provide warmth, attention, supervision, normal living experiences; VERBAL—excessive yelling, belittling, teasing; SEXUAL—incest, rape and other sexual activity (Anonymous 1976, emphasis and ellipsis in original).

The press continued describing new forms of physical abuse (e.g., the shaken-baby syndrome), but it also examined neglect and emotional, psychological, and verbal abuse. And the claims-makers quoted in these articles insisted that abuse need not be physical to be serious (e.g., emotional abuse is "probably the most heinous form of child abuse") (Seligmann 1988, 48; Parachini 1984; Sanoff 1982).

INSTITUTIONALIZING THE BROAD DEFINITION

Child abuse, particularly when defined and typified in terms of physical brutality, was a "valence issue"—one that "elicits a single, strong, fairly uniform emotional response and does not have an adversarial quality" (Nelson 1984, 27). Policymakers proved very responsive to the early claims about battering; only five years after the publication of "The Battered-Child Syndrome," all fifty states had laws requiring physicians to report cases of suspected abuse (Nelson 1984, 78–83). In 1974, Congress passed Mondale's Child Abuse Prevention and Treatment Act, which made federal funds available to states with reporting laws that met federal standards. While only three states met those federal eligibility requirements in 1973, most states soon revised their statutes, so that forty-three states qualified by 1978 (Besharov 1985).

The new state laws expanded the official domain of child abuse in two ways. First, they required more categories of professionals to report cases of suspected abuse; in addition to physicians, the new laws typically named other medical professionals, educators, social workers, and law enforcement officers, while granting those reporting abuse immunity from criminal and civil charges. Second, the laws adopted a broader definition of child abuse, requiring reporting of suspected cases of neglect, emotional abuse, and sexual abuse, as well as physical abuse (Besharov 1985; J. Johnson 1985). And because the new laws defined child abuse as a social welfare problem rather than a criminal problem, they granted child-protection workers extraordinary powers to investigate cases, separate children from their parents, and the like.

The new laws' definitions of abuse, while broad, were often vague. Statutes used terms such as "neglect" without defining them. Nor did the professionals obliged to report abuse have clear standards for labeling instances of abuse (J. Johnson 1985). When researchers asked people from different professions, as well as the general public, to rate the seriousness of abusive behaviors described in brief vignettes (e.g., "The parent experimented with cocaine while alone taking care of the child"), they found overall consensus (e.g., sexual and physical abuse tended to be seen as more serious than other types of abuse), but there was a good deal of disagreement in the ratings of the less serious behaviors (Garrett and Rossi 1978; Giovannoni and Becerra 1979).

Not surprisingly, reports of suspected child abuse boomed under the new laws.[4] The number of reports—well over a million per year in the 1980s—exceeded the capacity of protective-service workers to conduct thorough investigations. A growing proportion of reports— roughly two-thirds in recent years—is designated "unfounded"; critics argue that this is because the reporting system generates unmanageable caseloads consisting largely of minor complaints, while the system's defenders suggest that more reports might be substantiated if only the system had more resources (Besharov 1985; Crewdson 1988; Meriwether 1986). Concerns about potential abuses of authority by protective-service workers have led critics on both the right (Pride 1986) and the left (Eberle and Eberle 1986; Wexler 1985) to call for a narrower definition of abuse.

SEXUAL ABUSE

During the 1970s, sexual abuse joined neglect within the domain of child abuse. Incest and child molestation were renamed; they were now child sexual abuse. The new name emphasized that sexual contacts were harmful, analogous to other ways of harming children. And, like battering, these were activities with few advocates. Claimsmakers—principally psychologists and social workers—had few problems building a consensus (Weisberg 1984). Again, the claimsmakers typified the problem with horrific examples (small children repeatedly forced to have sex, or former victims who continued to suffer as adults) while defining the issue in much broader terms.

Thus what might seem to be relatively minor offenses were classified as "sexual abuse" when they involved children. All three network news broadcasts covered Senator Paula Hawkins's revelation that she had been sexually abused, i.e., briefly fondled by a neighbor at age five (Hawkins 1986). An article in the authoritative *Encyclopedia of Social Work* asked: "Is a father who routinely walks around his house naked in front of his children sexually abusing them? This situation is ambiguous" (Conte 1977, 127). Other definitions included "touching assaults by relatively young boys" (L. Kelly 1988, 68) and "indecent exposure, obscene phone calls or peeping toms" (Anonymous 1981).

Claims-makers warned that even apparently minor episodes could have serious consequences. For instance, *By Silence Betrayed,* a well-received book about sexual abuse, begins a chapter of typifying accounts of victims with the story of Alison, who was fondled by an adult when she was eleven. Her autobiographical account continues into an adulthood marked by failed relationships, overeating, and depression—all presented as products of a single brief encounter (Crewdson 1988, 42–46).

By the mid-1980s, sexual abuse was a well-established social problem with its own broad definitions, frightening typifications, and astonishing statistics. Some claims-makers even seemed to equate child abuse with sexual abuse:

> Think of five children you know. One will become the victim of child abuse. That's a fact we are trying to change.
> About one in five children are [*sic*] sexually abused . . . typically not once but repeatedly over a period of months or years (Parents League of the U.S. 1986, 29—ellipsis in original).

At least in this example's rhetoric, sexual abuse loomed larger than its parent concept. And, just as the domain of child abuse had been expanded to include neglect and sexual abuse, the boundaries of sexual abuse were extended.

SEXUAL EXPLOITATION

While incest and molestation were central to the construction of sexual abuse, other frightening forms of sexual exploitation came to be seen as part of the problem. Child pornography came to public notice in 1977, thanks to psychiatrist-lawyer Judianne Densen-Gerber. She drew attention to commercial child pornography, saying she had "counted 264 different magazines produced each month that use children" and noting "the fact that many of our children have been sold for [sexual snuff films] abroad" (U.S. House 1977, 43). Popular magazine stories typified the problem with examples of commercial pornography featuring very young children (*Time* 1977, 55). Later claims-makers expanded child pornography's domain to include non-commercial materials (e.g., molesters' snapshots of their victims) as well as pornography featuring older adolescents.

Interest in adolescent prostitution also grew during the 1970s. Adolescent prostitution was nothing new; nearly half of the prostitutes in antebellum New York were under twenty-one (Sanger 1972, 452). However, nineteenth-century campaigns to save prostitutes paid little attention to the women's ages (Connelly 1980; Pivar 1973). In contrast, age became an important issue in the 1970s, when some feminists called for decriminalizing adult prostitution (James et al. 1977). There was no longer a consensus that "working women" needed to be saved, and antiprostitution crusaders began to focus on the exploitation of underage prostitutes of both sexes (Weisberg 1985, 1–12).

Claims-makers typified both child pornography and adolescent prostitution with examples of the most extreme forms of exploitation: young prostitutes, often fleeing from physical or sexual abuse at home, fell into the hands of brutal, exploitative pimps; child pornography was a highly profitable commercial enterprise featuring very young children; both pimps and pornographers probably had links to organized crime; and so on. Similarly, the missing-children problem was constructed with multiple links to the larger problems of child abuse and sexual exploitation: runaways fled abuse, only to fall into the hands of pimps and pornographers; parents abducted their own children in order to abuse them; and stranger-abductions were likely the work of pedophiles and/or people in the sex industry.[5]

By 1983, shocking new charges began to surface in Jordan, Minnesota, Manhattan Beach (the McMartin Preschool) and Bakersfield, California, and other communities. The new problem, eventually labeled "ritual abuse," involved groups of adults molesting groups of children. Accounts of orgies, Satanic rites, ritual killings of animals and infants, and other extraordinary activities appeared in the press. Critics argued that there was little evidence for the charges except the testimony of the victims—often very young children who only admitted being abused after extensive interviewing. Others countered that the lack of other evidence only demonstrated that a powerful conspiracy was at work (Crewdson 1988; Eberle and Eberle 1986).

While claims-making about ritual abuse and other forms of sexual exploitation helped keep attention focused on sexual abuse, the 1980s saw a wide array of other claims-makers hoping to use the child-abuse label as a springboard for success.

EXPANDING THE DOMAIN

Child abuse had become a well-established social problem. A 1981 Harris poll found that 62 percent of Americans rated child abuse a very serious problem (E. Brown, Flanagan, and McLeod 1984, 291). The child-abuse label was familiar and generally accepted, and that acceptance attracted new claims-makers who sought to link their causes to the problem of child abuse. Such claims-making aimed to expand further the domain of child abuse.

The debate over abortion policy offers the clearest example, as representatives of both sides tried to label the opposition abusive. For instance, some pro-choice advocates warned that children were more likely to be abused if they had been unwanted, so that limiting abortions would only increase child abuse. One book spoke of "birth abuse"—"the unconscionable giving birth to unwanted babies" (Anonymous 1987, 102). And Faye Wattleton (1987, 7), national president of Planned Parenthood, argued: "Whenever you hear people discussing the obscenity of child abuse, suggest to them that denying teenagers the ability to avoid pregnancy is *just that*—child abuse" (emphasis in original). In contrast, pro-life advocates pointed to evidence that few abused children had been unwanted; rather than deterring abuse, they argued, abortion fostered child abuse by diminishing the value of children and damaging the attachment between parent and child (H. Brown 1977; U.S. House 1983b, 155). They also portrayed abortion as inherently abusive: "Death by abortion is far more violent than most child abuse deaths" (Pride 1986, 33; Lippis 1982); consistency demanded that abortion be classified as a form of child abuse.

The readiness with which both pro-choice and pro-life forces incorporated references to child abuse in their rhetoric was not unique.

During the 1980s, policymakers often attached new social policies to existing child-abuse laws. For example, in 1982, Infant Doe—a severely disabled newborn who died after physicians withheld food and further medical care—came to public attention. The case, with its echoes of the ongoing abortion debate, aroused great controversy, and officials in the Reagan administration denounced the doctors' decision. Congress required "that states establish specific procedures for handling complaints of medical neglect of handicapped infants with life-threatening conditions" by amending the Child Abuse Prevention and Treatment and Adoption Reform Act of 1978 (Silver 1986; U.S. House 1983a).

Child-abuse laws provided a foundation for other proposed federal legislation. The title of the proposed 1988 Child Protection and Obscenity Act (S. 2033) emphasized the bill's child-pornography provisions, but most of the bill was devoted to extending federal powers against those trading in any obscene works (obscenity was not defined) to include extensive criminal forfeiture penalties. Similarly, U.S. Representative Mario Biaggi led efforts against fathers who failed to pay their child support: "Nonpayment of child support continues to [sic] or exacerbates a form of abuse which is just as heinous as physical abuse" (U.S. House 1983c, 3).

Similar processes were at work in state governments. A California Attorney General's (1984) opinion held that the state's child-abuse reporting laws required health professionals to report sexually active adolescents under the age of fourteen, although a court of appeal ruled that reports were not required unless there was other evidence of abuse (Planned Parenthood Affiliates of California v. van de Kamp, 1986). Florida amended its child abuse laws to cover infants born drug-dependent, and one expert advocated extending protection to "infants born suffering from fetal alcohol syndrome or legal drug toxicity" (B. Spitzer 1987, 884). The concepts "fetal abuse" and "fetal neglect" also began receiving attention (Manson and Marlot 1988; Parness 1986).

Policymakers were not the only ones seeking to expand the domain of child abuse. Other claims concerned:

- *Smoking.* Writing in the *New York Times,* a surgeon argued that smoking is a "form of child abuse" because smoking by a pregnant woman endangers the fetus, while breathing secondary smoke can harm growing children (Cahan 1985). In 1987, the American Cancer Society ran public service ads in magazines, featuring a photograph of a pregnant woman smoking, over the caption "Some People Commit Child Abuse Before Their Child Is Even Born." And in 1988, a Tennessee judge ruled that a mother could not smoke around her four-year-old: "Exposing a child whose lungs are still growing to passive smoke is another form of child abuse" (*Saratogian* 1988).

- *Explicit Rock Lyrics.* Susan Baker—a leader of the Parents' Music Resource Center—stated, "I really believe that the escalation of violence and sexuality [in lyrics] is a form of child abuse" (Cocks 1985, 71).

- *Circumcision.* An article in the *Journal of Family Law* argued that circumcision might fall within the legal definition of child abuse (Brigman 1984).

- *Illicit Drugs.* Former U.S. Senator Paula Hawkins (1986, 76) linked drug abuse and child abuse: "I can think of few forms of child exploitation or neglect that are worse than encouraging a youngster to use an addictive substance."

- *Inadequate Social Services.* In "The Community as Child Abuser," Harold Lewis, D.S.W. (1986, 18), charged that, in a community where social services are insufficient to protect children, "the community, which tolerates these conditions and chooses not to remedy them, is neglecting and abusing the children."

- *Federal Communications Policy.* When President Reagan pocketvetoed a bill requiring television stations to offer responsible children's programming, Action for Children's Television denounced the move as "another example of the ideological child abuse prevalent in the Reagan administration" (Harris 1988, 35).

- *Courtroom Procedures.* A pediatrician described courtroom procedures for examining child witnesses in sexual abuse cases as "an increasingly prevalent form of child abuse" (Crewdson 1988, 195).

- *Religious Fervor.* When an eleven-year-old boy attracted media attention for "disruptive preaching," his father's religious instruction—warning the boy that he was a sinner bound for hell—was

76

described as "child abuse" and "torturing his own child" (Salter 1988, G1).

- *Child Snatching.* A "parental kidnaping victim-parent" declared: "Parental kidnaping is the highest degree of child abuse" (U.S. Senate 1986, 263).
- *Traditional Sex-Role Socialization.* "Dr. Joyce Brothers, the television pop-psychologist, . . . says she was abused when she was told, as a child, that little boys did some things better than little girls" (Elshtain 1985, 24).

No doubt other claims-makers made analogous arguments, that this or that behavior "was really a form of child abuse." Still others, promoting causes less clearly linked to endangered children, adopted similar rhetoric. Mothers Against Drunk Driving offers the most familiar example; although several of MADD's first members were parents whose children had been killed by drunk drivers, the organization quickly established a much broader base, while retaining the original name (Reinarmann 1988). Similarly, media coverage typified Parents of Murdered Children's campaign against criminal violence with examples of young children who had been killed, although many POMC members had lost adult children (Leerhsen 1982). In fact, movements of and for adults increasingly characterized their members as former child-victims—"incest survivors" or "adult children of alcoholics" (Rudy 1988). The powerful image of the threatened child began to be adopted by many different causes.[6]

Clearly, it became possible to label almost anything that might harm children as child abuse. And anyone could play this game; scholars, activists, and institutions all chose to locate additional issues within the ever-growing domain of child abuse. Why? Because domain expansion offered advantages over trying to establish a new social problem through claims-making.

DOMAIN EXPANSION IN THE NATURAL HISTORY OF SOCIAL PROBLEMS

The child-abuse label evolved to cover an ever-broader domain. Originally used to describe parents' physical brutality against small children, the term came to encompass neglect, sexual contacts, and—

77

at least according to some claimants—a miscellany of other acts that might harm young people. Child abuse no longer is limited to parents and guardians; noncustodial relatives, teachers, medical personnel, and even other children are considered potential offenders. And, where once the victims were thought to be those too young to explain what had happened to them, now older children and adolescents are viewed as at risk.

Other social problems show a similar process of domain expansion. We can, for instance, trace the genealogy of claims-making about discrimination over the last thirty years. The struggle against segregation in the South evolved into a broader campaign for civil rights, which in turn spawned movements aimed at discrimination against women, homosexuals, and the disabled. And each of these movements expanded its focus to address a growing range of issues. Thus, within the women's movement, initial claims about rape led to more specific attacks on marital rape and date rape, and the definition of sexual harassment became broader and more subtle. There is nothing unique in the way other claims-makers built on the foundation of successful child-abuse claims.

What accounts for the choice of domain expansion as a claims-making tactic? Why don't claims-makers simply campaign to bring new issues to public attention? Very simply, domain expansion offers a competitive advantage in the social problems marketplace.

Claims-makers find themselves in competition, bidding for public awareness, official recognition, program funding, and other scarce resources. Successful claimants capture attention; their problems become the subjects of congressional hearings, *Time* cover stories, Oprah Winfrey programs, and Ann Landers columns. These successes have consequences. Because only a limited number of problems can receive attention, each successful campaign means that other, competing claims will fail to gain recognition. Moreover, successful claims-makers find themselves at a competitive advantage for the future. They are now insiders with experience, visibility, certified expertise, contacts with reporters and policymakers—resources that can make future campaigns easier.

Claims-making's competitive nature accounts for the frequency of domain expansion. Domain expansion occurs in the natural history of many social problems.[7] This process can be divided into three stages.

Stage 1: Initial Claims-making. The greatest challenges claims-makers face occur when they are outsiders, at the beginning of their first campaigns. Novice claimants find themselves competing against insiders from institutionalized pressure groups who are promoting well-established social problems and have substantial funding, professional staffs, and links to key officials.

Of course, new claims have one potential advantage—novelty. A fresh topic stands a better chance of receiving attention than one that has become all too familiar. But new claims risk being too novel. Thus Schoenfeld, Meier, and Griffin (1979) argue that environmental activists in the 1960s found it difficult to get press coverage because their claims did not seem to belong to any of the standard reporters' beats. It helps if a new claim fits one of the standard frames used to classify social problems.

Dramatic claims also have a competitive advantage. Life-and-death issues, tales of heroism or villainy, and stories that compel emotional reactions are more likely to gain attention, sympathy, and action. This is where typification becomes important. Using compelling examples to illustrate a social problem shapes our reaction, not just to those cases, but to the larger problem they supposedly represent. Often, of course, these examples can be coupled with statistics showing that the problem affects large numbers of people, that it is spreading rapidly, and so on.

It is easy to see why the initial claims about the battered-child syndrome were successful. It was a novel topic, one which had received minimal attention for several decades. Presented as a medical discovery—a new disease—it fit neatly into a standard frame for news and public policy. And, typified by stories of parents' extraordinary physical brutality against tiny children, it was the stuff of high drama.

This example suggests that typification plays a central role in initial claims-making. New claims cannot afford to be abstract. Claims-makers must use examples to show what the problem is about and why it must receive attention. These examples are probably more important than the definition assigned to the problem, although initially claimants may find it useful to define the problem narrowly and include only the most dramatic cases.

Stage 2: Validation. Claims-makers succeed when others validate the claims, giving attention to the problem, expressing concern about it, and establishing policies to deal with it. Validation depends upon various contingencies: how many (and which) people claims-makers reach; how effectively the claims are presented; the number and nature of competing claims; and so on.

In the case of child abuse, validation came relatively quickly following the publication of "The Battered-Child Syndrome." The research report appeared in a leading medical journal, major magazines repeated the claims, and new state and federal laws were drafted and passed (Nelson 1984). We might speculate that this success reflected, in part, fortunate timing. Within a few years, Americans would become preoccupied with civil rights, Vietnam, the War on Poverty, crime in the streets, ghetto riots, student demonstrations, drug use, and other social issues. Had the first reports of the battered-child syndrome come a few years later, claimants might have found it more difficult to command attention. As it was, child abuse had the advantage of being established and relatively uncontroversial at a time when debates raged over other issues. The consensus regarding child abuse—the fact that it was what Nelson (1984) calls a valence issue—made it easier to validate the early claims.

Stage 3: Domain Expansion. Once the initial claims have been validated, they offer a foundation upon which additional claims can be constructed. These new claims can be linked to the established problem: claims-makers present the new, peripheral issues as "another form of," "essentially the same as," "the moral equivalent of," or "equally damaging as" the original, core problem. In turn, some of these claims are validated, offering an even broader foundation for further rounds of claims-making.

Insiders already associated with a problem provide an important source for domain expansion. If the initial claims-making led to new social policies, there may be a growing sector of activists, professionals, and officials specializing in the problem. Domain expansion fosters growth in this sector in several ways. Problem specialists may come into contact with cases that had previously gone unnoticed. Thus, once people began talking about battered children, many additional cases surfaced. If there are no adequate records predating the initial claims, then the records kept by problem specialists will seem to reveal an extraordinary increase in the problem's incidence. In the case of child abuse, a series of new laws compelled an expanding array of professionals to report instances of suspected abuse, insuring that the incidence of reported child abuse would increase. Of course, as the problem's "true magnitude" stands revealed, specialists can justify requests for additional resources (more personnel, new laws, and so on), beginning a cycle in which increases in the problem's reported incidence can justify increased resources which then can foster increased reports.

Their growing caseloads also bring specialists into contact with the fringes of the problem's domain. Thus early child-abuse professionals found themselves encountering neglect and sexual abuse. Not only do these specialists come to know something about these fringe phenomena, but they have incentives to expand the borders of their domain. For one thing, expanding the domain is a standard way of advancing within the specialists' world; the individual who identifies a new form of child abuse stands to gain recognition and other rewards. Moreover, an expanded domain calls for greater resources and authority, giving the specialists a competitive advantage in the struggle over social policy turf. And, of course, successful claims-makers have experience in constructing social problems; with their contacts and their grasp of the claims-making process, they stand a better chance of success in the social problems marketplace. For all these reasons, domain expansion becomes an attractive tactic for insiders.

But domain expansion also offers advantages for outsiders— would-be claims-makers from outside the specialists' world. Established social problems serve as common reference points: there is general agreement that something must be done about X. Outsiders may try to link their cause to that consensus. Thus Susan Baker

81

(quoted above) says, in effect: Since we all agree that child abuse is bad, if we can only recognize violent rock lyrics as a form of child abuse, then we should be able to agree that something needs to be done about rock lyrics. Piggybacking new claims upon established social problems increases the chances that the new claims will receive validation.

This suggests that domain expansion depends upon consensus. Because the child-victim offered a powerful symbol around which people could rally, and because the public had validated claims about child abuse, claims-makers sought to expand the problem's domain. This consensus suggests comparisons with other contemporary social movements. Lofland (1988) contrasts traditional social movements grounded in politics and conflict with what he calls "consensus movements," which combine "fresh-minded and attitudinal idealism and emotional joy and good will" with "ideas that are vacuously consensual and embracing and seemingly devised to mute obdurate differences in objective social interests." Although the rhetoric of claims about threats to children often emphasized consensus (e.g., children as priceless innocents), the new child-saving movements do not fit Lofland's description. The constructions of the various threats to children featured villains, with children menaced by brutal parents, pedophiles, pimps, Satanists, and other deviants. Thus, the threats-to-children crusaders call upon those emotions—"jaded cynicism, anger, and fear"—which Lofland argues characterize traditional conflict movements. These claims-makers often describe themselves as children's advocates, but they are also opponents—attacking those who would harm children.

As campaigns to expand the domain of child abuse increased, some of this consensus collapsed. The battered children at the problem's core remained uncontroversial, and claims-makers continued to use physical brutality against very young children to typify child abuse. But as the problem's boundaries expanded, controversy grew. Consider spanking. Some conservatives worried that broader definitions of child abuse made no distinction between brutality and corporal punishment. Their concerns were well founded. Many child advocates saw spanking as abusive: "Most [sexual-abuse] prevention programs . . . quietly but directly advance the view that spanking is a form of child abuse" (Gilbert 1988, 8); and Gelles and Straus (1988, 55) define "routine spankings, normal pushings, and seemingly harmless grabbings . . . as part of the problem of intimate violence." Corporal punishment in schools came under attack (Corrigan 1989). Other critics warned that strict reporting laws and broad definitions of abuse led to flooding child-protection agencies with trivial complaints, making it more likely that serious cases would be overlooked (Besharov 1985). And a debate arose among youth workers over whether police ought to detain runaways (a central recommendation of the U.S. Attorney General's Advisory Board on Missing Children [1986] and the President's Child Safety Partnership [1987]) or whether the youths should have better access to noncustodial shelters and other social services (U.S. House 1986b, 141–81).

Claims-making about sexual abuse became particularly controversial. Crusaders warned that traditional criminal justice procedures made it unreasonably difficult to convict offenders, and they promoted various reforms. Their critics countered that evidence in sexual-abuse cases was often weak—that therapists "brainwashed" children until they confirmed that they had been abused, that physicians' examinations for signs of abuse relied on ambiguous evidence, that arrangements to protect child witnesses (e.g., letting the child testify from another room via television) violated the principle that defendants should be able to confront their accusers, and so on. After most of the charges were dropped in the two most heavily publicized ritual-abuse cases (Jordan, Minnesota, and the McMartin Preschool), critics argued that the prosecutors' failure either to find physical evidence or to gain confessions to corroborate the children's charges indicated that the cases were without substance, while those disappointed by the prosecutors' decisions not to pursue the cases warned that the lack of corroborating evidence merely revealed the strength of the abusers' conspiracies. Charges of sexual abuse became an increasing common element in child custody disputes, and critics warned that these charges were often without foundation. Organized opposition in the form of Victims of Child Abuse Laws (VOCAL) emerged, and the press began questioning the basis for sexual abuse prosecutions (see Crewdson 1988; Eberle and Eberle 1986; Gorney 1988; Hechler 1988; Mawyer 1987; Nathan 1987, 1988).

Even child pornography—long the target of unanimous condemnation—became the focus of debate, with critics charging that postal inspectors used entrapment to make arrests: "The largest child-pornography ring in the United States is run by the Government" (Stanley 1988, 41).

In fact, there was surprisingly little agreement about the definition of sexual abuse. A 1985 national survey conducted by the *Los Angeles Times* gave a series of vignettes (see table 4.1) and asked respondents whether they would define each vignette as "an example of child sexual abuse, or an example of something else."[8] Table 4.1 reveals a con-

TABLE 4.1   PUBLIC DEFINITIONS OF CHILD SEXUAL ABUSE

Vignette	Percent Defining as Child Sexual Abuse
Fourteen-year-old boy seduced by fourteen-year-old girl	11
Fourteen-year-old boy seduced by eighteen-year-old girl	54
Fourteen-year-old boy seduced by twenty-two-year-old woman	85
Fourteen-year-old girl seduced by fourteen-year-old boy	16
Fourteen-year-old girl seduced by eighteen-year-old boy	61
Fourteen-year-old girl seduced by twenty-two-year-old man	88
Fourteen-year-old boy used physical force to have sex with fourteen-year-old girl	65
Fourteen-year-old girl seduced twenty-four-year-old man	34
Fourteen-year-old girl consented to have sex with twenty-four-year-old man	43
Twenty-two-year-old man had sex with fourteen-year-old prostitute	40
Adult made indecent remarks or sexual suggestions to a child	77
Adult took photographs of a naked child	88
Adult exposed himself or herself to a child	83

Source: Los Angeles Times National Poll, July 1985. *n* = 2,627

84

siderable range, extending from vignettes that only a small minority saw as sexual abuse to some that the great majority viewed as abusive. After a decade of public discussion and domain expansion, the boundaries of sexual abuse remained unclear.

In short, while there might be consensus about the core images of child abuse, the problem's periphery featured active debates over what should be considered abuse. Domain expansion efforts are not always validated. This is not surprising. Claimants usually begin their campaigns by typifying problems in especially compelling ways. Domain expansion extends the claims into more controversial territory, often challenging existing arrangements. But a society which circumcizes most male children is unlikely to reverse itself and validate a claim that circumcision is really child abuse. There are limits to how far any domain can expand.

THE THEORETICAL IMPORTANCE OF FAILED CLAIMS

Typification and domain expansion are part of the rhetoric of claims-making. Throughout the evolution of child-abuse rhetoric, whenever claims received validation, claims-makers sought to expand the problem's domain. At least until very recently, their efforts had considerable success, and successful claims-making, in turn, encouraged further domain expansion. Success also attracts analysts. Virtually all of the recent case studies of social problems construction concern successful claims-making campaigns. Failed efforts have received little attention, and, worse, analysts often take both success and failure for granted.

The prevalence of domain expansion reminds us of the reality of failure. A relatively large share of successful claims-making seems to build upon earlier successes. Presumably claims-makers choose domain expansion because many independent claims fail: they are addressed to the wrong audiences, or ineptly formulated, or encounter too much opposition, or whatever. Even the histories of successful claims commonly reveal records of earlier failures—unsuccessful efforts to mobilize concern around an issue that would later receive

85

validation. We need to know a good deal more about these failures if we are to understand how and why other problems are constructed successfully.

For outsider claims-makers, success usually depends upon getting the mass media to repeat claims. Validation first requires that claims are heard, and the media are obviously able to disseminate the claimants' messages. Getting the media's attention and shaping their treatment of claims therefore become key issues.

5

Network News as Secondary Claims

Amos Cummings of the old *New York Sun* is said to have been the first newspaperman to see the news value of the lost child. When children were lost their parents, the neighbors, and the police were involved, but it was not supposed to concern the general public. No one thought it was appropriate to the public prints, since they were devoted to the interests of politics and business and paid no attention to the domestic sphere.
—Helen MacGill Hughes, *News and the Human Interest Story*
(1940, 200–1)

Most claims-making begins with victims, activists, or experts—people with special knowledge about some social condition—making claims about that condition. These *primary claims-makers* must compete within the social problems marketplace, bidding for public awareness, official recognition, program funding, and other scarce resources (Hilgartner and Bosk 1988). The competitors bring very different resources to this marketplace; lone crusaders find themselves competing against institutionalized pressure groups.

Press coverage helps make claims-makers competitive. For outsider claims-makers with limited resources, media attention may be essential. By reporting claims, the press can bring an issue to general public attention, generating concern about the problem and support for the claimants' cause. Policymakers are more likely to act on claims if the public seems responsive to news stories about a problem, and, of course, the press itself may urge policymakers to action. This means that claims-makers compete for press coverage less as an end in itself than for the advantages it offers in the social problems marketplace.

87

Coverage should not be taken for granted. The press cannot cover all claims; it has limited resources, e.g., the minutes of broadcast time or column inches available for news, the number of reporters, the available budget, and so on. These set the media's "carrying capacity"—in effect, the number of social problems that can be covered (Hilgartner and Bosk 1988). Since not all claims can receive coverage, the press makes choices, placing a premium upon novelty, drama, and other elements it values in stories. The result is the "issue-attention cycle," in which social problems rise to public attention then drop from sight (Downs 1972). In turn, crusaders struggle to get—and hold—press attention. Those with enough money may hire a professional staff with press contacts, knowledge of how to organize press kits and press conferences, and experience in packaging claims for the press (McCarthy and Zald 1977).

But the press does more than repeat primary claims and transmit them to a larger audience. Research on the news media shows that a variety of conventions and constraints shape the construction of news stories (Altheide 1976; Epstein 1973; Gans 1979; Molotch and Lester 1974; Tuchman 1978). The press does not merely transmit claims; it translates and transforms them. The media are *secondary claims-makers*.

Secondary claims are efforts to persuade, subject to rhetorical analysis. While journalists invoke standards of objectivity and speak of reporting rather than persuading, every news story seeks to offer a convincing construction of reality. Most often, stories about claims-making accept the essential accuracy of the primary claims being reported. But reporting about primary claims is shaped by the conventions and constraints of news work, and the rhetoric of the resulting secondary claims deserves examination. After all, most claims reach most people through the mediation of the press, not through direct contacts with primary claims-makers.

Certainly, claims-making about threats to children needed press coverage. There were no large social movements promoting these issues. Most campaigns featured a relatively small number of primary claims-makers—usually a combination of interested professionals, parents and others with personal experience with the problem, and

88

political figures. These claimants depended on the press—and television in particular—to bring their claims to wide public attention (Eliasoph 1986; Fritz and Altheide 1987; Gentry 1988).

CHILD-VICTIMS ON THE NETWORK NEWS

Television news plays an important role in contemporary claims-makers' attempts to gain recognition. Many people believe that television is an especially influential medium, that televised images are more compelling than written words. Although television presents claims through dramatic programs, talk shows, public service announcements, and local newscasts, discussions of television's influence usually focus on the network news. In part, this reflects the news programs' large audience; on a typical evening, each of the three network broadcasts draws tens of millions of viewers—far more people than read any newspaper. Moreover, surveys find that substantial proportions of the population express trust in newscasters and report getting most of their news from television broadcasts.[1]

Time is scarce on network news broadcasts. Minus the minutes set aside for commercials, each broadcast lasts only about twenty-three minutes. Not surprisingly, the focus is "hard news"—the president, other political stories, foreign affairs, and economic news. Most studies of the network news concern coverage of major hard news stories (see Barkin and Gurevitch 1987; Hallin 1986; Hallin and Mancini 1984; Hart et al. 1984; Nimmo and Combs 1985).

The nature of most claims-making precludes intensive coverage on the network news. The networks focus on established political leaders, while claims-makers are often outsiders, trying to make their voices heard. Although a few social issues find a central place on the national political agenda (e.g., civil rights in the early 1960s), most remain on the periphery. On a typical day, there is little chance that a story about claims-makers will appear among the hard news items that lead the broadcast, but claims-makers may be the subject of an occasional feature story later in the program. Such coverage is infrequent; months or years may pass between features on a particular topic, and, when coverage does occur, the story must be compressed within two to five minutes. Still, because the broadcasts have a huge audience—and because the very fact of being chosen for the network news helps validate claims—this coverage presumably plays an important role in claims-making campaigns.

In order to identify network news stories about threats to children, I examined *Television News Index and Abstracts* for 1969–87.[2] I found 646 relevant stories (with a total broadcast time of twenty hours, fifty-four minutes). Spread over nineteen years, this coverage reflects modest concern with threats to children. In comparison, Barkin and Gurevitch (1987) identified 253 network news stories about unemployment broadcast during the first six months of 1983. The networks covered threats to children, but never with comparable intensity.

Coverage of threats to children rose in the 1980s. The network news averaged 16.4 stories per year during 1970–80 but 66.6 stories per year during 1981–87. If we eliminate all stories focusing on particular cases (e.g., the Atlanta child murders or the recovery of a particular missing child), the shift is equally striking. Stories with a broader focus (e.g., runaways or campaigns to fingerprint children) averaged 4.2 per year during 1970–80 and 16.6 per year during 1981–87.

The remainder of this chapter focuses on a sample of 101 network news stories about threats to children. I selected nearly six hours of videotaped stories, trying to pick broadly focused pieces that discussed particular social problems as a whole. (The 101 stories include the vast majority of pieces judged to meet this criterion.) Relatively few of these stories involved hard news—reports on something that had happened the day of the broadcast. Most were feature stories. They tended to be relatively long as television news stories go; all but 13 ran at least two minutes (median = 3:00). Few of the stories appeared early in the program, among the major hard news pieces; four-fifths began at least ten minutes into the broadcast. Nearly three-quarters appeared during 1981–87. Studying these stories reveals some rhetorical characteristics of network news coverage and, more broadly, secondary claims-making in the press.

FORM

Television news means to entertain, as well as inform. Each program is a construction of remarkable complexity; shots of the anchorperson are interspersed with more than a dozen stories from around the world, each featuring an array of still photos, filmed action, interviews, charts, and the like.[3] The camera shifts every few seconds, demanding that the viewer watch the screen.

But this complexity exists within a framework of conventions. Network news stories are assembled from a standard set of elements; exceptions are extraordinarily rare. The anchorperson's introduction is followed by the story itself. Typically, stories contain a combination of filmed action accompanied by a soundtrack or the correspondent's narration, interviews with individuals, charts and other graphics, and "stand-upper" shots of the correspondent in the story's setting.

Interviews: Who Talks

There were only two "tell stories" (the anchorperson merely reads an item) in my sample; ninety-nine pieces featured film, and all but two of these had a correspondent narrating the story. Typically, the correspondent's comments alternated with remarks from individuals connected with the story. These remarks might be part of the filmed action (e.g., President Reagan speaks at a ceremony), but more often they came from on-camera interviews. New speakers appeared at a rate of more than one per minute; feature stories routinely presented remarks from five to ten individuals.[4]

Building a story around the remarks of several people has a rhetorical effect. It suggests that the correspondent has gone to some lengths to get the story. Stories often include interviews with people who might be expected to have very different perspectives on the topic. Thus an ABC (16 November 1984) piece on the prevention of child molesting featured interviews with two child molesters, a father and two mothers of victims, a psychologist, a physician, a deputy sheriff, an instructor and a student in a children's self-defense class, and a former incest victim. The range of voices implies that the coverage is thorough and balanced.

TABLE 5.1   SOURCES SHOWN SPEAKING ON NETWORK NEWS STORIES
ABOUT THREATS TO CHILDREN, 1969–87

Type of Source	ABC (%)	CBS (%)	NBC (%)	Total (%)	
Federal Officials	14	10	2	8	
Other Officials	10	12	9	10	} 44
Other Authorities	24	22	30	26	
Child-Victims	16	7	19	14	} 29
Victims' Relatives	16	16	13	15	
Alleged Offenders	9	12	12	11	} 11
Others—Adults	9	14	10	11	} 16
Others—Children	2	7	6	5	
Total	100	100	100	100	
(Total Sources)	(140)	(121)	(147)	(408)	

Notes: An individual who spoke more than once in the same story was counted as one source. However, an individual who appeared in two stories was counted twice.

Who speaks in these stories? Table 5.1 shows that the 101 stories contained 408 appearances by sources. The networks turned most frequently to authorities of one sort or another.[5] Government officials—either representatives of the federal government (e.g., the president, senators, FBI agents) or state or local officials (e.g., judges, prosecutors, police officers)—accounted for over one-fifth of the sources on ABC and CBS, and for one-tenth of those on NBC.[6] When we combine these officials with other experts (e.g., physicians, psychologists, lawyers, activists, and others with special knowledge), the proportion of authorities being quoted is between 40 and 50 percent on all three networks. Victims—both children (usually interviewed as adults, recalling their childhood experiences) and parents or grandparents of child-victims—were the next largest group of sources. Alleged offenders—a category that included both acknowledged deviants and people who had been accused (and sometimes acquitted)—accounted for about one-tenth of the interviews. A residual category of others—most often interviews with ordinary people expressing concern about threats to children—outnumbered the alleged offenders; on CBS, these others even outnumbered victims.

These different sources conveyed three sorts of information. First, interviews with authorities offered information about threats to children: this is what happens and why; this is what needs to be done; and so on. Most authorities represented the federal government, the criminal justice system, or some sort of therapeutic perspective. Relatively few experts approached their topics from academic perspectives; there were, for instance, only two sources identified as sociologists. Second, both victims and alleged offenders personalized the issues behind threats to children. Individuals testified about their first-hand experiences, often revealing deep hurt. Feature stories about threats to children often drew their emotional impact from these interviews. Finally, interviews with ordinary people brought the issues home: a small boy tries to explain why he has been fingerprinted; a mother worries about protecting her children. In this way, a problem that has been intellectualized by experts and personalized by victims becomes the viewer's own.

Scenes and Settings: The Role of Film

With some exceptions (e.g., stories that conclude by returning to the studio, where the anchorperson makes a closing comment or, on rare occasions, conducts a live interview with an authority), everything that follows the introduction to a story is filmed. Audiences are thought to prefer film to the "talking heads" of newscasters, and some critics argue that television news distorts its priorities by favoring filmed stories over important pieces for which no good film is available (Epstein 1973; Gans 1979). Certainly the networks are unlikely to broadcast feature stories without compelling film.

The stories about threats to children used various sorts of film in addition to interviews. Some was *stock footage* (e.g., shots of streetwalkers), identifiable because the same shots appeared in more than one story. Several stories about self-protection programs for children showed *clips* from educational films used in the programs. One correspondent filmed a *simulated event* (a runaway calling a national hotline and leaving a message for her family), coupled with an explicit statement that this was a simulation. Four stories featured reporters staging *exposes*, entering the sexual underworld to talk with

93

pimps or pornographers while filming with hidden cameras. But most film showed events. Usually these were what Boorstin (1964) calls *"pseudo-events"*—occasions such as press conferences, demonstrations, and bill-signing ceremonies—staged, at least in part, in order to get press coverage, or other *predictable moments* a film crew could be assigned to cover, such as congressional hearings, prisoners being escorted through the halls of justice, or courtroom activity. Most remaining film showed *mundane scenes*—police on patrol, young people walking on city sidewalks, and so on. Finally, of course, many stories featured *stand-uppers*—shots of the correspondent speaking from a setting related to the story (e.g., outside a congressional hearing room or in front of a pornographic theater).

Like interviews, these filmed scenes and the settings within which they occur serve rhetorical purposes. They command our attention; camera angles, like sound bites, shift every few seconds. They also can be edited to tell stories. For instance, one NBC (28 November 1974) piece on runaways contained a brief sequence of six shots: while the correspondent talks about young people running away to big cities, we see a bus pull into a depot, young people climbing down from a bus, two shots of adolescents riding an escalator, a boy at a fast-food counter, and, finally, a shot of young people in the depot lobby. Sometimes the story presents drama (as when witnesses and congressional investigators exchange sharp words) or contrast (clips of interviews with child molesters interspersed with clips of therapists or victims of molestation). And, of course, all film demonstrates the efforts of the network news. When we see several interviews or scenes, often shot in different states or even, on occasion, in other countries, we know that the networks are on the job, hunting down the news. Stories that combine several types of film seem more convincing.

CONTENT

The form for network news stories, then, is predictable: an anchorperson's introduction followed by a mix of filmed events, interviews, and shots of the correspondent in the field. This standard form reflects the technology and economics of news gathering, the deadlines within which stories must be assembled, and the limited broadcast time available. We might imagine that the stories' contents would show far more variation. But conventions also govern content. Feature stories about threats to children adopted a fairly standard formula. Brief introductions located the stories within the larger context of the day's news. Most stories concentrated on describing the problem, devoting less attention to either explanations or solutions.

Introducing the Story

Consider the first network news story about the missing-children problem. On 3 June 1981 ABC's Frank Reynolds began:

> Democratic Representative Paul Simon of Illinois today introduced a bill to make use of the FBI's computer system to trace missing children. [video: Simon speaking before the House] Simon told the House children who disappear are not now given the same nationwide police attention as stolen automobiles or jewelry. [video: Reynolds with a background logo—a drawing of a child's face] Tonight Al Dale begins a special assignment series on the problem—or tragedy—of missing children. Here is his first report.

Almost all network news stories start this way. Backed by a logo (and less often a bit of film), the anchorperson's speech pegs the story and identifies its theme.

The logo symbolizes and classifies the story to come. Typically, logos for stories about threats to children featured the expressionless face of a child or two, as well as a brief title—"Child Abuse" or "Missing Children." The logos, like the stories that followed, personalized these issues; these were stories of individual children, not faceless statistics. The networks reuse logos in a deliberate attempt to give stories continuity (Westin 1982, 49–51). Occasionally a logo may misclassify a story, as when ABC's initial story on the McMartin Preschool (where staff members allegedly had molested dozens of children) used the logo "Pornography Ring."

A peg makes a story topical. Hard news reports appear immediately after the event. In theory, feature stories—like ABC's series on missing children—can run any day when there is enough time available for the piece. In practice, newscasters prefer to broadcast these stories when there is a peg, such as Simon's House speech (Gans 1979, 168–69). Pegging a story turns a feature into news.

Simon's speech placed missing children on the federal government's agenda. Evidence of federal concern—congressional hearings, reports by federal commissions, the president signing bills, and so on—was a common peg for pieces about threats to children. But local events, such as arrests, child-fingerprinting programs, or the recovery of a particular missing child, also served as pegs. In some cases, pegs had little to do with what followed:

> Once one of the secret horrors of our society, child abuse is now getting a great deal of public attention. In Nashville last night, for instance, country and western star Hank Snow organized a sell-out concert to aid victims of child abuse, after disclosing that he had been seriously mistreated as a youngster. As Fred Francis reports on Segment 3 tonight, child abuse remains a major problem, but there is encouraging progress (NBC, 1 September 1978).

The Nashville peg had little to do with the story, which concerned a Denver program to predict which parents might become abusers.

Pegs need not be events. Some stories were pegged to descriptions of a problem, identifying new problems or noting trends: "There's evidence of another kind of crime [child pornography], showing up all over the country and just now getting some attention" (ABC, 14 February 1977). Virtually all the stories I examined were pegged, either to descriptions of this sort or, more often, to particular events. Other, potentially adequate pegs seldom appeared. For instance, demonstrations or press conferences by activists almost never served as pegs. Such claimants sometimes appeared in the stories themselves, but the events that qualified as pegs were actions by officials, not outsiders. Thus pegs helped frame threats to children within a context of official action.[7]

Pegs can, but need not, reinforce a story's theme. Thus both Simon's speech and the ABC story which followed depicted missing children as a neglected issue, but Hank Snow's concert was unrelated to the Denver child-abuse program. Newscasters do, however, try to organize their stories around coherent themes, giving order to the events they report (Altheide 1976; Epstein 1973; Gans 1979). The introduction usually gives the viewer a sense of where the story is headed.

Description

Feature stories about threats to children emphasized description. Typical features identified a previously neglected problem, used examples to typify it, assessed its magnitude, and presented experts' views of the problem. However, because network news stories must be short, the resulting descriptions inevitably simplified—and distorted—their topics.

Typification. Following the anchorperson's introduction, the story begins with pictures, accompanied by the correspondent's voice:

> [video: woman walking through an airport] Cynthia Vargas is an American. She flew to Mexico City one day last week in hopes of seeing her two children for the first time since August, when her Mexican husband took them away from their home in San Francisco. [video: woman runs up to girl, hugs her, and cries] She found her four-year-old daughter walking with the maid. (CBS, 20 January 1987)

Network news features routinely begin with particular individuals, chosen to illustrate the report's topic. As the example suggests, these openings can be quite powerful, forcing an emotional response from viewers.[8] In a few seconds, we are forced to acknowledge that international child snatching is a serious problem.

In addition to grabbing our attention, these openings serve another important rhetorical purpose: they typify the problem. We see a mother's reunion with her daughter; for the rest of the story, those particular people become our touchstone, our referent. We interpret the abstract statistics, causal models, and expert prescriptions that follow in terms of how the problem has been typified.

Network news stories almost inevitably typified threats to children in ways that emphasized the seriousness of the threat. The examples featured young children: battered infants and preschoolers, prepubescent victims of child pornographers or kidnappers. Young children are dependent, vulnerable, innocent; their exploitation is especially horrifying. Similarly, the examples portrayed especially serious cases: children who died from battering, missing children who permanently disappeared, or other child-victims whose respectable, protected backgrounds proved no defense (e.g., adolescent prostitutes who had run away from upper-middle-class homes). Such examples add drama to the newscast, but they distort the nature of the problem being portrayed.

In addition to describing what a problem is, typifications may suggest what it is not. Thus some stories explicitly denied that a problem was concentrated within a particular segment of the social structure: "[Incest shows] no apparent relationship with race, economics, or social class" (NBC, 7 February 1981). If there is no pattern to risk, then no child is safe. In several interviews, parents of victimized children warned that it could happen to anyone.

Statistics. Having typified a problem, feature stories usually assess its magnitude. Estimates are commonplace:

> More than a million children are victimized each year by abuse or neglect. . . . Authorities say that as many as three thousand children were killed by their own parents last year in America (CBS, 1 December 1975).

> It's been estimated that as many as two million American youngsters are involved in the fast-growing, multi-million-dollar child-pornography business (NBC, 23 May 1977).

> Police say the number of boy prostitutes may be as high as a million (NBC, 25 October 1977).

These estimates usually originate with primary claims-makers, and the network news reports these figures with care, doing what Tuchman (1978, 90) calls "relocating facticity." That is, the stories attribute the statistics to some source (e.g., "authorities say"), insuring that the correspondent's statement is correct. It remains true that authorities gave statistic X, even if X is a wild exaggeration.

Consensus and Conflict. Child saving is an honored tradition in American reform, just as the hero rescuing a threatened child is a standard plot in our popular culture. We understand that children—in fact as well as fiction—are vulnerable; they need protection. Threats to children fall within Hallin's Sphere of Consensus, where "journalists do not feel compelled either to present opposing views or to remain disinterested observers" (1986, 117). Network news anchorpersons were not afraid to locate their topics within this sphere: "Here is something on which there can be no disagreement: the horror of young people selling their bodies, on the streets and in the film studios" (ABC, 9 July 1986).

Analysts argue that television news builds its stories around conflict and drama (Hart et al. 1984). Relatively little open conflict appeared in network news stories about threats to children, and the clashes that did occur sometimes seemed tangential (e.g., a member of the House berating a witness for bringing examples of child pornography to a hearing, where they might be filmed for television [ABC, 23 May 1977]). Of course, the real conflict was off-camera. Stories about threats to children were stories about society's struggle with deviants—child beaters, incestuous fathers, pimps, and pornographers. The typification of human tragedy, the frightening statistics, and the explicit statements of consensus made these stories about moral conflict.

Occasionally, there were schisms within this consensus. Early stories acknowledged, but minimized, counterclaims that the missing-children threat had been exaggerated and distorted: "Some say these statistics are overblown and create undue alarm among parents and children, but that's hard to convince the grandmother of Danny Davis, who was four when he was grabbed in a grocery store thirteen months ago" (NBC, 10 December 1982). But once the *Denver Post* ran its 1985 "numbers gap" articles, this issue entered Hallin's (1986) Sphere of Legitimate Controversy. All three networks dealt with this controversy, although they did not adopt the same approach.

CBS addressed the issue first. Two weeks before the *Post* published its first piece, CBS (29 April 1985) broadcast a missing-children story that included an interview with an Indianapolis prosecutor, who estimated that there were one hundred to two hundred stranger-abductions per year. A few weeks later, another story focused on the controversy. The final portions of that story deserve examination:

> CORRESPONDENT STEVE YOUNG: Dealing in actual cases, not estimates, the FBI says the number of children kidnapped by strangers last year was sixty-seven. The National Center for Missing and Exploited Children [NCMEC] says that's wrong, the number could range up to twenty thousand because it counts incidents not reported to the FBI, such as children kidnapped for less than twenty-four hours. But state and local police in California, Colorado, New York, and Massachusetts say the twenty-thousand figure for stranger-abductions just doesn't add up.
>
> [Interview with a representative of the Massachusetts State Police, who says none of the nineteen hundred missing children in their files were abducted by strangers. Excerpt from a commercial for a warning buzzer that can be attached to a child's clothing.]
>
> WILLIAM TREANOR (American Youth Work Center): [9] I think the market for virtually all those products would collapse tomorrow if the American public understood that out of sixty-two-and-a-half million people under the age of eighteen, less than a hundred are abducted every year by a stranger.
>
> YOUNG: Exact figures are in dispute, but child abduction by strangers appears relatively rare (CBS, 2 July 1985).

The CBS story was careful, yet critical. It spoke of contacting several official agencies and tried to show how these sources might reach such different figures. The correspondent's conclusion hedges but suggests that the NCMEC's critics are correct. A third story, pegged to an announcement that there would be a federal study to measure the incidence of missing children, included interviews with Treanor and the director of a shelter for runaways; it, too, concluded that stranger-abductions were relatively rare (CBS, 14 December 1985).[10] In contrast, ABC ignored the debate until 8 April 1986, when

Peter Jennings introduced a piece of child fingerprinting with "some clarification of what we're talking about." Noting that "there is still no real centralization of information," he offered statistics from "our fact file," citing the NCMEC as the source. The center, he said, estimated that four thousand to twenty thousand children were "abducted by total strangers" each year. Four months later, ABC covered a hearing by a House subcommittee about the conflicting estimates.[11] ABC's treatment of this hearing is worth quoting at length:

ANCHOR TOM JARRIEL: Two years ago, the government established a national center to cope with what was then thought to be a growing crisis. Now, however, some people are asking questions. Was the problem exaggerated, and were many parents and their children victims of scare tactics?

[The story's first moments do not address the conflict, then correspondent Bettina Gregory returns to the story's theme.]

GREGORY: In fact, there are serious questions whether the problem of missing children is nearly as big as the nation has been led to believe. . . . Today at a congressional hearing, the director of the center drastically revised the estimate of kidnapped children. [video and audio clip: NCMEC director Jay Howell estimates four thousand to twenty thousand cases] The national center and its numbers came under blistering attack.

WILLIAM TREANOR: Instead of meaningful diagnosis, the center has aided and abetted one of the most outrageous scare campaigns in modern American history.

GREGORY: The center has staunch defenders. . . . [video and audio clip of a mother of a murdered child acknowledging the center's help] But Congressmen questioned officers of the national center about the numbers since the FBI says it has only about seventy open cases of child kidnappings on its books.

BUD MEREDITH (NCMEC): These are little, helpless citizens of this country, being held hostage, scared to death, totally unable to take care of themselves, being held hostage by terrorists. What is it with the "only," sir?

101

GREGORY: The Justice Department is working on a study to determine how many children are kidnapped each year, but today they said that study won't be completed until 1988 (ABC, 4 August 1986).

This is what passes for debate in a forum of ten-second sound bites. ABC did make the debate the theme of a story, and it did quote one critic (Treanor). However, the missing-children movement, as embodied in the NCMEC, received most of the attention—and got the last word. ABC, apparently uncomfortable with the controversy, ended its story with the suggestion that the Department of Justice study would resolve the matter.

On this particular issue, then, the networks presented very different interpretations of one legitimate controversy. ABC acknowledged the debate but affirmed the NCMEC's perspective. In contrast, CBS and NBC challenged the NCMEC's figures—and their reports complemented other stories about exaggerated fears of threats to children. But this difference in coverage was exceptional, reflecting efforts to probe beneath an issue's surface. The networks rarely subjected primary claims-making to such critical examination; instead, their coverage emphasized the deviant nature of threats to children, about which there could be only consensus.

Explanation

By devoting most of their time to describing threats to children, network news stories inevitably shortchanged explanation.[12] How can we understand threats to children? Why do deviants menace children? If these dangers are indeed increasing, what accounts for the rise? While these questions might seem obvious and important, the network news gave them little attention. The explanations that did appear were simplistic: deviants usually emerged as flawed individuals, less often as conspirators, and only rarely as people affected by social forces.

Individualization. When network news stories tried to account for threats to children, they normally located the cause of deviance in the individual offender. In this model, "child beaters" or "abusive parents" strike out when frustrated or pressured. Molesters prey on children because they care unable to maintain satisfactory adult relationships but can control children. Runaways cannot resolve their conflicts with their parents or cannot cope with ongoing abuse.

These accounts may seem unexceptional. Both everyday and academic explanations of deviance often refer to qualities of the offender. Specific theories about feeble-mindedness, body types, and extra chromosomes may have been discredited, but the general model endures. In late twentieth-century America, it often takes the form of medicalization, where deviance is seen as a disease, exhibiting symptoms and requiring treatment by medical authorities (Conrad and Schneider 1980). Network news stories regularly medicalized threats to children; many of the experts interviewed were physicians, clinical psychologists, or psychiatrists. These experts presumably had the therapeutic tools needed to help offenders and their victims.[13]

Correspondents frequently reported that threats to children bore no relationship to race, class, or other social variables. Only one characteristic—childhood experiences—set offenders apart: child beaters had been beaten; molesters had been molested; and so on. This claim had rhetorical appeal. It could be endorsed by a wide range of experts, because the mechanism by which one generation transmitted abuse to the next was not specified. The claim was consistent with almost any biological, psychological, or sociological theory of social life. At the same time, the claim defined a population at risk; viewers who had not been abused as children could tell themselves that they were unlikely to become offenders. And, of course, the claim demanded action. Coping with this cycle of abuse required a dual effort: offenders needed therapy to help them understand and control their impulses; and victims needed treatment both to repair the damage done to them and to keep them from harming the next generation.

Conspiracies. While the network news held individual pathology responsible for most threats to children, the stories assigned some deviants a more sinister role. Stories about molestation, runaways, and child pornography often alluded to a sexual underground where deviants conspired to exploit children. For most of the twentieth cen-

103

tury, psychiatrists have portrayed the child molester as a socially isolated, sexual psychopath (Freedman 1987; Weisberg 1984). Contrast that image with the description from an early interview with a prosecutor in the McMartin Preschool case:

> There's a substructure of people who are child molesters, and through that substructure of life, that underworld of life, people can be brought in, recruited for the school, and people who do not come from that subculture or that particular underworld would not be hired for that school (NBC, 19 April 1984).

Or consider the discovery of the "Minnesota Connection": one correspondent described pimps coming to Minneapolis "from across the country to recruit the young women whose bodies they hope to sell in large cities across America" (ABC, 22 November 1977). Similarly, stories on child pornography ignored molesters with collections of personal snapshots, describing instead a highly lucrative market for commercial pornography, while several correspondents ended pieces on runaways by filming stand-uppers in front of pornographic theaters.

The fear that organized conspiracies of deviants exploit children is central to contemporary concerns about threats to children. Comparisons between some of the earlier stories in my sample and more recent stories on the same topics reveal very different interpretations. For instance, NBC (7 July 1974; 11 November 1974) broadcast two stories on runaways (set respectively in Berkeley and Haight-Ashbury) which included shots of street musicians playing guitars—perhaps the last pieces to link runaways to the hippies. In contrast, stories from the 1980s implied that runaways usually sold far less innocent services on the streets. Two early stories described terrible, inexplicable instances of young children who had disappeared; one correspondent puzzled that "no ransom demand was ever received" (CBS, 18 June 1975; NBC, 19 May 1974). Eight years later, after the construction of the missing-children problem, the mother of a vanished child had a ready explanation: "I basically feel that our son was kidnapped, and more than likely it was for some very organized effort for profit" (NBC, 12 October 1983).

Conspiratorial interpretations may have peaked with the construction of ritual abuse as a social problem. Several child-molestation cases involving multiple arrests with dozens of individual charges (e.g., the McMartin Preschool and Jordan, Minnesota, cases) brought allegations of widespread ritual perversion, featuring Satanic worship, human sacrifice, and commercialized child pornography. The network news showed some restraint in covering these stories. For instance, none of the stories in my sample about the McMartin or Jordan cases spoke of Satanism. But the initial stories repeated without challenge claims that organized conspiracies were at work.[14]

The focus on conspiratorial explanations is another form of typification. Research suggests that highly organized exploitation of children is very rare. Sex rings typically consist of a single adult and a few children, and most child pornography involves pictures taken for the offender's personal collection or traded with other collectors (A. Burgess 1984), but the network news invariably emphasized commercial child pornography. And, while research shows that young prostitutes typically choose that way of life (see Luckenbill 1985; Weisberg 1985), the network news spoke of runaways forced into vice by violent, manipulative pimps. The child molesters who appeared in the networks' own interviews were clearly social isolates, yet claims about molestation conspiracies were repeated without challenge. Just as the stories chose the most serious cases to typify threats to children, the emphasis on conspiracies of deviants revealed a preference for the most dramatic explanations.

Absent Social Forces. Because network news stories devote little time to explanations, they leave unanswered questions. Take one correspondent's explanation for child abuse: "For a parent who feels unloved and alone, a minor incident—anything from spilled milk to a crying child—can trigger a violent outburst leading to child abuse" (ABC, 8 December 1976). But, assuming this account is correct, why do some parents feel unloved and alone? In several interviews, runaways spoke of conflicts with parents, of feeling pressured; later in the same stories, correspondents insisted that a million or more children run away each year. Do a million children experience similar pressures? Why? What features of the social construction of adolescence create this problem? Such questions are never addressed. The network news simultaneously argues that threats to children are commonplace and that the causes of those threats may be found in the characters of flawed individuals.

Network news stories rarely display a sociological imagination. The only important exception to this rule suggests why the stories usually ignore the role of social forces. Several stories about child abuse stated that hard times fostered abuse, that unemployment increased the pressures on adults, leading to frustration and family violence. The problem with such accounts is that they contradict the typification that child abuse bears no relationship to race, class, and other social variables. If threats to children display patterns, and if poor children run far greater risks, then threats to children may no longer seem to be everyone's problem, to be the viewer's problem. The more distance between the viewer and the story, the poorer the story's chances for breaking into the network news. Just as domestic disasters command far more coverage than disasters in foreign countries (Adams 1986), threats that can strike anyone—including people just like us—make better stories than threats to someone else.

Solutions

Having described and explained threats to children, the network news offered solutions. In several cases, a particular solution provided the story's theme: "In New York, there is a new program to teach children how to avoid becoming victims of [child molestation]" (CBS, 12 November 1983). This particular story concerned self-defense classes for children, but other pieces focused on shelters and toll-free hotlines for runaways, child-fingerprinting campaigns, programs to distribute pictures of missing children on milk cartons and utility bills, child-safety programs in schools, and assorted therapy and self-help groups for child-victims, their families, and offenders.

The network news did not oversell these solutions. Most reports concluded that the program in question was promising, that it might help—or at least could not hurt. Nor were the solutions inappropriate, given the stories' individualistic explanations for threats to children. If troubled people cause threats to children, then therapy seems an appropriate response.

106

The networks' solutions reflected their descriptions and explanations and had some of the same limitations. In focusing on rare but extremely serious cases, the stories ignored less serious albeit more common problems. In child abuse, for instance, cases of severe battering are relatively uncommon; most reports involve neglect, not abuse. Yet none of the news stories described programs for dealing with neglect. And while runaways account for the lion's share of missing children, few stories about missing-children programs concerned runaways.

By locating the cause of threats to children in flawed individuals, the networks precluded any discussion of ideologically charged solutions to these problems. If problems reveal no social patterns, then they have no social causes and require no social solutions. That children raised in poverty are more likely to be victimized, that changing family structures contribute to sexual abuse, that adolescents hold social and economic positions that make running away and entering prostitution relatively attractive options to some—these are explanations that exist outside the network news. As a consequence, the news had no need to explore liberal or radical solutions focused on changing class, family structure, or other social arrangements. Similarly, the networks ignored conservative social analyses linking threats to children to moral breakdown, declining religious and parental authority, or government interference in private lives. The solutions covered in the news stories said nothing about moral instruction, strengthening family ties, or reducing governmental authority. Explaining threats to children in terms of individual deviants meant that the solutions to these problems could be nonideological and, therefore, noncontroversial—just another element in the consensual vision promoted by the network news.

SECONDARY CLAIMS AND THE NEWS MEDIA

In sum, network news stories reveal patterns of form and content. The stories' form combines a set of standard elements—including logo, peg, theme, interviews, and film—in ways that serve to make each story entertaining and credible. The stories' content concentrates on description, while explanations and solutions receive less attention. Overall, stories aim to persuade the viewer, to demonstrate both that a story is newsworthy, meeting the standards of objective, factual broadcast journalism, and that the problem under examination warrants public concern and can be resolved without fundamental changes in American society.

Claims undergo a transformation when they are reconstructed as news. Reporters repeat—and revise—what they hear from their sources. For instance, the network news stories about particular threats to children featured the same elements: they personalized the topic, using frightening, dramatic examples to typify the problem; they emphasized the problem's scope and societal consensus about the threat; they explained the problem in terms of individual failings or conspiracies of deviants; and they recommended individualistic solutions. Such secondary claims are selective, repeating some, but not all, primary claims. Although criticism of the FBI's reluctance to investigate missing-children cases was a central theme in the early rhetoric of missing-children crusaders, such criticism was muted in network news coverage of the issue.

Inevitably, network news stories distort the problems they explore. The conventions of news work impose severe constraints on prospective stories: it must be possible to tell the story in a few minutes; the story must be important enough and visually interesting enough to be selected over competing topics; the story should be told in a way that protects the network from criticism and legal action; and so on. Moreover, the reporters who cover these stories rarely have more than a superficial grasp of the issues. Few social problems become important enough to have correspondents assigned to the topic on an ongoing basis. Television news crews are assigned to major hard news stories (e.g., presidential campaigns), institutions (e.g., the Senate), or localities (e.g., Los Angeles). To the degree that these assignments bring the crew into contact with a small circle of reliable sources (e.g., candidates, their press secretaries, and campaign strategists), coverage may get beneath the surface. But feature stories about social problems currently deemed newsworthy do not produce such contacts—or such coverage. Finally, critics often argue that an implicit ideology governs the network news, that stories are grounded in a taken-for-granted consensual perspective (Gans 1979; Hallin 1986). For all of these reasons, network news stories rarely succeed as social analysis.

Such constraints shape the news media's coverage of claims-making. For instance, some sociologists have criticized the press's treatment of the missing-children problem. Fritz and Altheide (1987, 481) argue that television news in particular created an "informational context" for interpreting the issue: "This imagery reinforced a crisis definition of the problem, and interactively joined public and private discourse by labeling all major varieties of absent children as 'missing,' and by implication, abducted." [15] For Eliasoph (1986, 9), press coverage succeeded in bringing missing children to public attention but failed to provide a coherent interpretive frame:

> The news media are crucial tailors, then, of the moral fashion show that passes for the American public sphere. . . . Newsmakers always need new, decontextualized fragments to wrap up in their invisible cloak of common sense. They cannot continue to harp on a single issue, no matter how worthwhile.

Headley (1986) criticizes the Atlanta press for downplaying racial and class issues in covering that city's child murders. Such analyses characterize press coverage as ideologically constrained sensationalism. But while press coverage may be especially visible and influential, claims-making rarely begins with the media; the press usually covers other, primary claims-makers, and its coverage is a secondary claim.

What impact does press coverage have on the larger claims-making process? The network news stories about threats to children suggest that there are patterns in the ways the press transforms claims. Primary claims-makers who already occupy positions of authority (e.g., U.S. senators) have easier access to press coverage than outsiders. The network news favors stories that can be pegged, and officials' actions offer ready-made pegs (e.g., introducing a bill in Congress or holding a congressional hearing). In contrast, activists' demonstrations and press conferences rarely serve as pegs. Activists' efforts only become pegs when the claimants, rather than their claims, have become the issue. Thus, Gitlin (1980) argues that the coverage generated by the antiwar movement tended to treat the movement itself, rather than the war, as the issue.

Still, primary claims-makers almost always welcome network news coverage because it can confer prestige, legitimacy, and a place on the national agenda. And while they cannot control the coverage they receive, they can help shape it. Like public relations people, many activists have come to realize that understanding and attending to the press's needs tend to produce more favorable coverage. They know that the press favors stories that promise to capture the audience's attention—stories with elements of novelty and drama (and, for television, stories that lend themselves to filming). So long as claims feature these elements, there seems to be little respectable opposition, and the claims-makers avoid becoming the issue, there is a good chance that the press will repeat the claims it hears without challenge. We might imagine that the press is most likely to repeat—and primary claims-makers seeking coverage will therefore try to present—claims that are constructed so that the problem seems newsworthy, the problem seems serious, there seems to be a consensus among knowledgeable, interested parties, and the explanations and solutions offered are consistent with existing institutional authority (see Hilgartner and Bosk 1988). Of course, radical demands for social change cannot meet the latter two criteria, and it is not then surprising that radical claims rarely surface on the network news.

The evening network news is an especially competitive arena for primary claims-makers. Feature stories are short, and they receive a relatively small share of the limited broadcast time. Newspapers and news magazines cover a broader range of stories in greater depth (Gans 1979; Tuchman 1978). And television's other news programs—the networks' morning shows (e.g., "Today" [Hallin 1987]), prime-time magazine-style shows (e.g., "60 Minutes" [Campbell 1987]), and the syndicated talk shows (e.g., "Donahue")—devote substantial time to covering claims-makers. In particular, weekday talk shows typically address a different topic each day, and a large proportion of those programs are hour-long discussions of social problems. The growing number of competing talk shows means that

110

this television genre has a considerable, ongoing appetite for new claims, that at least this one arena has a very large carrying capacity.

But talk shows rarely figure in discussions of the press's role in social problems construction. Most analysts focus on the prestige press, particularly the print media. This focus may make sense when discussing how economic or foreign policy is made, but public attitudes toward social problems draw on a broader range of sources. These include the less prestigious elements within the press—and even those media presentations usually viewed as "mere entertainment."

6

Popular Culture as Secondary Claims

"We never used to have this kind of stuff—this child abuse, this incest, and stuff—when I was younger. You never heard a thing about it, now it's all you *do* hear." It struck me as the most fatheaded comment I'd heard in months . . . but I'd learned the hard way never to express such opinions to outstate sheriffs, especially when I'm in their counties.
—William J. Reynolds, *Moving Targets* (1986, 298)

Most discussions of the mass media's role in social problems construction focus exclusively on the press. But social issues also become subjects for movies, popular novels, episodes of television series, and the other forms of commercial entertainment we call popular culture. Like the news, popular culture presents secondary claims. Just as the press reshapes primary claims to fit the constraints of news stories, each popular cultural form makes its own demands on subject matter. Popular culture genres treat social issues—when those issues can be made to fit the genres' dramatic conventions.

Secondary claims-making in popular culture has become more common since the 1960s, when popular culture came under attack for being irrelevant. Some genres are notorious for finding plot lines in claims-making, e.g., "disease-of-the-week" TV movies. Such secondary claims receive praise for being educational as well as entertaining; defenders of soap operas routinely refer to the valuable information conveyed through plots about social problems. However, like the news, popular culture offers a constricted interpretation of these issues. Popular culture rarely presents social problems as products of a flawed social system; rather, the emphasis is on individ-

112

ual problems—troubled interpersonal relationships or deviant individuals (Cantor and Pingree 1983; Gitlin 1983).

In plots featuring troubled families or menacing deviants, threats to children are easily portrayed as individual problems, and they have received extensive treatment in recent popular culture. Most of this chapter concerns two popular fiction genres—horror and crime novels—chosen for their frequent secondary claims about threats to children. However, during the 1980s, threats to children also were the topic of at least one hit song ("Dear Mr. Jesus"), several movies (e.g., *The Golden Child, The Lost Boys, Nuts, Big*), many docudramas and made-for-television movies (e.g., "Something About Amelia," "Adam," "Adam: His Song Continues"), and countless episodes of television series (e.g., a stranger-abduction on "St. Elsewhere," a child snatching on "L.A. Law"). Horror and crime fiction, then, merely offer a place to begin.

The two genres treat threats to children differently.[1] Horror fiction seems to have discovered threats to children earlier, and the theme was, for a time, central to the genre. Because most of these books feature monsters, demonic forces, and other supernatural elements, their treatment of threats to children as social issues is oblique. The monster that devours children stands for other threats that we imagine actually endanger children. These books turn upon our fears, but only after making them fantastic. In contrast, the crime novel seems grounded in realism; resorting to supernatural explanations breaks the genre's rules. The detective confronts incest, child abuse, molestation, and abduction—the subjects of primary claims-making. However, detective stories also transform these claims, because the genre's conventions demand that evil be portrayed in particular ways.

HORROR FICTION: THE CHILD-MONSTER AND THE CHILD MENACED

It is easy to forget how recently horror fiction acquired its mass audience. Until the late 1960s, horror novels had marginal status, even among popular culture genres. Bookstores stocked *Frankenstein* and *Dracula* among the classics and kept the odd volume by Robert

113

Bloch or Richard Matheson with the science fiction; only gothic romances merited a section of their own.

The turning point came with the 1967 publication of Ira Levin's *Rosemary's Baby*. The book became a best seller in both hardcover and paperback, although *Publishers Weekly* had trouble classifying it, calling it a "mystery" and a "suspense novel." It took four years for horror to return to the hardcover best-seller list; in 1971, both *The Exorcist* and *The Other* were among the year's ten best-selling novels.[2] Stephen King's first novel, *Carrie*, appeared in 1974; *'Salem's Lot* (1975), *The Shining* (1977), and *The Dead Zone* (1979—King's first book to rank among the year's ten best-selling hardcover novels) followed. Significantly, a child is at the center of each of these books (except *The Dead Zone*, in which a child's murder is a key event).

These were not the first appearances of children in horror fiction. Many of the Grimm brothers' stories feature mistreated children (Tatar 1987), and several horror motifs involving children have long histories (Bussing 1987). But the key novels in establishing horror's mass audience were *all* about children. Today, a visit to a bookstore's horror section—and most bookstores have one—makes it evident that children remain important to the genre. One paperback cover after another juxtaposes a child or a toy with a skull, a scythe, or some other symbol of death.

Some obvious questions arise. Why did horror fiction find its mass audience when it did, in the late 1960s and early 1970s? And why did the plots that achieved mass popularity focus on children? One early answer by a horror aficionado speaks of an "almost obligatory theme[:] . . . children involved in murder and possession[,] . . . which, by outraging maternal instincts, appeals to the predominently matronly audience for best-selling novels" (Daniels 1975, 225). A discussion of the place of children in Stephen King's work concludes that "they are victimized by the inherited sins of an older world. . . . The children are constrained to pay for the mistakes of their elders" (Magistrale 1985, 49), while a critic of recent horror films argues that "the connection of the Family to Horror has become overwhelmingly consistent: the psychotic/schizophrenic, the Antichrist and the child-monster are all shown as products of the family, whether the family itself is regarded as guilty . . . or innocent" (Wood 1978, 28). But such explanations fail to account for the timing of horror's rise from marginality to popularity. The genre was not new; why did horror—and particularly plots featuring children—suddenly become popular?

In addressing this question, we need to consider how horror novels depict children. Bussing (1987) suggests that children play three roles in horror fiction: the child-monster, the evil innocent, and the child-victim. All three motifs depend upon the dramatic contrast between evil and childhood innocence.

Child-monsters and evil innocents embody both innocence and evil within a single child. Child-monsters are evil by nature; for instance, *Rosemary's Baby* is the Antichrist. In contrast, evil innocents have the sympathetic qualities (i.e., goodness and innocence) of children, but they are possessed by evil forces (*The Exorcist*) or provoked into destructive actions (*Carrie*). The contradiction of the evil child provides a foundation for several plots. Unable to think the unthinkable, adults may fail to discover the child-monster; the young murderess in John Saul's *Suffer the Children* (1977) goes undetected. More commonly, the theme is parental ambivalence toward the evil child. Rosemary knows she has given birth to the Antichrist, but she can't help feeling a mother's love toward the infant. Similarly, parents in Stephen King's *'Salem's Lot* and *Pet Sematary* (1983) surrender themselves to children who have become vampires and zombies, respectively. Other books feature sympathetic children who release their destructive supernatural powers after extended provocations by fellow students (*Carrie*), government agents (King's *Firestarter* [1980]), or a sadistic foster brother (Wood's *Amy Girl* [1987]). Each of these plots finds dramatic tension in the apparently innocent child's evil powers.

In contrast, novels about child-victims focus on children's vulnerability; here the child is not the monster, but the monster's target. Often the parents' failings contribute to the child's vulnerability. The parents of Stephen King's child-victims are abusive (*The Shining, It* [1986]), caught up in their own careers or extramarital affairs (*Cujo* [1981]), or neglectful and unwilling to confront what menaces the children (*It*). In Dan Greenburg's *The Nanny* (1987), the parents bring a demon into their home to care for their infant. But the evil that menaces the child-victim need not be supernatural. V. C. Andrews's *Flowers in the Attic* (1979) features a sadistic grandmother who abuses the four Dollanganger children while their mother refuses to protect them; later books in the five-volume tale trace the family's legacy of incest and hatred. Not all books about child-victims dwell on parental shortcomings; some focus more narrowly on the threat to children. Thus Stephen Gresham's *Midnight Boy* (1987) concerns a demented ex-POW killing boys on a junior-high-school basketball team, while *Baby Grand* (1987), by Joseph E. Keene and William W. Johnstone, features a spectre that periodically kidnaps, rapes, and tortures teenaged girls.

In general, the early horror novels that attracted a mass audience to the genre—*Rosemary's Baby, The Exorcist, The Other,* and *Carrie*—concerned child-monsters or evil innocents, while books from the late 1970s and the 1980s tend to feature child-victims. This pattern may reflect changing concerns about children in the larger society.

The link between the horror novel's rise and the social crises of the late 1960s and early 1970s seems obvious. It is probably inevitable that parents worry as their children mature, hoping, trying to insure that the child will choose to follow the parent's path. The 1960s seemed to offer an especially imposing array of temptations for the young, including drugs, sexual freedom, and political radicalism. None of these temptations were new, but they were more accessible; suddenly it seemed that every college campus featured pot, the pill, and political activism. Pundits worried, not just about friction between parents and their children, but about the gulf between society and its youth—the generation gap. Something horrible was happening to the next generation; they were turning their backs on the old ways. They were becoming monsters.

The new horror novels spoke to these fears. The stories usually were told from the parent's perspective, not the child's, and parental ambivalence toward evil children was an important motif. The novels captured a larger sense of ambivalence toward the young, ambivalence that combined love, repugnance toward—or at least suspicion of—the new youth culture, and fear that the untainted young might become corrupted. And where the young rebels blamed adults for the world's ills, these early horror novels located evil in the child:

> Almost as if to relieve ourselves of the responsibility, we claimed it was not Dr. Spock but the Devil that made them act that way. . . . We also like to pretend that the child can be an independent perpetrator of evil, simply a mistake—no fault of our own (Twitchell 1985, 300).

Parents' ambivalence toward the youth culture was mirrored in young people's reluctance to join the adult world. The generation that boasted "we are not our parents" was in no hurry to have children; from 1970 to 1976, the number of live births per 1,000 population fell from 18.4 to 14.6. The youth culture had its own ambivalence toward children, and stories about child-monsters complemented young people's decisions to delay starting families.[3]

Similarly, horror fiction's more recent focus on child-victims corresponds to contemporary fears about threats to children. These fears gave the youth culture new meaning. By the late 1970s, the problem of teenage runaways was being reconstructed; where earlier discussions had portrayed runaways as youthful rebels, off to Haight-Ashbury to join the hippies, now they were seen as fodder for the vice industry, innocents from the Midwest, turned out as prostitutes on New York's "Minnesota Strip." And there seemed to be other horrible consequences of sexual freedom—child pornography, incest, child molestation, and AIDS. Public attention now focused on horrible things that happened to children, rather than horrible things children did.[4]

The novels about child-victims revealed ambivalent attitudes toward families in general, and parents in particular. The books' fictional parents want to protect their children, but they cannot. Often they are self-centered and neglect their responsibilities; sometimes they are simply powerless in the face of evil. If the child-monster books blamed children, the child-victim tales found the parents guilty. This message matched primary claims about society's failure to confront various threats to children. Other claims-makers warned that would-be parents might be unable to have children, that an "infertility epidemic" threatened those who had postponed starting

117

families (Scritchfield 1989). Children now seemed endangered, perhaps unattainable, and horror fiction's shift from child-monsters to child-victims reflected the public's changing concerns.

Even horror novels depicting fantastic, supernatural evils often portray, or at least mention, realistic threats to children. *Suffer the Children* opens with a father raping and murdering his daughter; her spirit later possesses the novel's central character—a girl who murders other children. Some of Stephen King's characters explicitly compare supernatural threats to real mass murders of children in Houston (*'Salem's Lot*) and Atlanta (*It*), and the children in his books experience realistic episodes of physical and sexual abuse (*Carrie, The Shining, It*). Other realistic dangers may be portrayed indirectly; at least one critic argues that the adult-child relationships in *'Salem's Lot* and *Firestarter* are sexual (Reino 1988), and it is possible to make analogous interpretations for other novels (e.g., Straub's *Ghost Story* [1979]). Similarly, realism intrudes when the 1987 movie *The Lost Boys* reveals what happens to missing children—they become vampires. Thus the reader's knowledge of and fears about real threats to children frame even the most fantastic horror tales.

DETECTIVE FICTION: CONSPIRACIES, CORRUPTION, AND KIDS

While horror fiction is overtly fantastic, the detective novel pretends to realism. Book jackets promise readers believable stories and gritty authenticity. Plots often follow the headlines, and the villains have real-world counterparts; recent novels match their heroes against terrorists, serial killers, corporate criminals, and other contemporary deviants. Not surprisingly, plots centered around threats to children have become common.[5]

Most often, the threatened children are older—teenaged prostitutes or other adolescents—than the preadolescents common in horror fiction. The horror novel uses the young child to represent goodness and innocence; the child-victim usually recognizes that an evil force is at work, even when adults fail to see that something is wrong. In contrast, the adolescents in detective fiction are past innocence; they are old enough to know better. These stories tend to have an erotic charge, with the plot revolving around a teenager's sexual corruption.

Some detective heroes seem to specialize in these cases, confronting threats to children throughout the volumes in their series. Jonathan Kellerman's hero, Alex Delaware, is a child psychologist whose investigations center around molestation, incest, or other child abuse. Andrew Vachss's Burke is an ex-convict matched against Manhattan's sexual underworld of molestation, child pornography, and child prostitution. Benjamin M. Schutz's Leo Haggerty is a private eye whose first two cases concerned missing children. (It is worth noting that all three of these authors give biographical statements that suggest they may bring special knowledge to their books: Kellerman and Schutz are clinical psychologists, while Vachss is "an attorney in private practice, specializing in juvenile justice and child abuse cases.")[6] While Robert B. Parker's popular detective, Spenser, has dealt with a broader range of cases, troubled adolescents figure prominently in the series; five books concern child snatching, runaways, or juvenile prostitutes.

Parker's series offers a place to begin, because the Spenser books were among the first to address these issues. Like the plots in horror fiction, these reveal changing attitudes and emerging fears about threats to children. In *God Save the Child* (1974), the second book in the series, Spenser investigates a runaway boy's disappearance. Although Spenser learns that the boy is in a homosexual relationship with a bodybuilder, the book does not view it as a predatory relationship; Spenser sees the boy's self-indulgent mother as the cause of the problem. Spenser's next case, *Mortal Stakes* (1975), involves tracing the background of a young woman. He discovers that she had a troubled adolescence—"kind of restless, not really happy, . . . first girl in class to smoke, the first to drink, the first to try pot" (66)—and, at eighteen, ran away from her indifferent, impoverished family. Her boyfriend took her to New York, where she became a prostitute. *Early Autumn* (1981) begins with Spenser finding a boy who has been snatched by his father; the novel portrays both parents as self-indulgent and unconcerned with their son's well-being.

In these early books, the children make their own decisions; both runaways are sexually involved with young adults, but neither rela-

119

tionship is described as predatory. In contrast, the young people in Parker's later books are more clearly victims. In *Ceremony* (1982), it first seems that a rebellious high-school senior left her upper-middle-class suburban home to become a prostitute, but the plot unfolds to reveal that a state education official with ties to organized crime has been recruiting troubled adolescents for the vice industry. Spenser encounters another young prostitute in *Taming a Sea-Horse* (1986)—an incest victim whose father sold her to a brothel when she was fourteen. In short, Parker's treatment of runaways and adolescent prostitutes has evolved; while the early books portray young people whose unhappy family circumstances lead them to choose deviance, the youths in the more recent books are pawns of sinister conspiracies.

Several other recent books feature conspiracies of child molesters, child pornographers, or other deviants involved in systematic exploitation of children. Jonathan Kellerman's *When the Bough Breaks* (1985) concerns a conspiracy of wealthy men who molest the residents of a large facility for retarded children. Faye Kellerman's *Sacred and Profane* (1987) has the Loving Grandpas—"a club of old, rich pervs who beat up runaways" (274). In Robert Campbell's *In La-La Land We Trust* (1986), wealthy men have a more informal arrangement:

> [Warsaw] had a taste for little boys between the ages of nine and ten, some of whom he got from Walter Cape when Cape was done with them. . . . Quon had a taste for little boys between the ages of ten and eleven. . . . Warsaw passed the children he got from Cape on to Quon. And Quon passed them on. Each pedophile had a taste for children of the age they'd been when they'd had their innocence taken from them. Now they traded in lost innocence, passing the children from hand to hand as they grew older, until they were so old that there was nothing left to them. (29–30)

Vachss's *Flood* (1985) and *Strega* (1987) depict child molesters and child pornographers living in comfortable—even opulent—surroundings. The principal pornographer in *Strega* has a wealthy clientele: "She guarantees all her stuff is so-called collector's items. No reproduction—every picture is one of a kind. . . . She gets a minimum of five thousand dollars a picture. . . . She produces pictures to order" (319). In James N. Frey's *The Long Way to Die* (1987), a human-potential movement leader operates a preschool—actually a front for molestation and child pornography—and supplies a runaway girl as a sexual companion for a powerful politician. Mike Lundy's *Baby Farm* (1987) features a scheme to impregnate kidnapped runaways and sell their babies. In each of these books, conspiracies of wealthy, powerful men are behind child exploitation.[7]

The villains in other books do not conspire with one another, but there are elaborate webs of evildoing. The young woman at the center of Jonathan Kellerman's *Blood Test* (1986) was conceived in an affair between her mother and another man and sexually abused by both her mother's husband (with the mother's knowledge) and her biological father. "Nona had been turned into a weapon, an instrument of vengeance, abused and twisted until sex and rage were inexorably intertwined, then launched and aimed at a world of weak men" (348). She becomes involved with a killer—a young man who was sexually abused by his wealthy father, with his mother's knowledge. Kellerman's *Over the Edge* (1987) features a series of murders of homosexual prostitutes—part of an elaborate plot to frame a young man and deny him his inheritance. Barbara Wilson's *Sisters of the Road* (1986) concerns a young prostitute who is sexually abused by her father as a young child, then by a stepbrother in adolescence; the stepbrother, a former male prostitute, becomes her pimp. Like the conspiracy novels, these books, with their interlocking exploitative relationships, depict worlds in which child-victims are commonplace.[8]

A few villains act alone, but their motives make them terrifying. The serial killer in Benjamin M. Schutz's *Embrace the Wolf* (1985) has kidnapped, tortured, and murdered more than forty children. He confesses his crimes to a priest (in order to torment the priest with his knowledge), explaining:

> But it's those silent parents out there. Those wishes, dreams, so fiercely held that I was after. Think of it. Each death radiating out in a lattice of guilt and rage, fear and sorrow without end. . . . The missing ones like black holes torn in the fabric of families (48)

Here we are given an especially terrible motive. The missing-children movement frequently described the parents' pain, the awful uncertainty about what had happened to their children. And Schutz's villain makes it clear that he deliberately inflicts that pain. Extraordinary evil provides a focus for all these books, evil in the form of great conspiracies, spreading corruption, or the work of terrible, cruel villains.

The serial killer in *Embrace the Wolf* denies having been abused as a child. This sets him apart. Jane Caputi (1987) notes that novels about serial murders routinely depict a male who kills women and that these crimes are blamed on childhood abuse inflicted by the killer's mother. Thus Parker's *Crimson Joy* (1988) ends by revealing that the killer was a victim of mother-son incest. Similarly, revelations of childhood abuse—physical or sexual—are commonplace in detective stories about threats to children. Adolescent prostitutes of both sexes regularly turn out to have been incest victims. Several books feature female characters toward whom the reader is made to feel ambivalent; in addition to those mentioned above, the title character in *Strega*, the young prostitute in Katherine V. Forrest's *Murder at the Nightwood Bar* (1987), the masochist daughter in William J. Reynold's *Moving Targets* (1986), the lesbian film director in S. F. X. Dean's *Nantucket Soap Opera* (1987), and the runaway girls in *The Long Way to Die* and Schutz's *All the Old Bargains* (1987) have both sympathetic and deviant qualities. In each case, the confusion is explained through a revelation—probably intended to be dramatic but, given the frequency with which the scene occurs in these books, in fact trite—that the character was a victim of sexual abuse.[9]

In sum, the detective stories seem to offer realism, a graphic portrait of a corrupt world that we prefer to deny exists:

> The twenty-four-hour news station was saying something about another baby beaten to death; this one in the Bronx. So many cases like that now, all they do is give you a daily body count. (*Strega*, 38).

> The rain had washed all the baby prostitutes and twangy boys, the chicken hawks and queer bashers, the gonifs and petty grifters off the four corners of Hollywood and Vine. (*In La-La Land We Trust*, 11)

Yet the villainy in these books is not realistic. Researchers routinely find that child molesters are socially marginal figures; in detective novels, they become men of wealth, power, and prestige. Most sex rings involve a single adult and several children, not vast conspiracies of pedophiles. Most child pornography is homemade, for personal consumption, rather than the product of highly profitable commercial operations. Inevitably, the detective story makes crime larger than life.

Of course, these outsize villains serve the author's purpose. As the villains become more powerful, more numerous, and more sinister, the hero's stature rises: it takes a great hero to conquer great evil. This must be especially true in novels about threats to children. Children are weak, vulnerable. A villain who harms children commits terrible crimes but need not be a frightening figure. Being strong enough to hurt children does not make a villain worthy of the hero's attention. So authors make their villains powerful, part of vast conspiracies, in order to insure that the books involve sufficiently dramatic conflict.

OTHER GENRES: HEROIC MOTHERS, ADOLESCENT SUPERHEROES, AND STRANGER DANGER

The need to match villains to the hero's powers becomes evident when we compare the treatments of threats to children in detective stories with their treatment in related genres. For instance, several recent novels seem to straddle the border between the crime story and the romance. Written by women, apparently for a largely female audience, these books feature mothers, rather than detectives, as the central characters. The typical heroine is a successful professional, a divorced or widowed mother of a kidnapped child. Although she may be aided by (and even fall in love with) a police detective, it is the mother's unyielding determination that leads to the child's recovery, and the books focus on her fears, inner strength, and efforts in the child's behalf.[10] In Beth Gutcheon's *Still Missing* (1981) and Gloria Murphy's *Bloodties* (1987), the kidnapper remains offstage. In Samantha Chase's *Postmark* (1988), Marjorie Dorner's *Nightmare* (1987), and Murphy's *Nightshade* (1986), the heroine confronts the kidnapper and uses sex, violence, or cunning—stereotypical forms of female power—to defeat him. Often the villain combines several threats to children; Dorner's Jack Ryter deals in child pornography, as well as kidnapping, molesting, and killing children. But these are working-class villains (Ryter works in a factory making toilet seats), not the powerful conspiracies faced by detective heroes (although Murphy's *Nightmare* [1987] concerns a mother who saves her children from an Orwellian government plot). In the conventions of popular culture, any man represents enough power to make the heroine an underdog.

Comic books portray threats to children in a similar fashion.[11] Comics present child molesters, child pornographers, kidnappers, and serial murderers as marginal loners. Conspiracies tend to be limited to organized criminals exploiting runaways—using them to distribute illegal drugs (*New Teen Titans*) or to test new addicting substances (*Peter Parker*). Compared to the detective novels' powerful villains, comic-book villains seem mundane. But these villains do not confront Superman or other adult superheroes. Instead, the heroes in comic-book tales about threats to children are women without superpowers (Lois Lane, Ms. Tree), or adolescent (Cloak and Dagger in *Peter Parker,* the Elementals' Monolith, the New Teen Titans) or child superheroes (Power Pack).

These comic books mean to inform. When reporter Lois Lane investigates the missing-children problem, she interviews the head of a child-search agency, the parents of several missing children, and the director of a shelter for runaways; the resulting dialog becomes a forum for secondary claims-making. The comics present runaways and other child-victims as rounded characters with diverse, credible experiences. In addition to what is conveyed through the story, many of the comics contain editorial matter—two or three pages of fine print—examining the social issues depicted in the stories. The comics' secondary claims include the usual background information (e.g., Lois Lane learns that "there are more than two million children reported missing each year"), but they also offer their young readers a good deal of advice on avoiding or recovering from victimization.

But children—and concerned adults—need not turn to comic books for guidance in these matters. During the 1980s, a small industry emerged, supplying educational materials about child-victims for educators, therapists, and parents. The 1988 catalog for Kidsrights ("Distributors of Materials About Childrens' [sic] Moral and Legal Rights") is eighty pages long and lists hundreds of books, pamphlets, videotapes, and the like. For instance, one can order anatomically correct dolls—used in sexual abuse investigations— "complete with open mouth and separate bendable fingers," in child, adult, and grandparent models for both sexes, with light, Hispanic, Oriental, or dark skin tones.

Other products are marketed directly to parents. By 1986, parents could find fingerprint/identification kits in drugstores, and bookstores carried a variety of child-safety guides designed to help parents protect their children from abduction and sexual abuse. Some of these books addressed worried parents (Hull 1986; Kraizer 1985), but most were meant to be read to or by children. A typical book presents a series of brief stories in which children encounter and get away from troublesome adults. Presumably the books teach children how to behave in such situations.

These self-help books offer their own constructions of threats to children. In particular, they associate strangers with danger. I examined seventy-four stories taken from eight books (Berenstain and Berenstain 1985; Berry 1984; Boegehold 1985; Lenett 1985; Lenett and Barthelme 1986; Meyer 1984; Newman 1985; Wachter 1986); thirty-nine of the stories involved children confronting complete strangers, twenty-nine featured people familiar to the child, and only six concerned family members. Threats, then, come from outside the family and the child's circle of acquaintances—a typification that runs counter to primary claims that child snatchings outnumber stranger-abductions and that most sexual abuse involves family members or people known to the child. Moreover, the stories feature adults who may be trying to lure or trick children (e.g., asking for directions or help finding a lost puppy). These adults rarely use force, nor do they gradually ingratiate themselves to the child. Again, this does not match primary claims that sexual abuse often involves a lengthy seduction (Lanning 1987). Finally, the books seem to promise that children will be able to recognize and control dangerous adults. A father in one story explains, "No stranger can get you if you are careful and stay away from him" (Boegehold 1985, 16); another book assures children: "Once you understand what to watch for and how to act, no nasty stranger should be able to outwit you . . . ever" (Newman 1985, 16—ellipsis in original).

Thus child-safety guides typify threats to children as tricky strangers who can be outwitted and controlled. This is a comforting message: it equates deviance with outsiders and describes the threats as easy to recognize and manage. Like the lone detective who overcomes a powerful conspiracy, the properly trained child can handle stranger danger. Popular culture usually delivers happy endings, and child-safety guides are no exception.

THE JAILBAIT PARADOX

The treatments of threats to children in recent detective fiction, comic books, and child-safety guidebooks self-consciously evoke themes raised by primary claims-makers. By the mid-1980s, child-victims had become stock characters in several popular cultural genres. While each genre's dramatic requirements shaped its depiction of threats to children, they all shared a revulsion toward the deviants who menace children. Popular culture had no trouble depicting kidnappers, child molesters, child pornographers, and serial murderers as evil predators. However, these typifications stand in contrast to other popular cultural images.

For instance, popular culture presents child molesters as predators, adults who sexually abuse and exploit children and adolescents. But other popular culture images celebrate sexual relationships between adolescents and adults. Dozens of recent movies involve the sexual initiation of adolescent boys by older women (e.g., *Risky Business, Class, My Tutor, In the Mood, Vision Quest*) or, less often, sexual relationships between adolescent girls and older men (e.g., *Manhattan, Blame It on Rio, Smooth Talk*). And "jailbait songs" about sexually tempting underage women abound in rock music (Huffman and Huffman 1987). Thus popular culture draws a distinction between molestation—typified as an extremely exploitative activity—and adolescent-adult sexual relationships—which may be shown as romantic, sensual, or comic.

Some claimants charge that such popular cultural images cause or exacerbate the sexual abuse problem. Mawyer (1987, 107) argues that *Playboy, Penthouse,* and *Hustler* cartoons "use young children and their fairy tales to portray youngsters as enjoying sex with other children and with adults and as the objects of extreme violence." Crewdson (1988, 71) suggests the "mythology" created by movies and novels about older women initiating boys into sex makes officials less likely to take seriously complaints about women abusing boys. He also warns that when pedophiles "see advertisements that use suggestive pictures of adolescent and even preadolescent girls to sell clothing, perfume, and shampoo, they might be forgiven for concluding that the same society that condemns them so loudly is speaking in more than one voice" (248–49).

The use of sexualized images of children and adolescents reflects the young audiences that consume some forms of popular culture. Those who go to the movies and listen to popular music tend to be under twenty-five, and popular culture producers concentrate on pleasing their young audience. One result is the proliferation of movies about youths, including such subgenres as mad-slasher pictures, sexual coming-of-age pictures, and teenage vice pictures. The content of youth culture may go unnoticed, thanks to the age segregation within the popular culture audience, until attention is drawn to it. Thus the ready availability of music videos on MTV led to the Parent's Music Resource Center's campaign against "porn rock" (Gore 1987; Gray 1989). Sexualized images of youth attract the youth audience, but claims-makers worry about the effects on the young—and on those inclined to prey upon the young.

In short, popular culture that explicitly addresses threats to children assumes a societal consensus against those who menace children. Society stands united against raincoat-garbed molesters lurking around schoolyards. But other popular cultural images that present children as sex objects reveal an underlying ambivalence within the larger culture (Sonenschein 1984).

POPULAR FICTION AND PUBLIC ISSUES

Two apparently contradictory themes run through studies of popular culture. The first is that popular culture affects its audience. The concern that the experience of consuming popular culture is somehow harmful lies behind much social research and a good many calls for new public policies. The strongest statements of this position warn that popular culture causes deviant behavior: watching televised violence leads to violence, reading crime comics to delinquency, and viewing pornography to sex crimes. Weaker versions identify more subtle shifts in attitudes: people who watch thousands of televised crimes develop an exaggerated fear of crime, and viewers of mad-slasher movies become less sympathetic toward rape victims.

The second theme is that popular culture reflects its audience. In this view, popular culture mirrors society's values. By examining popular cultural texts—using content analysis to skim the surface or psychoanalysis to probe the depths—we can discover what the audience believes. The decline of the Western and the rise of the cop show seem to reveal an audience with new tastes or, at some deeper level, new fantasies.

Of course, the contradiction is apparent, not real. Popular culture influences its audience, and the audience's tastes also shape popular culture's content. Thus far, I have emphasized popular culture as a reflection of the larger social mood, arguing that the emergence of themes about threatened children in horror and detective fiction and other popular cultural genres corresponded to growing public concern about threats to children.

No doubt these popular cultural treatments of threats to children were inspired by primary claims-making campaigns against child pornography, sexual abuse, and the like. Authors may have become aware of ongoing claims-making and decided to incorporate elements from current claims into their plots. But there may have been other processes at work as well. That old pop culture standby—the damsel in distress—has become unfashionable. In an era of feminist sensibilities, the audience may be offended if helpless, vulnerable women have to wait for the rescuing hero to arrive.[12] The advantages of substituting the child-victim for the now controversial woman-victim may have encouraged some novelists to develop plots revolving around threats to children.

But what of popular culture's effects? Does reading horror novels or detective fiction about child-victims have consequences? We have no good way of identifying the people who were exposed to popular culture about threats to children, let alone proving the link between such exposure and their opinions. Still, it seems obvious that popular cultural content becomes part of the mix of influences on people's attitudes. The audience knows that the news is "factual" and that novels are "fictional." But, while they understand that both Derry, Maine, and the monster living below the city are figments of Stephen King's imagination, they may accept that some elements in the story—such as the depiction of the abusive relationship between Beverly and her father—are realistic. This acceptance seems particularly likely for detective fiction, where the reader takes a tour of a largely unfamiliar urban underworld. The reader may be uncertain which elements in this fictional underworld are realistic and which are fictional devices designed to heighten a story's dramatic impact. Some readers may well come away from such books accepting, say, the existence of large, powerful conspiracies to victimize children.

Thus popular culture plays a part in the claims-making process. Like the press, popular culture transforms primary claims into secondary claims that help spread—and shape—awareness of social issues. Of course, the distinction between crusaders' primary claims and the media's secondary claims is overly simple. The media often rely on prior media reports, as when a novelist bases a plot on information taken from news stories. And secondary claims can become raw material for new primary claims: the heavily publicized series of child murders in Atlanta led to the television docudrama "The Atlanta Child Murders," which in turn led the Atlanta press to criticize the program's content (Boles and Davis 1988). Or consider the postmodernist career of John Walsh. The father of a murdered child, Walsh became a leader within the missing-children movement, inspiring two docudramas about his struggles in that movement, then went on to become a television host on "America's Most Wanted"— "part action adventure crime show, part live newscast, and part telethon"—a series that reenacts crimes and invites viewers to help locate the fugitive criminals (Weinstein 1988). Such transformations make the limitations of the distinction between primary and secondary claims obvious.

Similarly, the border blurs between what is factual and what is fictional in popular cultural content. Secondary claims range from self-conscious attempts to disseminate information (e.g., child-safety manuals) to material presented as "pure" entertainment. But even the most informative material reflects the demands of its genre, just as the most entertaining material affects the audience's understanding of social problems.

7

Fears and Folklore

"Okay," he said. "This is a wonderful story about how your
worst nightmares can come true at any moment, with no warning
at all."
"Good," I said. "Let's hear it. I like these stories. They speak to
my deepest fears."
—Hunter S. Thompson, *The Curse of Lono* (1983, 37)

Making claims, even having one's claims repeated in the media, is
not enough. People make claims in order to make a difference; successful claims-makers evoke a response. Most claimants hope to
affect social policy. But while insider claims-makers may go directly
to policymakers, outsider claims-makers usually have to take a more
roundabout path, first gaining media coverage, then shaping public
opinion, before finally influencing policymakers.

A major consequence of secondary claims-making, then, is its
effect on public perceptions of the issue raised by primary claims-
makers. Discussions of the media's powers sometimes assume that
this is a straightforward process: the media pass along a message, and
the public takes that message to heart. Of course, this is too simple.
Generations of researchers have found that the media have far less
influence than is commonly imagined (Gamson 1988). But some
messages are accepted—perhaps because they tell the audience what
it wants to hear.

Clearly claims-making about threats to children found a receptive
public. This chapter and the next examine contemporary public attitudes about threats to children and try to account for their emergence.
Chapter 8 examines a traditional source for sociological data—

131

public opinion polls. This chapter's focus is less conventional—contemporary folklore.

A HOLIDAY FOR SADISTS?

The 1970s witnessed the discovery of a frightening new deviant—the Halloween sadist who gave dangerous, adulterated treats to children. Each year, Halloween's approach brought warnings to parents:

> That plump red apple that Junior gets from a kindly old woman down the block . . . may have a razor blade hidden inside (Klemesrud 1970).

> If this year's Halloween follows form, a few children will return home with something more than an upset tummy: in recent years, several children have died and hundreds have narrowly escaped injury from razor blades, sewing needles and shards of glass purposefully put into their goodies by adults (*Newsweek* 1975).

> It's Halloween again and time to remind you that . . . [s]omebody's child will become violently ill or die after eating poisoned candy or an apple containing a razor blade (Van Buren 1983).

Various institutions responded to the threat: legislatures in California (1971) and New Jersey (1982) passed laws against Halloween sadism; schools trained children to inspect their treats for signs of tampering; merchants promoted the shopping mall as a scene for safe trick-or-treating; hospitals offered to x-ray children's treats; and some communities tried to ban trick-or-treating (Trubo 1974).

By the 1980s, most people apparently took the threat of Halloween sadists for granted. According to press reports, many parents restricted their children's trick-or-treating, examined their treats, or arranged parties or other indoor celebrations (Klemesrud 1972; Thackrey 1982). Doubts about the threat's reality rarely appeared in print, and surveys suggested that concern was widespread. A 1985 ABC News/*Washington Post* poll found that, among respondents who planned to let their children go trick-or-treating, 60 percent reported being afraid of Halloween sadism (ABC News Polling Unit 1985; *USA Today* 1988; Wemhaner and Dodder 1984).

Like other threats to children, Halloween sadism involved random, vicious, unprovoked attacks against small children. The attacks seemed irrational, and the attackers routinely were described as disturbed or insane. These "child-haters" were theorized to "have had a really deprived childhood"; having been "abused as children," they became "frustrated and filled with resentment against the world in general" (Isaacs and Royeton 1982, 69; Klemesrud 1970; Trubo 1974; 28). Law enforcement officials and the media reaffirmed that the threat was real, urging parents to protect their children against sadistic attacks.

As with other threats to children, there are no reliable official statistics on Halloween sadism. Minor incidents, particularly those that do not involve injuries, may never be reported to the police. Cases that are reported may be classified under a wide range of offenses, and there is no centralized effort to compile cases from different jurisdictions. Moreover, the circumstances of the crime—the young victim, the unfamiliar assailant, the difficulty in remembering which treats came from which houses—make it unlikely that offenders will be arrested.

While the true incidence of Halloween sadism cannot be measured, newspaper reports reveal changes in public reaction to the threat. I reviewed the coverage of Halloween sadism in four daily newspapers between 1958 and 1989. I checked all entries under "Halloween" in the *New York Times*'s annual indexes for information about Halloween sadism. The *New York Times Index* proved to be unusually complete, listing even short items of a sentence or two.[1] The published indexes for two other major regional newspapers, the *Chicago Tribune* and the *Los Angeles Times,* were less thorough, so for each year I read both papers' issues for the first three days in November. Finally, I examined all Halloween stories in the files of the *Fresno Bee*. I found stories about seventy-eight alleged incidents of Halloween sadism which included at least the community where the incident occurred and the nature of the attack.[2] Table 7.1 shows the number of incidents reported in each year.

Obviously, the seventy-eight incidents identified through this procedure are not a complete list of cases of Halloween sadism. However, there are several reasons why it is unlikely that I overlooked

133

TABLE 7.1 REPORTED INCIDENTS OF HALLOWEEN SADISM, 1958–89

Year	Number of Incidents	Year	Number of Incidents
1958	0	1974	1
1959	1	1975	2
1960	0	1976	2
1961	0	1977	0
1962	1	1978	0
1963	1	1979	3
1964	3	1980	0
1965	1	1981	0
1966	5	1982	12
1967	4	1983	1
1968	3	1984	0
1969	7	1985	0
1970	10	1986	1
1971	14	1987	0
1972	1	1988	1
1973	4	1989	0

Source: Incidents reported in the *Chicago Tribune, Fresno Bee, Los Angeles Times,* and *New York Times.* All reports specified incident location and type of contamination.

many serious incidents—involving deaths or serious injuries. First, the papers' coverage was national. The seventy-eight reported incidents came from fifteen states and two Canadian provinces; while each of the four newspapers concentrated on incidents in its own region, all reported cases from other regions. All four included at least one case from the South—the only major region without a newspaper in the sample. Second, the seventy-eight reported cases were generally not serious. Injuries were reported in only twenty cases, and only two of these involved deaths. It seems unlikely that newspapers would choose to print accounts of minor incidents while ignoring more serious crimes. This impression is bolstered by the frequent appearance of stories—often from different states—about other Halloween tragedies: children struck by cars and other accidental deaths; people murdered when they opened their doors, expecting trick-or-treaters; racial disturbances; vandalism; and so on. At least two of the newspapers carried reports on each of the two deaths attributed to Halloween sadists. It is therefore unlikely that the list of seventy-eight incidents excludes any fatal instances of Halloween sadism.

Table 7.1 reveals two peaks in the pattern of reporting. Thirty-one of the seventy-eight incidents occurred in the three years from 1969 to 1971. This wave of reports fostered recognition of Halloween sadism as a threat. As a holiday when millions of children venture out at night, Halloween has a long history of tragic accidents. Newspapers and magazines routinely print lists of safety tips, warning parents against flammable costumes, masks that obscure the wearer's vision, and the like. A systematic review of such lists found no mention of the danger posed by sadists before 1972; but, from that year on, lists of safety tips almost invariably warned parents to inspect their children's treats for signs of tampering. At the same time that these warnings spread, reports of Halloween sadism fell to a few per year until 1982, when there was a dramatic increase. Of course, this reflected the fear caused by the Tylenol murders. A month before Halloween, seven people died after swallowing poisoned Extra-Strength Tylenol capsules. In the weeks that followed, there were hundreds of reports of "copycats" adulterating food, over-the-counter medications, and other household products. As Halloween approached, the media repeatedly warned parents that trick-or-treaters would be in danger (Nimmo and Combs 1985, 185–95).[3] After raising the specter of Halloween sadism, the press naturally covered the incidents that were reported. A year later, however, coverage fell to pre-Tylenol levels.[4]

Examining the reports of the seventy-eight incidents leads to three conclusions. First, the threat of Halloween sadism has been greatly exaggerated. There is simply no basis for *Newsweek*'s (1975) claim that "several children have died." The newspapers attributed only two deaths to Halloween sadists, and neither case fit the image of a maniacal killer randomly attacking children. In 1970, five-year-old Kevin Toston died after eating heroin supposedly hidden in his Halloween candy. While this story received considerable publicity, newspapers gave less coverage to the follow-up report that Kevin had found the heroin in his uncle's home, not in his treats (*San Francisco Chronicle* 1970). The second death is more notorious. In 1974,

135

eight-year-old Timothy O'Bryan died after eating Halloween candy contaminated with cyanide. Investigators concluded that his father had contaminated the treat (Grider 1984). Thus both boys' deaths were caused by family members, rather than by anonymous sadists.[5] Similarly, while the newspaper reports rarely gave detailed information about the remaining eighteen cases in which injuries were reported, most of the victims were not seriously hurt. Several incidents involved minor cuts and puncture wounds; what was apparently the most serious wound required eleven stitches (but see Conforti, Smego, and Kazarian 1987). In short, there were no instances in which an anonymous sadist caused death or a life-threatening injury; the data offer no justification for the claim that Halloween sadism stands as a major threat to U.S. children.[6]

A second conclusion is that many, if not most, reports of Halloween sadism are of questionable authenticity. Children who go trick-or-treating know about Halloween sadism; they have been warned by their parents, teachers, and friends. A child who "discovers" an adulterated treat stands to be rewarded with the concerned attention of parents and, perhaps, police officers and reporters. Such a hoax is consistent with Halloween traditions of trickery, just as the fear of sadists resembles the more traditional dread of ghosts and witches (Santino 1983). The seventy-eight reported incidents included two cases that were identified as hoaxes at the time, and it seems likely that other cases involved undiscovered fraud. After all, it is remarkable that three-quarters of the children who reported receiving contaminated treats had no injuries. Systematic efforts to follow up reports of Halloween sadism have concluded that the vast majority were fabrications. After Halloween 1972, *Editor and Publisher* (1973)—the trade magazine of the newspaper industry—examined several papers' efforts to trace all local reports of Halloween sadism; it concluded that virtually all the reports were hoaxes. Ten years later, in the wake of the Tylenol scare, the confectionary industry tried to reassure potential customers in a "white paper" on Halloween candy tampering in 1982 (National Confectioners Association et al., n.d.). The report noted that "more than 95 per cent of the 270 potential Halloween 1982 candy adulterations analyzed by the Food and Drug

Administration have shown no tampering, which has led one FDA official to characterize the period as one of 'psychosomatic mass hysteria.'" Further, a confectionary industry survey of police departments in "24 of the nation's largest cities, as well as smaller towns in which highly-publicized incidents were alleged to have occurred, found two reports of injuries—neither requiring medical treatment—from among the hundreds of claims of candy tampering."[7] Thus, not only does a survey of press coverage reveal fewer reports of Halloween sadism than might be expected, but there is good reason to suspect that many of these reports are unfounded.

Third, the press is not solely responsible for the widespread belief that Halloween sadism poses a serious threat. While the news media can manufacture "crime waves" by suddenly focusing on previously ignored offenses (Fishman 1978), the press gave Halloween sadism relatively little publicity. Many of the seventy-eight reported incidents received minimal coverage in news stories of only two or three sentences. Often the reports were part of larger stories, such as a wire service summary of Halloween news from around the country. Nor did popular magazines highlight Halloween sadism; before 1982, only two short articles focused on the problem. The absence of authentic cases of serious injuries caused by Halloween sadism undoubtedly explains this limited coverage. While the publication of annual warnings to parents to inspect their children's treats, as well as occasional short items reporting minor incidents, may help keep the fear of Halloween sadism alive, the media do not seem to be the principal channel by which people learn of the danger. Rather, knowledge of Halloween sadism apparently spreads by word of mouth.

URBAN LEGENDS AND CHILD-VICTIMS

The belief in Halloween sadism as a serious threat can be understood using a concept developed by folklorists: Halloween sadism is an *urban legend*. Urban legends are contemporary, orally transmitted tales that "often depict a clash between modern conditions and some aspect of a traditional life-style" (Brunvand 1981, 189). Whereas traditional legends often feature supernatural themes, most urban legends "are grounded in human baseness" (Fine 1980, 227). They describe

137

criminal attacks, contaminated consumer goods, and other risks of modern life.[8] Thus Halloween sadism features contaminated food, a motif in several urban legends, including the mouse in the soft-drink bottle, the Kentucky Fried Rat, and poisoned hamburgers (Brunvand 1981, 1984, 1986, 1989a; Fine 1979, 1980, 1985; Turner 1987). These legends, like that of the Halloween sadist, are told typically as true stories. They "gratify our desire to know about and to try to understand bizarre, frightening, and potentially dangerous or embarrassing events that *may* have happened" (Brunvand 1981, 12). Urban legends may even have a factual basis; soft-drink manufacturers have been sued by people claiming to have found mice in their drinks (Fine 1979). Whether a legend begins with a real incident or as a fictional tale, it is told and retold, often evolving as it spreads. On occasion, urban legends appear in newspaper stories, reinforcing the tale's credibility (Brunvand 1981, 1984, 1986, 1989a). The belief in Halloween sadism is maintained through orally transmitted warnings about the dangers contemporary society poses for the traditional custom of trick-or-treating. These warnings, which greatly exaggerate the threat, are an urban legend. That some incidents of Halloween sadism have occurred, and that the media have reported such incidents, does not disqualify the warnings as legends.[9]

Endangered children appear in more than twenty contemporary urban legends. Some of these tales are decades old, or they feature standard urban legend motifs—the boy who innocently mistakes baby copperheads for worms, the girl whose ratted hair becomes infested with black widow spiders, or the babysitter pursued by a homicidal maniac (Brunvand 1981, 1986). But other urban legends seem more clearly linked to recent claims-making about threatened children.

There are, for instance, tales of children endangered by parental neglect. In "The Baby on the Roof," a young couple drives off, forgetting that they had placed their infant on the car roof. Parents leave their infant with "The Hippie Babysitter" who, while under the influence of drugs, cooks the baby in the oven. "The Mother's Threat Carried Out" involves a mother who utters a terrible threat, warning her young child what will happen "the next time"—only to have her older child carry out the threat. Each of these legends offers the obvious message that parents must always attend to their young (Brunvand 1981, 1984, 1986).

Physical abuse and the limitations of protective services are the themes in a tale of a little girl who takes a hammer to the family car; her father then hammers her hands until they must be amputated, and, when the girl's mother refuses to press charges, the hospital must return the child to the parents' custody (Brunvand 1989b).

But most of the current legends feature children menaced by strangers. The Halloween sadist, for instance, resembles the pushers who distribute LSD ("Mickey Mouse Acid," "Blue Star Acid") in the form of stamps, stickers, or lick-on tattoos "designed to promote new addicts through appeal and enslavement of children" (Pogue 1987; Arax and Billiter 1987; Brunvand 1989a; Ellis 1989; Kantrowitz 1986; Kolata 1988). In "The Body on the Car," a drunk driver hits a child and does not notice; later, the body is discovered "embedded in the grill of his car" (Brunvand 1989a). Another popular legend concerns a young boy who is castrated in a public restroom; the attackers are often described as motivated by racial hatred (Carroll 1987; Ridley 1967). A parallel tale involves a young girl who narrowly escapes being abducted by white slavers from a shopping-mall restroom (Odean 1985). This story is only one of several contemporary child-abduction tales, which include the child abducted from an amusement park, a clown who kidnaps children, and an attempted abduction from a department store (Brunvand 1981, 1984, 1985, 1986).[10]

Satanists are blamed in another widespread abduction rumor. This legend warns that Satanists plan to kidnap children (in different versions, one hundred children or a blonde, blue-eyed virgin) for human sacrifices (Collins 1987; Robrahn 1988; Victor 1989). A related tale concerns "altar babies"—infants conceived and born in secrecy so that they can be sacrificed without detection (Lyons 1988). The legend that candles used in Satanic rites are made from human fetuses (Lyons 1988) seems related to the tale that some cosmetics have the same base (Brunvand 1986). Some analysts argue that claims about ritual abuse of children by Satanists are best viewed as an urban legend (Charlier and Downing 1988; Lyons 1988).[11]

The various legends about threatened children resemble another contemporary folklore genre—the dead baby joke cycle (Dundes 1979). These riddles feature babies suffering grotesque fates, e.g., "What's red and sits in a corner? A baby chewing on razor blades." Dead baby jokes emerged in the early 1960s, somewhat earlier than most of the urban legends about threatened children, but they remained popular throughout the 1970s and 1980s. Other, less well-documented joke cycles (e.g., jokes about serial killer John Wayne Gacy and the Atlanta child murders) also circulated (Goodwin 1989).

These jokes and legends are not about children, they are about *threats* to children. The children in the urban legends are featureless, generic children. They have no personalities; they are not curious or disobedient or troublesome. They might as well be valuable objects. The emotional punch in these legends comes from the villains—people so awful that they do despicable things to innocent children, children chosen effectively at random. Often these villains seem to lack rational motives—they kidnap, castrate, poison, and peddle drugs to preschoolers for no clear reason. Or, of course, their motives derive from their involvement in Satanic rites: they do terrible things to children because, presumably, those are the sorts of things Satanists do. In urban legends, as in melodrama, the villains have all the good lines.

In most respects, these villains resemble their counterparts in traditional tales featuring endangered children (e.g., Hansel and Gretel, Little Red Riding Hood), albeit with updated trappings (Tatar 1987). The dark forest has been replaced by the shopping mall, the enchanted apple by the contaminated treat, the witch or wolf by the criminal or Satanist. Urban legends are expressions of anxiety; they articulate contemporary concerns.

URBAN LEGENDS AND SOCIAL STRAIN

Identifying Halloween sadism as an urban legend helps explain why the belief became widespread when it did. News reports of Halloween sadism are not new (see *New York Times* 1950).[12] But the general perception that Halloween sadism is a serious threat dates from the early 1970s. This was when the press began reporting more incidents and warning parents to inspect treats, and legislatures began passing laws against Halloween sadism. While it is usually impossible to identify the moment when a particular legend began to spread, folklorists suggest that "The Castrated Boy" became widespread in the early 1960s (Carroll 1987), the stories about shopping-mall white slavers and children abducted from amusement parks or shopping malls in the late 1970s (Brunvand 1981; Odean 1985), "Mickey Mouse Acid" around 1980 (Brunvand 1984), "Blue Star Acid" in 1986, and tales of Satanist kidnappers in 1987 (Victor 1989). Some of these legends managed to spread widely within a relatively short time. A few weeks after "Blue Star Acid" reached Fresno, I called a random sample of the city's preschools and elementary schools. The legend was known at every school; in several cases, schools had circulated warnings to each student's parents. In short, legends about threatened children flourished during the same period that claims-makers launched various campaigns against threats to children.

In general, urban legends are products of social tension or strain. They express fears that the complexities of modern society threaten the traditional social order (Fine 1980, 1985). Urban life requires contact with strangers who—the legends suggest—may be homicidal maniacs, unscrupulous merchants, voyeurs, or otherwise threatening deviants. By repeating urban legends, people can respond to social strain, expressing their doubts about the modern world.

While it is obviously impossible to establish a causal link between particular social tensions and the spread of a particular urban legend, folklorists typically examine a legend's elements for clues about its roots (Brunvand 1981, 1984; Fine 1980). Some legends feature a transparent message, but others are more difficult to interpret. In the case of Halloween sadism, a plausible argument can be made that the legend's flowering in the early 1970s was tied to the heightened social strains of that period. The late 1960s and early 1970s were years of unparalleled divisiveness in post–World War II America. The media exposed several serious crises to the public, including an increasingly unpopular war, ghetto riots, student demonstrations, and increased drug use. It was a period of intense social strain. Three forms of strain that emerged or grew during these years seem related to the growing fear of Halloween sadism.

Threats to Children

The form of strain that seems most clearly linked to a belief in Halloween sadism was the growing sense that children were no longer safe in the United States. Physicians and social workers began promoting child abuse as a major social problem in the early 1960s. Their rhetoric emphasized that all children were potential victims, but even parents who remained confident that their children would never be abused could worry about losing their children to other threats. Older children might adopt radical political views or experiment with illegal drugs.[13] Other parents found their grown children facing a less symbolic threat—death in Vietnam. The social conflicts that marked America during these years must have left many parents wondering if their hopes for the next generation would be fulfilled.

Since the emergence of the belief in Halloween sadism, the generation gap seems to have narrowed, but threats to children remain visible. Perhaps the clearest link between threats to children and the fear of Halloween sadism appeared during the series of child murders in Atlanta. In 1980, STOP, an organization of the victims' parents, argued that "the city should organize Halloween night events that will minimize dangers to the children" (Sheppard 1980).[14]

Fear of Crime

Other forms of strain involved more general threats. Survey data reveal that the fear of crime grew substantially between the mid-1960s and the early 1970s (Erskine 1974; Stinchcombe et al. 1980). Although violent crimes often involve offenders and victims who are acquainted, the fear of crime focuses on the threat of an anonymous attacker.[15] The threat of an unpredictable, unprovoked criminal attack parallels the Halloween sadism menace.

Mistrust of Others

Survey data also reveal rising expressions of general mistrust during the early 1970s. The proportion of Americans who agreed that "you can't be too careful in dealing with people" rose from 45.6 percent in 1966 to 50.0 percent in 1971 to 54.3 percent in 1973 (Converse et al. 1980, 28). Studies of urban dwellers in the 1970s found high levels of mistrust for strangers (Fischer 1982; Merry 1981; Suttles 1972). While warnings about the collapse of the neighborhood in the anonymous modern city have proven exaggerated, the belief that people now live in greater isolation remains widespread. The social conflicts of the 1960s and early 1970s may have encouraged doubts about the trustworthiness of other people. Such doubts provided another form of strain during the period when the belief in Halloween sadism spread.

These sources of strain—threats to children, fear of crime, and mistrust of others—provided a context within which the concern about Halloween sadism could flourish. The Halloween sadist emerged as a symbolic expression of this strain: the sadist, like other dangers, attacks children—society's most vulnerable members; the sadist, like the stereotypical criminal, is an anonymous, unprovoked assailant; and the sadist, like other strangers, should be met with suspicion, rather than trust.[16] Placed in the context of the late 1960s and early 1970s, the spread of Halloween sadism is easily understood.

Other analysts offer analogous interpretations linking particular urban legends or joke cycles to strain produced by changes in the larger society. For instance, Dundes (1979) argues that dead baby jokes reflected uneasiness about the spread of the pill and legal abortion, while Carroll (1987) views "The Castrated Boy" legend as a reaction to changing women's roles. Victor (1989) notes that rumors about Satanists apparently found their most receptive audience in rural America, and he suggests these tales were a reaction to a threatened rural economy. In contrast, Bromley (1988) interprets stories about Satanists as a response to parents' uneasiness over their increasing need to share responsibility for child care. The fact that several urban legends about threatened children circulated during a period when claims-makers were denouncing child abuse, child pornography, sexual abuse, missing children, and the like—a period when both the press and popular culture were offering dramatic treatments of these issues, asserting that deviant individuals and conspiracies of deviants were to blame—suggests that there must have been a general sense that children were in danger, a sense that contributed to the legends' popularity.

If sources of strain account for the legends' spread, what explains

143

their persistence? The extraordinary social conflicts of the early 1970s have moderated, yet the belief in Halloween sadism remains. Why? First, some of the same sources of strain continue to exist: concern about threats to children and the fear of crime and strangers remain high.

Second, and more important, Halloween sadism is now an established urban legend; it can remain as a taken-for-granted, if dormant, part of American culture. The survey of newspaper stories found only five reports of Halloween sadism from 1976 to 1981—less than one per year.[17] However, warnings about sadists continued to appear during these years, and, of course, the Tylenol poisonings in 1982 led to both predictions and reports of Halloween sadism.

Third, folklorists have traced the evolution of some legends over centuries (Brunvand 1984). Legends seem most likely to persist when they have a general, underlying message (for instance, warnings about trusting outsiders) that can be tailored to fit new situations. Thus the dangers of eating commercially prepared food were detailed in nineteenth-century stories about cat meat in baked pies and, more recently, in tales about rats sold at fried-chicken franchises (Simpson 1983; Fine 1980). Like other urban legends about homicidal maniacs, the Halloween sadist legend expresses fears about criminal attacks. Given the general nature of this threat, the legend may persist as long as the custom of trick-or-treating.

URBAN LEGENDS AS UNCONSTRUCTED SOCIAL PROBLEMS

Where do urban legends fit within the broader framework of sociological theory? The case of Halloween sadism suggests (1) that urban legends may be viewed as a form of unconstructed social problem, (2) that collective hysteria, urban legends, and social problems construction offer alternative responses to social strain, and (3) that the emergence of a particular response to strain reflects social organization.

At first glance, the fear of Halloween sadists resembles some of the instances of collective hysteria in the collective-behavior literature. The Halloween sadist can stand beside the "phantom anesthetist" of Mattoon (D. Johnson 1945), the "phantom slasher" of Taipei

144

(Jacobs 1965), the "June bug epidemic" in a southern textile plant (Kerckhoff and Back 1968), and the windshield pitting in Seattle (Medalia and Larsen 1958) as a focus of exaggerated fears. Studies of collective hysteria usually account for the emergence of hysterical beliefs as a response to social strain: the Mattoon episode occurred during wartime; the workers in the textile plant were putting in heavy overtime, and so on. In response to this strain, there emerges a belief in some threat, "an ambiguous element in the environment with a generalized power to threaten or destroy" (Smelser 1962, 82). This threat is credible, frightening, and difficult to protect oneself against:

> Instead of simply having a feeling that something is awry, the belief in a tangible threat makes it possible to *explain* and *justify* one's sense of discomfort—instead of anxiety, one experiences fear, and it is then possible to act in some meaningful way with respect to this tangible threat rather than just feeling frustrated and anxious. (Kerckhoff and Back 1968, 160–61—emphasis in original)

However, some of this model's key features do not fit the emergence of the belief in Halloween sadism and other urban legends. Collective hysteria is bounded in time and space. Hysterical beliefs are short-lived; they typically emerge, spread, and die within the space of a few days or weeks. Further, they are typically confined to a restricted locality—a single region, town, or facility (Lofland 1981). In contrast, the belief in Halloween sadists appears to have spread more slowly, over a period of years, and to have become an established, taken-for-granted part of the culture. Nor has the belief observed the normal geographic limits of collective hysteria—reports of Halloween sadism have come from throughout the country, suggesting that the belief is nationwide. If the Halloween sadist resembles the threats identified in instances of collective hysteria, the dynamics of the belief's spread do not fit the hysterical pattern.

The constructionist perspective offers an alternative framework for understanding the fear of Halloween sadism. Of course, most studies of social problems construction focus on visible, well-organized claims-making campaigns. Constructionists rarely ask why other social conditions with the potential to be defined as social problems never reach this status. Emergent or unconstructed social problems receive little attention (Troyer and Markle 1983, 1984). However, it is useful to think of urban legends in these terms.

While the belief in Halloween sadism is widespread, it never led to effective claims-making activities. On brief occasions, Halloween sadism occupied the attention of legislators, city officials, journalists, and PTA associations, but the belief spread largely outside institutionalized channels. The press never reported more than a handful of incidents in a given year, and most of these reports were very short; the belief spread informally, by word of mouth. Similarly, there was no especially visible response to the threat. By the mid-1970s, the press reported a few organized attempts to thwart sadists—hospitals offering to x-ray treats, communities organizing alternative celebrations, and municipalities passing ordinances against trick-or-treating.[18] But most of these efforts remained localized; they received little publicity and did not lead to a broader, organized response to Halloween sadism. (Similarly, organized campaigns by the confectionary industry to expose fabricated reports of Halloween sadism also failed to attract widespread recognition [*Editor and Publisher* 1973; National Confectioners Association et al., n.d.].) While it is possible to trace the claims-making activities by which many social problems are constructed, this is not true for Halloween sadism. Although the belief spread widely, it moved largely through informal channels, and the principal reaction—parents restricting their children's trick-or-treating—was equally informal.

This suggests that collective hysteria, urban legends, and social problems construction are alternative responses to social strain. Social strain is a product of changing conditions that alter existing social relationships; it is a sense that something is awry in the social world. Strain prods some people to act, to express their concerns. These expressions can take different forms. Claims-making of the sort constructionists usually study is one—political—response: individuals identify an issue and make claims about it, mobilize support, and press for policy changes.[19] But strain also can become manifest in essentially symbolic forms—the threats that are the subjects of collective hysteria and urban legends.

Social organization affects the response to strain. In compact, homogeneous collectivities, collective hysteria can spread quickly. In larger, more diffuse collectivities, it takes longer to draw attention to the threat and to mobilize concerned individuals. Typically, in social problems construction, some individuals take the lead in organizing claims-making activities, while urban legends spread through informal contacts. In other words, collective hysteria, urban legends, and claims-making all seem to emerge from a sense of social strain. Urban legends, then, are a form of unconstructed social problem, an alternative to claims-making which appears under some circumstances.

The example of Halloween sadism suggests some specific factors that may affect the response to social strain. Reports of Halloween sadism did not lead to collective hysteria for two reasons. First, the belief spread throughout the country, rather than within a compact collectivity. Second, this spread could occur relatively slowly, given the limited nature of the threat. Reports of sadistic incidents posed no threat to other children for another year. There was no urgency to the news; the tale could be disseminated slowly, through informal channels.[20] Although a few organizations began claims-making activities directed at Halloween sadism, little came of their efforts. In part, this may have been caused by the absence of serious, documented sadistic incidents; without genuine atrocities to typify the problem and demonstrate the need for action, claims-makers had trouble making a convincing case. Further, potential social movements aimed at Halloween sadism lacked a well-organized natural constituency; while no one approved of Halloween sadism, no group found it in its interest to mount a sustained campaign against the threat. Again, the fact that the danger was limited to one evening a year may have inhibited the construction of Halloween sadism as a social problem. Nor was it clear how collective action might stop Halloween sadism; parents who worried about the threat found the best protection in individually curtailing their children's trick-or-treating or inspecting their treats. Thus the diffuse collectivity, the infrequency of the reported attacks, the absence of convincing evidence, the lack of interested individuals willing to commit extensive

147

time to the cause, and the difficulty of devising solutions meant that Halloween sadism became the focus of neither collective hysteria nor elaborate, organized claims-making. Yet, retaining considerable symbolic power as an expression of social strain, Halloween sadism endures as an urban legend.

The Halloween sadist legend spread before most contemporary claims-makers began their campaigns against threats to children. If claims-making and urban legends are alternative responses to social strain, we might imagine that, once claims about threatened children were widespread, the related urban legends would begin to drop from circulation. While there is no good way to measure shifts in the popularity of particular legends, it seems clear that folklore about threats to children continued to flourish in the mid-1980s. In particular, the various legends about Satanists' crimes against children and "Blue Star Acid" spread at the same time claims-makers were especially active. These new primary claims and the media's secondary claims—both emphasizing the threats posed by deviants—must have contributed to the larger sense that children were in danger, reinforcing the social strain that encourages telling legends. In at least one instance, folklore borrowed directly from popular culture's treatment of threats to children: a rumor spread—at Halloween time—that a man dressed as Jason (the killer from the *Friday the 13th* movies) was stalking a suburb (Schechter 1988, 152–53). Perhaps the legends spread among people who remained relatively unaffected by claims-makers' efforts. While it seems obvious that urban legends are one aspect of the public's reaction to claims about threatened children, the dynamics of that reaction remain uncertain.

IMPLICATIONS: CUSTOM AND CONCERN

Like all folk customs, holiday celebrations reflect the larger culture. The events celebrated, as well as the customary ways of celebrating, reveal the society's values and structure. And as society changes, its holidays often take on new meanings consistent with the altered culture. Where earlier American celebrations were communal, ceremonial, and often religious or patriotic, contemporary observances tend to be individualistic, materialistic, secular occasions, marked largely by unstructured leisure time (Caplow 1982; Caplow and Williamson 1980; Hatch 1978).[21]

Gregory P. Stone's (1959) "Halloween and the Mass Child" developed this thesis. Stone traced the evolution of Halloween activities in his lifetime, from the elaborate pranks of adolescents in the 1930s to the playful trick-or-treating of young children in the 1950s. He found the 1950s children did not understand the extortionate premise of trick-or-treat; for them, Halloween was merely an occasion to receive candy. Stone interpreted this shift as consistent with the changes in American values described in Reisman's (1950) *The Lonely Crowd:*

> Reisman's character type of "other-direction" may, indeed, be a *prototype* of American character and not some strange mutation in the northeast. Consumption, tolerance, and conformity were recognizable in the Halloween masquerade of a near-southern town. Production, indignation, and autonomy were not (Stone 1959, 378—emphasis in original).

Thirty years after Stone's analysis, the fear of Halloween sadism has further altered the meaning of Halloween. While Stone saw trick-or-treating as a part of the emerging culture of consumption, folklorists view Halloween as among the least commercialized of modern holidays (Grider 1984; Santino 1983). But this informality has been labeled dangerous by those who warn against Halloween sadists. Children are urged to refuse homemade treats and accept only coupons or mass-produced candy with intact wrappings, as though commercialism offers protection.[22] Long celebrated through vandalism and extortion, Halloween has been a symbolic expression of disorder. Today, the Halloween sadist has become an annual reminder of the fragility of the social bond—an expression of growing doubts about the safety of children, the trustworthiness of strangers, and the strength of the modern urban community.

Suspicion of others, fear of the unknown, and conservative moral messages are standard elements in urban legends. Such tales offer one way ordinary people can make sense of a complex, changing world. Too often, analysts seem to assume that mass media determine the public's understanding of social issues—the media describe social problems, and the public passively accepts those descriptions. But just as the constraints of media work lead to the transformation of primary claims into secondary claims, people modify the media's secondary claims, even as they respond to those claims. Thus media warnings about threats to children serve to inform citizens about child abuse, but they also foster urban legends about Halloween sadists and other villains. Folklore, then, is one—often oblique—response to claims-making. But people also respond in more straightforward ways: the media's messages shape individuals' attitudes, which are, in turn, reflected in public opinion.

8

Concern and Public Opinion

The public attention and donations this cause has generated is [*sic*] impressive—even alarming. Legitimate parental fears, particularly those of working women, have been skillfully manipulated through patently false statistics and oft-told, gruesome, heart-wrenching stories about murdered children.
                    —William W. Treanor (U.S. House 1986b, 148)

That more than twenty contemporary urban legends depict endangered children suggests that public concern about threats to children is widespread. But how widespread? What proportion of people—and which people—have heard these stories? And what proportion—and which people—believe them? Folklorists rarely ask such questions, and the standard methods of collecting folklore offer no good way to answer them.

Fortunately, there are other ways to assess the extent of public concern about social problems. Sample surveys can reveal the proportion of the population concerned about a particular issue, and they can help identify which people are most likely to have this concern. But public opinion is not the passive response of people accepting the mass media's messages. Like folklore, public opinion involves individuals actively constructing their own meanings for what they know, and we need to interpret survey data with this in mind (Gamson 1988). In the case of concern about threats to children, we can use survey data to learn the extent and social location of concern, how the public typified threats to children, and what people saw as solutions to the problem. In turn, the patterns in the survey data can help interpret the meaning of public concern.

151

IS CONCERN WIDESPREAD?

Several surveys taken in the mid-1980s indicate that most people viewed threats to children as serious social problems.[1]

As might be expected, those who might be directly affected—parents and youths—expressed considerable concern. Asked to compare sexual abuse and sexual exploitation of children to other national problems, 93 percent of Illinois parents rated it "very" or "quite" serious (Lavrakas and Rosenbaum 1987). Parallel questions gave other high ratings to stranger-abductions (89 percent), runaways (79 percent), and parental abductions (60 percent). A pre-Halloween national survey found that 60 percent of parents whose children would be trick-or-treating worried about contaminated treats (ABC News Polling Unit 1985). Similarly, when a national sample of youths aged eight to seventeen was asked to rate seven national issues, 79 percent reported that they personally were "very concerned" about the kidnapping of children and teenagers, and another 16 percent said they were "sort of concerned" (ACYP). This was the issue about which youths expressed the greatest concern; lower proportions said they felt very concerned about AIDS (69 percent) and the threat of nuclear war (67 percent). And fear of being abducted ranked first among five concerns listed on a questionnaire completed by 315 midwestern fifth-graders; 86 percent agreed that missing children were a major social problem (Price and Desmond 1987).

But parents and youths were not the only ones worried; surveys of the general adult population also revealed widespread concern. Asked "how serious is the problem of missing children today," 67 percent of Californians rated it "very serious," while another 29 percent said it was "somewhat serious" (CP). Another item asked whether stranger-abductions of children had "reached crisis proportions"; 29 percent strongly agreed, while another 31 percent agreed somewhat. Fifty percent of the adults in a national survey agreed that sexual assault was common within families; virtually all respondents argued that a ten-year-old sexually abused by an adult would suffer "very great harm" (79 percent) or "a lot of harm" (18 percent); and 73 percent said that sexual abuse would have great permanent effect (LATP). The same survey found that child sexual abuse was on people's minds; 69 percent reported having read or talked about it during the previous month.

The sense that threats to children were serious was coupled with concern that these problems were getting worse. The California Poll asked respondents whether the danger of four threats to children had increased over the past ten years; in each case, substantial majorities reported that things had gotten worse (see table 8.1). However, the *Los Angeles Times* Poll's national sample revealed less conviction that sexual abuse was on the rise. Asked what proportion of children in the respondent's community today were sexually abused, 21 percent estimated that more than 20 percent of children experienced abuse, and only 3 percent gave estimates that more than half of all children were abused. When asked a parallel question about sexual abuse in their community twenty-five years ago, the respondents were only slightly more optimistic; 16 percent said that more than one-fifth of all children had been abused, while only 1 percent thought that more than half of all children had experienced abuse. What is most striking, however, is the respondents' perception of extensive abuse occurring outside their communities. When asked to estimate the proportion of the nation's population that had experienced sexual abuse, more than two-thirds (68 percent) of the respondents gave figures over 20 percent, and 21 percent estimated over 50 percent.

There are other indications that people believe threats to children are something that affect other people's lives. People were more likely to rate their community's overall crime problem as serious than their community's sex crime problem (LATP). Asked to estimate the danger of "a child being abducted by a stranger," 38 percent of Californians said there was "a great deal" of danger, and another 47 per-

TABLE 8.1 PERCEPTIONS OF INCREASED DANGER TO CHILDREN

Danger Now Compared to Ten Years Ago	Child Abuse (%)	Kid-napping (%)	Sexual Molestation (%)	Child Pornography (%)
Much Greater	39	39	44	52
Somewhat Greater	24	26	23	22

Note: Number of respondents = 1,023.
Source: California Poll, September–October 1986.

153

cent said there was "some" danger (CP). However, when asked to assess the chance of a young child of theirs being abducted, only 6 percent said there was an "excellent" chance, and another 17 percent a "good" chance.

In sum, large proportions of survey respondents were ready to agree that threats to children were serious problems, and they had some sense that those problems were getting worse. Much of this concern seems altruistic, rather than self-interested. For most respondents, these were distant threats that did not intrude much into their lives or communities.

WHO IS CONCERNED?

While concern was widespread, it was not spread evenly throughout American society. There were patterns in the responses to the surveys' questions; some sorts of people were significantly more likely to express concern about threats to children. Here it will be useful to distinguish the responses of children and those of the adults who responded to the California Poll and the *Los Angeles Times* Poll.

Children's Responses

Among the fifth-graders responding to Price and Desmond's (1987, 813–14) questionnaire, "girls were significantly ($p < .01$) more likely than boys to be worried about becoming a missing child, to perceive themselves as susceptible to becoming a missing child, and to think more often about becoming a missing child." Similarly, 84 percent of the female respondents to the American Chicle Youth Poll reported being very concerned about kidnapping, compared to 69 percent of the males ($p < .001—v = .19$).[2]

Perhaps girls expressed more concern because they saw themselves as physically weaker than boys, and therefore more vulnerable to abduction. A sense of vulnerability might also explain why concern fell among older youths; 79 percent of the national sample's elementary-school students and 80 percent of the junior-high-school students said they were very concerned, but the figure dropped to 69 percent for high-school students ($p < .001—v = .10$) (ACYP).

The responses to the same survey show that concern was greatest among youths from relatively secure backgrounds. Those who described their home life as happy were more likely to express concern ($p < .05$—$v = .09$), as were those who described themselves as coming from the upper or middle—as opposed to lower—class ($p < .001$—$v = .11$) (ACYP). This might be another reflection of perceived vulnerability; perhaps young people who saw themselves as insulated from hardship worried more because they had less experience dealing with dangerous situations.

Responses to the California Poll

Consider the responses to three California Poll questions asking respondents to (a) assess the danger of a child being abducted by a stranger, (b) assess the chance of a child of the respondent being abducted by a stranger (this question was asked of all respondents), and (c) agree or disagree with a statement that stranger-abductions had become a crisis. Table 8.2 shows several patterns in the responses to these questions. In general, concerns about stranger-abduction were more likely to be expressed by:

- women;
- those over sixty-five;
- people living in households with a child under eighteen;
- blacks and Hispanics;
- less educated respondents;
- those with lower incomes;
- Protestants, Catholics, and those affiliated with other non-Jewish religions;
- people who consider religion important in their lives; and
- respondents who were not registered to vote.

Essentially the same patterns appear in the responses (not shown) to the four California poll items asking whether particular threats to children had increased over the previous ten years and to a question asking respondents to rate the seriousness of the missing-children problem. As might be expected, the responses to all eight items were interrelated; people who expressed concern about one threat to children were likely to be concerned about other threats.[3]

On the assumption that there is a generalized concern about threats to children, rather than unrelated opinions about a set of independent issues, I combined the responses to these eight questions to

155

TABLE 8.2 PATTERNS OF CONCERN ABOUT STRANGER-ABDUCTION

Characteristics of Respondents		Danger of Child Being Abducted by a Stranger[a]	Chance of Respondent's Child Being Abducted[b]	Stranger-Abductions Are Now a Crisis[c]
Sex		***[d] $v = .23$	*** $v = .19$	*** $v = .21$
Male	($n = 485$)	33	17	22
Female	(538)	42	28	35
Age		* $v = .08$	* $v = .08$	* $v = .08$
18–29	(274)	36	19	30
30–44	(337)	38	21	29
45–64	(262)	37	24	23
65+	(145)	41	30	36
Child Under 18 in Household		** $v = .11$	* $v = .10$	* $v = .10$
Yes	(373)	45	25	32
No	(643)	34	21	27
Ethnicity		*** $v = .12$	* $v = .08$	*** $v = .10$
White	(813)	33	21	26
Hispanic	(106)	60	33	46
Black	(52)	62	27	42
Asian	(28)	29	32	25
Education		*** $v = .20$	*** $v = .13$	*** $v = .17$
High School	(353)	51	30	41
Some College	(388)	38	23	27
College Graduate	(138)	20	15	18
Graduate School	(143)	22	11	14
Household Income		*** $v = .12$	*** $v = .12$	*** $v = .12$
<$20,000	(256)	47	35	38
$20–40,000	(374)	35	17	28
$40–60,000	(194)	35	22	25
$60,000+	(132)	25	14	19

156

TABLE 8.2 continued

Characteristics of Respondents		Danger of Child Being Abducted by a Stranger[a]	Chance of Respondent's Child Being Abducted[b]	Stranger-Abductions Are Now a Crisis[c]
Religion		***	*	***
		$v = .14$	$v = .09$	$v = .11$
Protestant	(452)	41	25	28
Catholic	(290)	42	25	35
Jewish	(32)	22	19	19
Other	(85)	44	28	30
None	(151)	21	10	22
Importance of Religion		***	***	***
		$v = .16$	$v = .12$	$v = .15$
Very Important	(434)	46	28	34
Somewhat	(357)	38	23	31
Not Very	(127)	27	17	17
Not Important	(98)	15	6	16
Marital Status			***	
		$v = .07$	$v = .10$	$v = .07$
Married	(586)	39	26	27
Separated/Divorced	(121)	40	26	31
Widowed	(76)	42	39	42
Never Married	(235)	33	16	29
Registered to Vote		***	***	**
		$v = .14$	$v = .13$	$v = .13$
Yes	(810)	34	22	27
No	(199)	51	26	36

Note: Number of respondents = 1,023.
Source: California Poll, September-October 1986.
[a] Percent responding "a great deal" of danger.
[b] Percent responding an "excellent" or a "good" chance of stranger-abduction.
[c] Percent responding "strongly agree."
[d] Chi-square significance: *—$p < .05$; **—$p < .01$; ***—$p < .001$.

create an Index of Concern. Responses to the index ranged from the fourteen people who expressed maximum concern about every item to the lone individual who expressed minimal concern for each. As expected, the index scores showed strong, significant relationships (not shown) with all the background variables that had earlier been found related to the eight component items. The most concerned respondents were more likely to be female, over sixty-five, living with a child, Hispanic or black, less educated, with lower incomes, more religious, and not registered to vote. However, a multiple regression analysis using the Index of Concern scores as the dependent variable, found that these background variables, taken together, explained only a modest share of the variance ($r^2 = .254$). The most important predictors were education (beta $= .235$), sex ($.205$), and religiosity ($.164$). The California Poll data, then, reveal patterns in concern, but they also show that concern was held fairly widely.

Responses to the Los Angeles Times Poll

We can compare the patterns in the California Poll responses to those for the *Los Angeles Times* Poll on child sexual abuse (see table 8.3). Several familiar relationships reappear, with concern highest among women; blacks and members of other non-Asian minorities;

TABLE 8.3 PATTERNS OF CONCERN ABOUT CHILD SEXUAL ABUSE

Characteristics of Respondents		Increased Attention Reflects More Abuse[a]	Estimate 40% of U.S. Children Abused[b]
Sex		***[c]	***
		$v = .13$	$c = .25$[d]
Male	($n = 1145$)	25	20
Female	(1481)	28	45
Age		***	**
		$v = .09$	$v = .09$
18–29	(634)	28	39
30–44	(904)	21	34
45–64	(713)	26	28
65+	(361)	38	34

158

TABLE 8.3 continued

Characteristics of Respondents		Increased Attention Reflects More Abuse[a]	Estimate 40% of U.S. Children Abused[b]
Ethnicity		*** $v = .09$	*** $v = .12$
White	(2242)	25	32
Hispanic	(77)	36	35
Black	(213)	45	52
Asian	(27)	27	22
Other	(53)	35	41
Education		*** $v = .16$	*** $v = .18$
High School	(1467)	35	40
Some College	(507)	20	34
College Graduate	(377)	13	24
Graduate School	(266)	12	16
Household Income		*** $v = .14$	*** $v = .15$
<$20,000	(830)	38	42
$20–40,000	(1107)	23	34
$40–60,00	(773)	19	24
$60,000+	(174)	16	24
Religion		*** $v = .09$	* $v = .08$
Strong, Moderate Protestant	(1423)	30	35
Nonpracticing Protestant	(244)	21	32
Strong, Moderate Catholic	(515)	25	35
Nonpracticing Catholic	(161)	20	26
Jewish	(69)	18	16
Other	(137)	21	36
Atheist	(52)	25	41

Note: Number of respondents = 2,627.
Source: Los Angeles Times National Poll, July 1985.
[a] Percent responding that there are more news stories about child abuse because "there is more child abuse going on today than there used to be."
[b] Percent estimating that over 40 percent of U.S. children have been victims of child sexual abuse.
[c] Chi-square significance: *—$p < .05$; **—$p < .01$; ***—$p < .001$.
[d] Contingency coefficient.

respondents with less education; and those with lower incomes. The patterns for some of the other variables are less clear. As we might expect, those over sixty-five were most likely to attribute the increased interest in sexual abuse to a real increase in abuse; however, respondents under thirty were most likely to estimate that a large proportion of American children had suffered sexual abuse. As expected, Jews and nonpracticing Protestants and Catholics expressed less concern, but those classified as atheists showed considerable concern.

Risk, Vulnerability, and Concern

Overall, the results from the two polls contradict one popular folk explanation for concern about threats to children. There is a perception that concern is concentrated among "baby-boomer" parents. The argument is that many people in this generation—particularly in the upper-middle class—delayed parenthood until their thirties or forties, so that their families are limited to one or two children in whom the parents have a particularly heavy emotional investment. The supposed result is a cohort of parents who are especially likely to worry about and seek to protect their children from all sorts of dangers. The problem with this argument, of course, is that it receives little support from the survey data.[4] It is impossible to stretch the notion of upper-middle-class, baby-boomer parents to fit the older, lower-income, less-educated, nonwhite respondents who are most likely to express concern.

The baby-boomer-parent hypothesis is one version of the more general argument that opinions derive from self-interest. Thus early sociological studies of fear of crime assumed that people's fear reflects their risk of victimization, and much work has gone into trying to explain the then puzzling finding that those who are in fact least likely to be victimized (e.g., the elderly) are often the most frightened.

But concern is not the same as fear. Typically, surveys measure fear of crime by asking respondents if they are afraid to walk at night near their homes. In contrast, only two of the questions about threats to children addressed such personal fears: Price and Desmond (1987) asked fifth-graders if they worried about being abducted; and the California Poll asked respondents to assess the chances of a child of theirs being kidnapped by a stranger. Most questions addressed more general, more abstract concerns.

Did respondents who expressed concern do so because they felt vulnerable, because they believed that children close to them were endangered? Before trying to answer this question, it may help to consider how the respondents typified the dangers.

OBJECTS OF CONCERN

The survey results not only reveal which segments of the population were concerned most about threats to children, they help reveal the nature of those concerns. I have argued that the rhetoric of primary claims-makers typifies social problems, and that the mass media's secondary claims present their own typifications. Presumably these primary and secondary typifications—as well as the images conveyed in other ways, such as jokes and urban legends—shape public opinion. Surveys can help reveal how the general public typifies social problems.

The California Poll included two items about the nature of the missing-children problem. Respondents were asked to agree or disagree with the statements: "Most missing children are runaways, not kidnapping victims," and "More kidnapped children are abducted by a separated or divorced parent who doesn't have legal custody than by strangers." Note that both statements are consistent with figures presented through both primary and secondary claims-making; virtually everyone involved with the missing-children problem acknowledged that runaways outnumbered abductions, and that child snatchings outnumbered stranger-kidnappings. However, both missing-children crusaders and the media *typified* the problem differently, emphasizing cases of stranger-abduction.

Interestingly, examining the responses to these items against the Index of Concern scores reveals that the least concerned respondents were most likely to recognize the relative importance of runaways and child snatchings (see table 8.4). They were also least likely to agree that "the news media are portraying an accurate account of the problem of missing children today." In other words, the respondents who expressed the greatest concern about threats to children were more likely to exaggerate the frequency of stranger-abductions—to

CHAPTER EIGHT

TABLE 8.4 CONCERN ABOUT THREATS TO CHILDREN AND TYPIFICATIONS OF THE MISSING-CHILDREN PROBLEM

	Percent Strongly Agreeing That		
Index of Concern (quartiles)	Most Missing Children Are Runaways	Parents Commit Most Kidnappings	Press Coverage Is Accurate
	***a	***	***
Most Concern (226)	16 $v = .16$	37 $v = .16$	30 $v = .16$
(266)	18	44	24
(224)	23	51	16
Least Concern (196)	32	69	8

Note: Number of respondents = 1,023.
Source: California Poll, September–October 1986.
aChi-square significance: $*—p < .05$; $**—p < .01$; $***—p < .001$.

grasp the problem in terms of its typification—and they were more likely to approve of press coverage of the problem—the press coverage that had helped establish that typification. These were the same people who, when asked about their sources of information about missing children, were significantly more likely to mention television ($p < .01—v = .11$).[5] This suggests that television coverage of social problems, which relies heavily on dramatic typifications, encourages viewers to define issues in terms of those typifications, which in turn produces higher levels of concern (CP).

Similarly, the *Los Angeles Times* Poll helps us understand how the public typified child sexual abuse. The survey asked several questions about typical features in molestation cases. For instance, when asked to give the age at which "children are most likely to be sexually abused," 73 percent of the respondents named ages from six to twelve. Most respondents agreed that both victims and offenders could come from either sex; only about a third of the respondents estimated that less than 30 percent of all victims were male, or that less than 20 percent of offenders were female. While only 12 percent of the sample stated that children were "usually molested" by strangers, only 22 percent named family members as the usual offenders; the most popular choice was acquaintance (43 percent). More than half (54 percent) of those responding agreed that child molesters generally use force or threats against their victims, and, when asked

162

why children submit to abuse, two-thirds of the respondents mentioned fear. Taken together, these responses suggest that the public typified sexual abuse in terms of a preadolescent—either male or female—compelled by an acquaintance and submitting from fear. The respondents saw this as a serious offense; asked to imagine a ten-year-old victim, 78 percent of the respondents said that sexual abuse would cause "very great harm."

The *Times* survey also sought to learn just what its respondents meant by sexual abuse. The poll included thirteen vignettes (e.g., "a fourteen-year-old boy was seduced by a fourteen-year-old girl"—all the vignettes are listed in table 4.1), and, in each case, respondents were asked whether the vignette was "an example of child sexual abuse, or an example of something else."[6] I combined the responses to these items into a Definition of Sexual Abuse Index. Respondents received a point for each vignette that they agreed involved sexual abuse, so that scores could range from zero to thirteen. Respondents with low scores presumably defined sexual abuse narrowly, while those with high scores had broad definitions.

We might expect that the tendency for claims-makers first to capture public support by using extreme cases to typify problems, before gradually expanding the problem's domain, would complicate public reactions. Do most people continue to define social problems in terms of the dramatic cases initially used to typify the problem? Or do they come to accept a broader definition of the problem?. Which people are most likely to adopt broad definitions, and how does the breadth of one's definitions affect how one views the problem?

The responses to the Definition of Sexual Abuse Index offer some clues. We might imagine that those most likely to express concern about child sexual abuse would also be more likely to define abuse broadly; to some degree, that is the case (not shown). For instance, 21 percent of those with incomes under twenty thousand dollars had broad definitions, versus only 13 percent of those with incomes over sixty thousand dollars. Similarly, broad definitions were more common among the less-educated, black, and non-Jewish religious respondents. But there were some surprises: broad definitions were more common among the youngest respondents and among whites (but not Hispanics). And there was no difference in the proportions of men and women holding broad definitions (LATP). In short, breadth of definition is not simply a reflection of concern.

Respondents' definitions of sexual abuse also affected some of their opinions about the problem (see table 8.5). Those who defined abuse broadly were significantly more likely to estimate that more than 40 percent of American children are abused, view sexual abuse as very harmful, and believe that child molesters force or threaten their victims. On the other hand, those holding broad definitions were not more likely to attribute the recent interest in abuse to an actual increase in offenses, nor did they hold distinctive views about the prior relationship between the victim and the offender, the proportions of males among victims and offenders, the most likely age of victimization, or whether victims submitted primarily due to fear (not shown). In short, those who defined sexual abuse broadly more often saw it as a serious, harmful offense, but they did not typify it differently from those who adopted narrower definitions.

Taken together, the data from the two surveys reveal a good deal

TABLE 8.5   DEFINITION OF CHILD SEXUAL ABUSE AND CONCERN

Percent Stating That	Definition of Sexual Abuse Index		Sig.[c]
	Broad Definition[a] (quintile)	Narrow Definition[b] (quintile)	
Increased Attention Reflects More Abuse	27	25	$v = .03$
Forty Percent of U.S. Children Are Abused	41	28	*** $v = .08$
Abuse of 10-Year-Old Causes Very Great Harm	84	70	*** $v = .09$
Molesters Generally Use Force or Threats	59	50	* $v = .06$

Note: Number of respondents = 2,627.
Source: Los Angeles Times National Poll, July 1985.
[a] Defined 10–13 vignettes as abusive ($n = 507$).
[b] Defined 0–4 vignettes as abusive ($n = 514$).
[c] Chi-square significance: *—$p < .05$; **—$p < .01$; ***—$p < .001$.

about the typification of social problems in public opinion. The California Poll data suggest that the media's use of dramatic examples to typify the missing-children issue shaped public attitudes. In particular, those who expressed the greatest concern about threats to children were more likely to exaggerate the danger of stranger-abduction, i.e., to emphasize the features of the problem that had been the media's focus. The public's typifications also appear in the *Los Angeles Times* Poll data; for instance, the respondents tended to view child sexual abuse as the work of non–family members who compelled victims to cooperate. The data also reveal considerable variation in the definition of sexual abuse, with those holding broader definitions generally viewing the problem as more serious.

ATTITUDES OF FORMER CHILD-VICTIMS

Claims-makers' warnings that threats to children are epidemic in modern America suggest that many adults must be former victims. The *Los Angeles Times* Poll attempted to identify those respondents who had experienced sexual abuse as children. Overall, 23 percent of the sample (15 percent of the males and 29 percent of the females) reported having been abused.[7] The great majority (74 percent of the males and 68 percent of the females) described a single incident of abuse. But 4 percent of the sample's male respondents and 9 percent of the females reported multiple experiences with abuse; 15 percent of the former victims described abuse extending over more than a year.

There were few differences in the backgrounds of former victims and the rest of the sample. Former victims were slightly younger (64 percent were under forty-five, versus 58 percent of the non-victims [$p < .001$—$v = .09$]) and slightly better educated (probably a reflection of their relative youth). There were no significant differences in ethnicity, father's education, or current religious affiliation or income. These findings support claims-makers' arguments that children throughout society experience sexual abuse. Not surprisingly, though, one difference stands out: 59 percent of the non-victims—but only 45 percent of those abused once and 32 percent of those abused more than once—described their childhood family life as "very happy" ($p < .001$—$v = .14$) (LATP).

Table 8.6 demonstrates that there were important differences in

165

the experiences of those abused once and those abused more often. As might be expected, repeated abuse was more likely to involve a family member and occur at home. Repeated abuse was also more likely to involve force or threats, although this remained relatively uncommon. Victims were less likely to report repeated abuse within one year after it began, and the report was less likely to be made to a family member ($p < .05$—$v = .17$). When asked to give "the most important reason why it happened," victims of repeated abuse were more likely to say that there was no one to whom they could turn for help (38 percent versus 13 percent for those abused once) or that they wanted to keep the offender's love (21 percent versus 4 percent).[8] In short, these two sets of experiences correspond roughly with the common-sense categories of molestation and incest.

Former victims typified sexual abuse differently than nonvictims (see table 8.7). Asked to account for the recent interest in sexual

TABLE 8.6 FORMER VICTIMS' EXPERIENCES WITH SEXUAL ABUSE

	Number of Abusive Incidents		
Characteristics of Abuse	One ($n = 391$)	Two or More ($n = 169$)	Sig.[a]
Abuse Occurred in Home	18%	42%	*** $v = .32$
Abuse Involved Force or			** $c = .13$[b]
Threats	14	25	
Abuser Male	94	93	$c = .01$
Abuser's Relationship to			*** $v = .38$
Victim			
Stranger	37	4	
Acquaintance, Friend	40	45	
Family Member	18	42	
Other	5	8	
Victim Reported Abuse			*** $v = .19$
Within One Year	48	32	
After One Year	16	32	
Never	36	36	

Note: Number of respondents = 2,627.
Source: Los Angeles Times National Poll, July 1985.
[a]Chi-square significance: *—$p < .05$; **—$p < .01$; ***—$p < .001$.
[b]Contingency coefficient.

166

TABLE 8.7 ATTITUDES OF FORMER VICTIMS AND
NONVICTIMS TOWARD CHILD SEXUAL ABUSE

Attitudes about Abuse	Number of Abusive Incidents			Sig. [a]
	Nonvictims $(n = 1973)$	One $(n = 391)$	Two or More $(n = 169)$	
Reason for Increased Interest in Sexual Abuse				* $v = .05$
More People Talking	37%	41%	46%	
More Media Coverage	35	36	35	
More Abuse	28	23	18	
Breadth of Definition				* $v = .05$
0–4 Vignettes	20	16	23	
5–9 Vignettes	62	59	54	
10–13 Vignettes	18	25	23	
Abuse of Ten-Year-Old Causes Very Great Harm	78	82	79	$v = .03$
Abuse Has Great Permanent Effect	73	74	70	$v = .03$
Usual Molester/Victim Relationship				*** $v = .11$
Stranger	14	6	6	
Acquaintance, Friend	58	55	51	
Family Member	19	32	31	
Other	9	7	12	
Molesters Generally Use Force or Threats	55	53	45	** $v = .05$
Forty Percent of U.S. Children Are Abused	29	44	57	*** $v = .18$
Sexual Assault Common in Families	46	59	72	*** $v = .16$

Note: Number of respondents = 2,627.
Source: Los Angeles Times National Poll, July 1985.
[c]Chi-square significance: *—$p < .05$; **—$p < .01$; ***—$p < .001$.

167

abuse, they were more likely to attribute it to increased candor ("more people are willing to talk publicly about child abuse today") and less likely to refer to an actual increase in abuse. At the same time, former victims were much more likely to estimate that over 40 percent of U.S. children are sexually abused. Former victims were less likely to agree that the usual molester was a stranger and more likely to name family members as likely offenders; similarly, they were far more likely to agree that sexual assault within families is common. In short, individuals who have personal experience with abuse are more likely to believe that abuse is widespread. However, when the Definition of Sexual Abuse scores of former victims are compared with those of nonvictims, there is no clear pattern: those abused once were most likely to hold broad definitions, but those abused more than once were most likely to have narrow definitions. Former victims do not necessarily define sexual abuse more broadly or more narrowly.

The experiences of former victims offer another way of assessing the way the public typifies sexual abuse. The offender in that typification is a stranger—often a woman—who relies on force and threats. In contrast, when former victims draw on their own experiences, they portray a large but hidden problem, the work of family members and other males known to the child-victims.

WHAT OUGHT TO BE DONE?

Given their widespread concern over threats to children, what social policies did the public advocate? Both the California Poll and the *Los Angeles Times* Poll included questions about what might be done.

The California Poll asked a series of questions in which respondents rated various steps parents might take to protect their children, using a scale from one (least important) to ten (most important). In most cases, there was great consensus on the importance of the different steps: 86 percent of the sample assigned a rating of ten to teaching children to report all cases of sexual abuse, compared to 78 percent for teaching children to beware of strangers, 72 percent for inspecting all Halloween treats for signs of tampering, and 23 percent for reading the lyrics on all records and tapes before allowing a child to listen to them. On a separate question, 88 percent of the respondents strongly agreed that children should be taught from an early age how to avoid kidnapping. While the California Poll data show consensus, there were patterns in the responses. Those who scored highest on the Index of Concern were significantly more likely to advocate all of the precautionary steps.[9]

Where the California Poll asked how parents could protect their own children, the *Los Angeles Times* Poll's questions focused on institutional responses to sexual abuse. Respondents were asked whether existing laws were "adequate to deal with the problem of sexual abuse," whether "people who work with children—like camp counselors, babysitters or scout leaders—should be required to be licensed and have their fingerprints checked," what was the appropriate punishment for sexual abuse (with choices ranging from the death penalty to probation—or a declaration that punishment was not the appropriate response), and whether "a person convicted of sexually abusing a child can be rehabilitated."

Table 8.8 demonstrates that those respondents who expressed the greatest concern about sexual abuse tended to take a harder line when crafting social policy. Those who attributed the increased interest in sexual abuse to an actual increase in abuse and those who estimated that a large proportion of U.S. children experienced abuse were significantly more likely to believe that people working with children should be registered, that the death penalty or long prison sentences were appropriate, and that rehabilitation was unlikely. Those who believed that sexual abuse had increased were more likely to say that existing laws were adequate, while those who believed that more candor or more press coverage had uncovered a previously hidden problem—and those estimating that a large proportion of children became victims—saw the need for new laws.

The *Times* Poll respondents' attitudes also depended upon how they typified the problem. In general, those who believed that sexual abuse was very harmful and those who said that molesters generally used force or threats took a harder line. However, Breadth of Definition Index scores were not related to most policy items, nor were the responses of former victims significantly different from those of nonvictims (not shown).

The data from both polls, then, suggest that respondents who re-

169

TABLE 8.8 CONCERN OVER SEXUAL ABUSE, TYPIFICATIONS,
AND ATTITUDES TOWARD SOCIAL POLICIES

Attitudes about Abuse	Laws Not Adequate[a] (%)	Register Workers[b] (%)	Death or 20+ Years[c] (%)	Rehab. Unlikely (%)
Reason for Increased Interest	$**c$	$***$	$***$	$***$
in Sexual Abuse	$v = .08$	$v = .10$	$v = .13$	$v = .07$
People Talking (948)	82	76	43	18
Media Coverage (867)	78	71	42	20
More Abuse (663)	74	82	58	28
Percent of U.S. Children	$*$	$***$	$***$	$***$
Abused	$c = .06^f$	$c = .11$	$c = .13$	$v = .09$
0–40 Percent (1507)	77	71	41	19
41–100 Percent (768)	82	82	55	25
Harm of Sexual Abuse to a	$**$	$*$	$***$	
Ten-Year-Old	$v = .08$	$v = .06$	$v = .07$	$v = .03$
Very Great Harm (2047)	80	77	48	22
A Lot of Harm (472)	77	72	42	20
Some Harm (82)	64	72	32	17
Molesters Generally Use Force		$***$	$***$	$***$
or Threats	$c = .03$	$c = .08$	$c = .19$	$v = .09$
Agree (1293)	77	78	55	24
Disagree (1107)	80	72	36	18

Note: Number of respondents = 2,627.

Source: Los Angeles Times National Poll, July 1985.

[a] Percent responding that existing laws are not adequate to deal with the problem of sexual abuse.

[b] Percent responding that people who work with children should be required to be licensed and have their fingerprints checked.

[c] Percent responding either that the death penalty or imprisonment for more than twenty years is the appropriate punishment for sexual abuse.

[d] Percent responding that it is very unlikely that a person convicted of sexual abuse can be rehabilitated.

[e] Chi-square significance: $*$—$p < .05$; $**$—$p < .01$; $***$—$p < .001$.

[f] Contingency coefficient.

vealed the most concern were more likely to favor taking additional measures to do something about threats to children.

THE MEANING OF CONCERN

We return to a basic question: why did concern about threats to children become widespread in the late 1970s and early 1980s? Most of the troubling behavior identified by the claims-makers had long histories—there was nothing new about physical or sexual abuse. What accounted for the new interest in old problems? And why did attention focus more or less simultaneously on several different threats to children?

To understand the meaning of this concern, we must focus on the objects of concern—the children—and consider the meaning of children for those who became concerned. Obviously, some people's concern must have centered on particular children. Some knew or had known endangered children; 15 percent of the respondents to a 1981 Gallup Poll said they personally were aware of serious instances of physical child abuse (*Gallup Report* 1982), and 19 percent of the *Los Angeles Times* Poll respondents reported having suspected someone of sexual abuse. Some had been victimized themselves. Some had broader concerns about their own children's safety (in the early 1980s, many parents mounted plastic caution signs in their car's rear windows, warning that there was a "Baby on Board"). Yet much of the concern about threats to children seems to have been diffuse, abstract; people worried about the safety of children in general.

And what do children—children in general—represent? At least two answers suggest themselves. First, children represent the future. American culture has been generally optimistic about the future, and American political rhetoric is filled with references to the children who are "our most precious natural resource," "the future leaders of our country," and "our nation's future." To do something for children is to do something for the future.

Second, children represent vulnerability. They are small, innocent, weak, inexperienced; they need protection. They are themselves vulnerable, but they also often serve as symbols of more general vulnerability. Mothers Against Drunk Driving used children's deaths to dramatize the social costs of drinking and driving. Or consider the

Vietnam-era antiwar slogan: "War Is Not Healthy for Children or Other Living Things." Drunk driving and war were not child-protection problems, but claims-makers found it useful to frame these issues in terms of children's (and therefore all people's) vulnerability.

The fact that children can represent both the future and vulnerability may explain some of the concern about threats to children. It seems no accident that this concern emerged in a period when Americans began to have considerable doubts about the future. The early 1970s saw a series of major shocks to the social system—defeat in Vietnam, the Watergate scandal and Nixon's resignation, flagging income growth, and the oil embargo and energy crisis. By 1980, Americans could choose among several apocalyptic visions of the future. There was a fresh, widespread movement against nuclear weapons, fueled by graphic warnings about the consequences of nuclear war. There was a growing sense that the American economy could no longer compete in the international marketplace and that the United States was—and would remain—in economic decline. Warnings about the terrible ecological consequences of population growth, resource depletion, and pollution continued. By the mid-1980s, there were claims that AIDS would become an uncontrollable global epidemic. As the end of the millenium came into sight, the only question seemed to be which bang or whimper would mark the world's end.

Survey data offer evidence of this pessimism about the future. In 1979, the Gallup Poll began asking the question: "In general, are you satisfied or dissatisfied with the way things are going in the U.S. at this time?"[10] From 1979 to 1983, substantial majorities (from 59 to 84 percent) expressed dissatisfaction. Dissatisfaction fell in the mid-1980s (with 48 to 60 percent expressing satisfaction in polls from 1984 to 1987), but large proportions of Americans continued to worry. For instance, an August 1987 poll found 45 percent satisfied and 49 percent dissatisfied, with dissatisfaction higher among women, nonwhites, and older, less-educated, and lower-income respondents (*Gallup Report,* 1987). Or consider the 1986 Gallup International Poll that asked respondents to estimate the chances of a world war breaking out within the next ten years. U.S. respondents were the most pessimistic, with 49 percent estimating that there was at least a 50 percent chance of war; in comparison, an average of 20 percent of respondents in eighteen European countries were equally pessimistic (*Gallup Report* 1986). For Americans in the late 1970s and early 1980s, the future was in doubt.

We might imagine that the ready availability of military, economic, ecological, and even medical apocalyptic scenarios was frightening. These were visions of uncontrollable, unpreventable cataclysm. Individuals could do little to protect themselves from these disasters. There was little to gain from talking about, or even thinking about, these awful futures. At the same time, the underlying anxiety about the future must have remained.

For some people, focusing concern on threats to children may have provided a solution to this psychological dilemma. Anxiety about the future could be expressed in terms of concerns for children's safety. This is a more manageable concern. After all, a very large proportion of adults are at some point responsible for the well-being of children, and most are able to protect those children from the worst of the world's dangers. Moreover, the threats to children that attracted concern were relatively manageable. These threats took the familiar form of deviant individuals, and there were established strategies for dealing with such deviants. Children could be taught to detect and avoid deviants, and the existing social control apparatus, both punitive and therapeutic, could presumably cope with these threats. From this perspective, the future might still seem endangered, but only by threatening individuals, not by systemic forces requiring extraordinary responses.

Note, too, that the people who worried most about threats to children were people who must have seen themselves as especially vulnerable in uncertain times. The survey data reveal that concern about threats to children was higher among categories of people who would seem more likely to feel socially vulnerable: women rather than men; blacks and Hispanics rather than whites; older—and to a lesser degree younger—people, rather than the middle-aged; the less-educated; and those with lower incomes. The same categories tend to show higher levels of fear of crime and concern about other social problems. For instance, the profile also fits the Gallup Poll respondents most likely to express pessimism about the nation's future.

Nor is it surprising that concern about threats to children was higher among those not registered to vote—who would presumably have greater feelings of powerlessness.

Anxiety about an impending, uncontrollable disaster should be greatest among those who see themselves as more vulnerable to whatever fate has in store. For some people, displacing their worries to threatened children might offer a means of coping with such anxiety. These adults might feel vulnerable, but children were even more vulnerable. The future might seem uncertain and threatening, but there were even clearer threats to the children who embodied the future. In this way, focusing on kidnappers, molesters, and other terrible threats to children offered a way of deflecting more frightening, less manageable fears.

This process, by which anxieties about the future are transformed into concerns for child-victims, is not unique to the United States in the 1980s. Case studies suggest that something similar has been at work in other times or other places. For instance, Barker's (1984) history of the mid-1950s British campaign against horror comic books notes that the crusaders' rhetoric emphasized the threat foreign (i.e., American) culture posed to Britain's innocent youths. He argues that the attack on comics emerged from the uncertainties of the postwar world. Similarly, Freedman (1987) describes two major twentieth-century American panics over sexual psychopaths: the first (1937–40) developed during the Depression, as the nation braced for the coming world war; the second (1949–54) occurred during the onset of the Cold War. While the comparative evidence is hardly conclusive, these examples suggest that claims-making about child-victims may be more common—and elicit a more enthusiastic response—during times when the future seems in doubt.

CLAIMS-MAKING AND PUBLIC REACTIONS

The recent public concern over threats to children was a product of the way the social problems marketplace operates. In the competition among claims-makers, those able to present claims in compelling rhetoric have an advantage, and the new child savers found it easy to define their cause in terms of threatened, vulnerable innocents. These emotion-laden images encouraged the mass media to incorporate threats to children into news coverage and popular culture; the media's treatment further emphasized the issue's dramatic elements. In turn, the portraits drawn by primary claims-makers and relayed through the media's secondary claims evoked reactions from the public. Some people helped spread urban legends—a sort of tertiary claim—but many other adopted new attitudes, concerns that can be seen in the responses to public opinion polls.

Obviously, there was a broader social context within which the public heard and responded to claims. There were social strains that made listeners more susceptible to claims about threatening deviants and, in particular, about deviants who threaten children. During the late 1960s and early 1970s, these strains included the generation gap and rising fear of crime and mistrust of strangers; a decade later, there were serious, widespread doubts about the nation's future. And, of course, established fears about endangered children fed new fears. Claims about battered babies served as a foundation for folklore and new attitudes, as well as further claims-making about other threats to children.

But, awful as the conditions described by the claims-makers might seem, there were attractive features to the problems they described. The new child savers saw, or at least typified, threats to children in terms of individual deviants—battering mothers, incestuous fathers, kidnappers, molesters, and child pornographers. These were flawed, dangerous individuals who had to be thwarted, restrained, rehabilitated, or otherwise brought under social control. Their offenses might be terrible crimes, but they could be seen as the acts of terrible individuals. It was easy to adopt this individualistic interpretation of threats to children, and more difficult to present the problems as systemic, requiring a general reform of children's place within the larger society. Claims-makers had little luck promoting systemic views of threats to children, but they had relatively little difficulty spreading warnings about predatory deviants. Not surprisingly, the public took these warnings to heart. Public concern focused on evil individuals without questioning the place of children in American society.

175

9

Competing in the Social Problems Marketplace

There's a big parade marching by, just outside your front door—a major movement, led by organizations, agencies, legislators, and private individuals who are committed to improving the safety of our nation's youngsters. What you have to do to enhance the protection of your own children and those of your neighbors is to step out and join in.
—U.S. Senator Paula Hawkins (1986, 107)

Every issue slows down.
—John Walsh (Uhlenbrock 1988b, 6)

Why do claims emerge and take hold when they do? The recent wave of public concern over threats to children began with the discovery of the battered-child syndrome in the 1960s, spread during the 1970s through campaigns against sexual abuse, adolescent prostitution, child pornography, and child snatching, and peaked with the missing-children movement in the 1980s. What brought these problems—each featuring children menaced by adult deviants—to public attention at roughly the same historical moment?

Case studies of social problems construction tend to finesse such questions.[1] Constructionist research often seems to assume that claims-making emerges from a constant pool of potentially articulatable claims. In this view, there was probably nothing new about adults beating children; would-be claims-makers might have objected to this practice at virtually any time in the past. That such claims emerged during the 1960s was simply a product of various contingencies—the Children's Bureau's decision to fund research, the modest professional status of pediatric radiologists, a paucity of

176

competing claims, and so on. While the specific contingencies vary from one claims-making compaign to the next, they deserve our attention. We need to understand what leads claimants to register their objections to particular social conditions, what causes the media to notice and ratify particular claims, and what makes the public respond with concern to some media reports about social problems.

In the case of the new child savers, the relevant contingencies can be found in the organization and culture of the contemporary social problems marketplace and in the appeal of the crusaders' message.

CONDITIONS IN THE CONTEMPORARY SOCIAL PROBLEMS MARKETPLACE

The claims-makers who sought to bring attention to threats to children operated within a social problems marketplace characterized by an established, ongoing wave of activism and reform, supportive institutional structures, and a conducive contemporary mood.

Waves of Reform Activity

American history reveals periods when claims-making activities seem particularly intense. For instance, during the decades before the Civil War, the abolitionist movement flourished, as did campaigns by anti-abolitionists, nativists, temperance and women's rights advocates, and other claims-makers. Half a century later, Progressive reformers attacked municipal corruption, vice, and a wide range of other urban social problems.[2]

As in these earlier reform waves, highly visible claims-making campaigns have characterized the late twentieth century. The civil rights movement of the 1960s marked the beginning of this wave, providing the model (and often the training ground) for activists who went on to join the student, antiwar, environmental, gay, and women's movements. By the 1970s, this model of protest was being adopted across the political spectrum; both the pro-life and the New Right movements borrowed methods and tactics from sixties leftists.

In short, a modern approach to claims-making developed. The public face of this reform wave was the televised demonstration, showing claimants marching, sitting in, having silent vigils, or otherwise engaged in forms of public protest. Claims-makers learned to copy one another's tactics, adopting methods that had attracted media attention to others' causes, but modifying those methods enough to insure that their demonstrations would be presented in a sufficiently novel fashion to make their own claims newsworthy (McAdam 1983). The less visible side of this protest tradition was the spread of experienced activists, people who had experience packaging claims, drawing media attention, and mobilizing public support. These were people who knew how to draft a press release and hold a press conference, how to generate funds through grant applications and direct-mail advertising, in short, how to make a cause competitive in the contemporary social problems marketplace. Many activists learned their basic skills in one movement, then applied them in the service of other causes (McCarthy and Zald 1977). And even those without claims-making experience could learn a great deal about organizing a campaign and promoting a cause by following media coverage of other crusaders.

The diffusion of both public and backstage claims-making skills was aided by technological developments. Activists found photocopiers and computers useful for mailing-list management, electronic bulletin boards, desktop publishing, and the like. It became increasingly possible for a small group of activists to gain publicity, attract members, generate funding, foster letter-writing campaigns, and otherwise comport themselves in the manner of large, well-established interest groups. Knowledge of new techniques quickly spread among those involved in the ongoing wave of reform.

Institutional Developments

The claims-makers who sought to draw attention to threats to children had the advantage of promoting their causes during a period when there was considerable receptivity to new claims. In part this was a product of the ongoing reform wave, which encouraged treating new claims as at least potentially legitimate, but it also reflected new institutional arrangements.

For instance, consider the evolution of television news coverage. Critics often charge that the quality of broadcast news is in decline, that the documentary has virtually disappeared from the networks' prime-time schedules, while the same networks' long-promised hour-long evening news broadcasts have failed to materialize. But this critique overlooks a remarkable expansion in other news (some might say quasi-news) coverage. The list of other forums for televised news includes not only the networks' morning shows (e.g., "Today"), prime-time news magazines (e.g., "60 Minutes"), and late-night programming (e.g., "Nightline"), but a wide range of syndicated news and/or public service programming (most obviously in the form of talk shows [e.g., "Donahue"]), as well as parallel programs on cable and public television. Relatively inexpensive to produce, such programs became increasingly attractive to broadcasters as the competition for viewers grew more intense. Whereas the evening network news tends to focus on hard political news and minimize coverage of social issues and other soft news, the morning shows, talk shows, news magazines, and other less prestigious programs regularly cover claims-making campaigns. The resulting proliferation of programs—each with broadcast time to fill, each searching for fresh material to hold the attention of an increasingly jaded audience—has made it far less difficult for claimants to gain access to television.

Or take the expansion of the corps of professionals concerned with child protection. Child saving did not begin with the discovery of the battered-child syndrome; rather, the Children's Bureau and other existing child-welfare organizations provided a foundation upon which claims about child abuse could be constructed. But the success of those claims—both in drawing public attention to child abuse and in creating new policies mandating that medical professionals, teachers, and others watch for and report instances of suspected abuse—made more people sensitive to the dangers children face. Foundations and government agencies funded research and pilot projects, universities began offering courses, professionals enrolled in workshops to learn to detect and deal with child abuse, and protective-services agencies expanded. There were now more people—many of them officials with greater resources and more broadly defined prerogatives—involved in child-abuse prevention and detection and in protective services. In turn, this new child abuse establishment became a base from which further claims-making could be staged, so that each successive movement against threats to children benefited from the support of a growing number of professionals and laypeople already concerned with child protection.

The Contemporary Mood

These institutional changes occurred within a broader cultural context. No doubt every age has its anxieties, but claims about threats to children seem to have emerged in relatively stressful times. Beginning in the mid-1960s, with their student protests, ghetto riots, and antiwar demonstrations, conflict has played an especially visible role in American society, and observers have voiced serious concerns about the strength of the family, the economy, and other central institutions. This has been a period of rising crime rates and widespread fear of crime. Political and social rhetoric has emphasized crises in the present and the prospect of collapse in the future.

This contemporary mood helped maintain the wave of reform sentiment, as claims-makers offered to diagnose society's ills and prescribe the needed cures. The mass media gave these claims attention and legitimacy. And, of course, doubt fed upon itself. If terrible things were happening, there must be something terribly wrong, and, if something was terribly wrong, it was no surprise to learn that even more terrible things were happening. In particular, if the very future seemed endangered, threats to the children who would inhabit that future made sense.

More specifically, it made sense to focus on the threat deviant adults posed to children. Deviance is an important theme in American culture. We prefer to blame social problems on flawed, deviant individuals, while paying little attention to the complex workings of the social system. Focusing on threats to children offered an outlet for some of the anxiety people felt about an uncertain future; it specified their fears and thereby made them more manageable. And defining threats to children in terms of child molesters, kidnappers, and other deviant adults made those fears more manageable still: if society could bring just a few villains under control, the threats would disappear, and the future could be secured. Deviants often serve as scapegoats in times of social crisis, and, particularly for those who perceived themselves as vulnerable in an uncertain future, the deviants who menaced children offered a sort of relief. They could represent not only the dangers faced by children, but all the uncertainties of the future.

THE MEANING OF THE CHILD-VICTIM

Because children seem to embody the future, doubts about America's future course translated easily into concerns about threats to children. Such concerns had nearly universal appeal because, while people may interpret problems involving threatened children in very different ways, the endangered child is a powerful symbol for almost all Americans.

Every society needs to replenish its membership, and almost all societies accomplish this through procreation. But no birth rate is ever high enough to insure that the society's membership will be reproduced, unless the young also learn to behave like their elders; they must be socialized. Not surprisingly, adults with a stake in a social order place great importance on teaching the young the correct lessons, just as those who hope to revolutionize society often establish their own programs to indoctrinate the young.

But Americans see childhood as more than simply the period when young people learn the ways of their elders. If the traditional view of childhood held that adults were primarily teachers who imparted information and moral standards to the young, a more sentimental perspective emerged during the nineteenth century and has been elaborated by child psychologists and other authorities during the twentieth (Wishy 1968; Zelizer 1985). This new view defined children as priceless innocents whose boundless potential is gradually constricted through contact with the adult world. No longer authoritative teachers, adults now became constraining agents or—at best—facilitators who let children develop to fulfill their potential. This sentimental portrait of children's limitless potential suited a culture that approached the future with optimism. But the portrait of the adult who constantly runs the risk of doing more harm than good has implications of its own. Deviants who menace children merely extend the role of harmful adult to its logical conclusion. In short, the notion that children are precious, that they need protection from a harmful adult world, is basic to contemporary understandings of childhood.

Child-victims play an important role in this sentimental view of childhood. Anthony Comstock and other nineteenth-century moral crusaders emphasized that vice threatened to corrupt children's innocence (Kendrick 1987). For over a century, child-saving rhetoric has described delinquents and other rebellious children as child-victims who should not be blamed for their offenses. More recently, as the women's movement has taken women off their traditional moral pedestal, children have become the last sacred category of innocents to require society's protection (Adler and Adler 1978). The image of the threatened child is quite powerful, and concern for child-victims can be made consistent with many different contemporary ideologies (Nathan 1987).

For instance, representatives of the New Right took an active part in denouncing several threats to children. In particular, fundamentalist Christians built much of their social agenda upon protecting the nuclear family and preserving parents' traditional authority over their children. Concern about threats to children meshed neatly with the fundamentalists' values. Warnings about a rising tide of sexual immorality were consistent with claims-making about child pornography, child molestation, and, of course, abortion. In this view, the principal dangers came from without, from strangers who might snatch children from the safety of the family circle. Stories of runaways turned prostitutes or ritual abuse in preschools and day-care centers revealed the risks to children outside the family's protection. This may have been the principal audience for claims about Satanic conspiracies involved in kidnapping, orgies, and human sacrifice. For the New Right, the basic lesson was that a society that turned its back on religion and traditional values endangered its children. They translated these concerns into policy recommendations, emphasizing the need to minimize and control strangers' contacts with children, while simultaneously arguing to restrict the authority of protective-services workers to interfere within families (Pride 1986).

But threats to children found a place on the social agendas of those well outside the New Right. Feminists—targets of much New Right criticism—also played important roles in claims-making about child-victims. The special ties between mothers and their children lay at the root of feminist concerns; women most often have the primary, day-to-day responsibility for protecting their children. And this responsibility seemed all the greater at a time when family violence was a hot topic. The 1960s campaign against child abuse had helped pave the way for claims-making about wife battering and, of course, incest. Feminist rhetoric tended to emphasize the violence of husbands and fathers, making all forms of family violence a women's issue. Feminist concern about other forms of sexual exploitation sparked interest in adolescent prostitution and child pornography. And, with a growing proportion of mothers working, fears about sexual abuse in preschools and day-care centers became an issue for feminists. In short, these critics saw dangers to children as one more consequence of a patriarchal society's misplaced values. Like followers of the New Right, feminists found that threats to children could be understood in terms consistent with their analysis of the larger society's problems.[3]

These two examples demonstrate that threats to children appealed to a wide range of claims-makers. Because the vulnerability of children was generally accepted, the child-victim offered a powerful symbol for almost any claimant addressing almost any audience. No one defended harming children. To be sure, the apparent consensus could be pushed too far; disagreement was especially likely to arise over policy recommendations. For instance, fundamentalists favored discouraging day care and abortion, while feminists supported both. But overall, campaigns against threats to children faced little overt opposition. The general sympathy for child-victims let claims-makers campaign on the basis of consensus, not conflict.

A DECLINE IN CONCERN?

By 1988, concern about missing children and other threats to children seemed to be waning. There were fewer pictures on milk cartons and utility bills, fewer congressional hearings, and fewer guidebooks on how to protect children from kidnappers for sale in shopping-mall bookstores. Mass fingerprinting campaigns had virtually disappeared. Instead of feature articles about the missing-children problem, newspapers began running stories about the fading missing-children movement (Ginsburg 1988; Uhlenbrock 1988a, 1988b). The success of Stephen King's *It* in late 1986 and early 1987 now seemed to mark the period when concern peaked and began to recede.

Not all campaigns follow the same trajectory through the social problems marketplace; even within the larger movement against threats to children, claims made very different impacts. The campaign against child abuse had great success. Constructed by people with links to the Children's Bureau, the child-abuse problem achieved widespread recognition and led to new policies which significantly expanded and strengthened the child-welfare establishment. Child abuse became a well-established social problem. In contrast, claims-making about ritual abuse—as typified by accounts of the systematic sexual abuse of preschoolers by Satanists—had less impact. The media proved reluctant to relay reports of Satanic rituals, and the prosecution's decisions to drop the charges against most of the defendants in the Jordan, Minnesota, and McMartin Preschool cases—the two most visible instances of alleged ritual abuse—raised public doubts. As the 1980s ended, the very term "ritual abuse" remained unfamiliar to most people.

The missing-children movement's impact fell between the substantial success of the campaign against child abuse and the limited effect of the crusade against ritual abuse. To be sure, the missing-children movement left a legacy. The federal government continued to fund the National Center for Missing and Exploited Children, new state and federal laws made searching for missing children more efficient, and dozens of organizations continued to help search for children and offer child-protection education. Looking for missing children had become one more institutionalized form of child protection. But the issue no longer held the spotlight; it no longer generated widespread horror and fear among the general public. Posters of missing children began to feature the words "Stranger Abduction" in bold print, assuring readers that *this* case was serious; the phrase "Missing Child" was no longer enough. The issue had lost much of its power.

The same could be said for other threats to children. They had become familiar problems; the public now knew something about the issues, and the earlier fears had been replaced by weaker emotions. Child abuse remained a well-established social problem, but it was no longer as likely to make the front page—although the heavily publicized trial of Joel Steinberg in 1989 demonstrated that the issue still had dramatic power.

In part, the decline of threats to children as prominent social issues reflected the influence of counterclaims. In the case of the missing-children movement, not only were the claims-makers' statistics challenged, but fund-raising scandals emerged, critics questioned the value of fingerprinting and other prevention programs, a debate developed over the appropriate policy toward runaways, and the media even began celebrating an "underground railroad" to help child snatchers get their children away from abusive custodial parents (Podesta and Biema 1989). In short, some of the complexities of the issue—complexities which had often been ignored during the initial wave of claims-making—became apparent. Similarly, critics began charging that the federal government's campaign against child pornography was misguided, that child-abuse reporting laws were generating an unmanageable load of trivial complaints, that charges of sexual abuse were being brought on insufficient evidence, that accusations of ritual abuse reflected a witchhunt mentality, and so on. Whereas early claims-making often builds consensus, invoking widely held values and typifying an issue in terms certain to gain widespread sympathy for the cause, this consensus cannot last. People find that competing interests are involved, and this discovery of complexity produces conflict (Downs 1972).

And, of course, established claims lack novelty. As the decade came to a close, threats to children faded in prominence, and a new set of social problems attracted media attention—a new drug menace (crack) and a new war on drugs, serial murderers, huge urban gangs linked to the drug trade and random violence, and AIDS were among the fresh issues receiving prominent coverage. The social problems marketplace puts a premium on emotionally charged issues, but it also values novelty. Problems surge to the top, are redefined as boring and overexposed, then fall from view, to be replaced by fresh topics.

The child-victim, then, seemed to slip from sight. The issues had become too complex, and they were no longer fresh and compelling. But they remained just below the surface. The enlarged child-protection apparatus meant that there were now more people with a stake in child safety, more potential claims-makers to mount campaigns against threats to children. And, of course, the child-victim remained a powerful symbol around which support could be mustered for new claims-making (as in the Steinberg case).

RHETORIC AND SOCIAL PROBLEMS CONSTRUCTION

Words make a difference. What we say about social problems is important. Claims define and shape problems, make them what they are. Therefore the rhetoric of claims-making deserves our attention.

But rhetoric must be located within its organizational context. In a recent paper, Mehan and Wills (1988, 364) state:

> The idea of competing over the meaning of ambiguous events rests on a view of language that can be understood by visualizing words in a territory or conversational space. If one conceptualizes conversational space in a personal sense, then one concludes that individuals own meaning, own the territory. Meanings are privately assembled by a solitary speaker and transmitted to a passively receptive hearer. . . . If one conceptualizes words in a dialogic sense, . . . then one concludes the territory is jointly owned.

We can understand claims-making as a dialog, but of a peculiar, complex sort. Some claims-making may be neatly bounded in face-to-face interaction, as when an apartment tenant asks the landlord to make repairs. But claims-making about the issues we customarily call social problems almost always spills well beyond the boundaries of a particular face-to-face encounter. Take a demonstrator arrested by a police officer. Their interaction is an instance of claims-making leading to a response, but the encounter's meaning depends upon each individual's connections to the larger world. Is the demonstrator part of a larger movement? Was there one arrest or hundreds? Was the police officer acting under special instructions, and, if so, who set the policy? Did reporters cover the arrest, and, if so, how did they describe what happened? Was there any public reaction, and what forms did it take—people flocking to support the demonstrator's cause, support for the police and criticism of the demonstrator, or what? Did policymakers take notice of the arrest or the reactions to the arrest? Most social problems are constructed through many interactions, some face to face (demonstrators being arrested, reporters interviewing activists, and so on), but most indirect (viewers watching a claims-maker interviewed on a talk show, policymakers reading public opinion poll results, and the like).

In other words, constructing social problems on the national stage—particularly when it is the work of outsider claims-makers—involves a dialog over meaning, but it is a dialog with many participants, a dialog mediated by the mass media. In a competitive social problems marketplace, some claims gain attention, while others fall by the wayside. Most often, media coverage separates the two groups: it is very hard for outsider claims-makers to succeed unless the media pay attention to their claims. But the media have their own standards for deciding whether to cover claims-makers; the press is most likely to select claims which seem important ("could mean the end of life as we know it"), authoritative ("a group of Nobel laureates warned"), novel ("a new danger"), and dramatic ("threatens small children"). Claims-makers who hope to capture media attention find it useful to package their claims to fit the media's criteria.

But media coverage is not sufficient. The media can bring claims to public attention, but that does not insure that people will attend to them. Of course, in relaying claims, the media emphasize those elements most likely to capture and hold their audience, so that secondary claims tend to focus on the problem's most dramatic features. There is, then, a rhetorical chain, beginning with the primary claims-makers, who must first define a social problem to their own satisfaction and then present their claims in a fashion likely to draw media attention. Next, the media transform those primary claims into secondary claims. Some of those claims are taken seriously: policymakers may decide on their own that an issue merits attention; or the public may come to see the issue as serious and, perhaps, pressure policymakers to act. But this is not a straightforward process. Just as the media have their own criteria in assessing the suitability of primary claims for coverage, so does the public evaluate secondary claims within a larger context. The general attitude toward social reform, the contemporary mood of crisis or contentment, and the cultural meaning of a claim's central elements (e.g., children) shape the public reaction.

The recent child-saving campaigns reveal some of the workings of the social problems marketplace. Claims-makers found effective ways to present these issues. The battered child, the kidnapped child, and the other typifications of child-victims—and the deviants who menace them—became familiar figures in Americans' constructions of social life. But such constructions have consequences. Public opinion and social policy depend upon how issues are defined. A society which is mobilized to keep child molesters, kidnappers, and Satanists away from innocent children is not necessarily prepared to protect children from ignorance, poverty, and ill health. Inevitably, some campaigns succeed in the social problems marketplace. Whether the most significant issues come to the fore is another question.

NOTES

CHAPTER ONE

1. Sociologists in the constructionist camp disagree over the assumptions which should guide their analyses (Best 1989, 245–49). *Strict constructionists* view constructionism as a form of phenomenological sociology (Spector and Kitsuse 1977; Woolgar and Pawluch 1985). They argue that the analyst should focus on how claims-makers present—and other members of society respond to—claims about putative conditions, and avoid evaluating the claims' content or otherwise making assumptions about empirical reality. Since all reality is socially constructed, an analyst who makes statements about reality is taking sides—trying to validate some constructions and discredit others. Strict constructionists say that analysts must not act as though they are privileged arbiters of reality; in this view, the sociologist is merely another claims-maker.

The analytic purity of strict constructionism comes at a cost. In effect, this theoretical stance declares some questions unanswerable, out of bounds. For instance, treating all claims as equal means that analysts may not differentiate among tales of flying-saucer abductions, declarations that sexual abuse is "epidemic," and the results of social surveys. Refusing to evaluate the content of these claims removes them from their social context.

In contrast, *contextual constructionists* argue that analysts can and should locate social problems construction within its context (Blumer 1971; Gusfield 1985). Flying-saucer reports and social surveys are both social constructions, but they are constructed by different sorts of people, operating within different social environments and addressing different audiences, and the sociologists need not be blind to these differences. Unless the analyst incorporates some background knowledge into the analysis, questions of how and why claims emerge cannot be addressed. In fact, contextual constructionists question whether a strict constructionist analysis is even possible; underlying assumptions about objective reality may be unavoidable.

This book's orientation is frankly contextualist. At various points, I use official statistics, the results of social research, and other background information to interpret claims about threatened children. My goal is to understand how and why concern about threats to children emerged, and I do not believe these questions can be answered without locating the claims-making within its social context.

CHAPTER TWO

1. Between 1979 and 1981, there were several congressional hearings on parental kidnapping. Although those testifying sometimes spoke of "missing children," they clearly meant child snatching. Neither runaways nor chil-

189

dren abducted by strangers figured prominently in these deliberations (U.S. House 1980, 1981a; U.S. Senate 1979). Sociological interpretations of the missing children problem's emergence include Eliasoph (1986), Fritz and Altheide (1987), Gentry (1988), and Joe (1988).

2. Occasionally claims-makers spoke of other categories of missing children, e.g., infants who had been given up for adoption and were now sought by a biological parent (U.S. Senate 1981, 189).

3. Like many child-search organizations, Child Find was established by the parent of a missing child—Gloria Yerkovich, whose daughter was snatched by the child's father. Kristin Cole Brown, Child Find's information director, handled press interviews and congressional testimony. The Dee Scofield Awareness Program was an early effort begun after a stranger-abduction. After 1981, John Walsh, who founded the Adam Walsh Child Resource Center in his son's memory, became the most visible claims-maker among the parents.

4. A noncontroversial issue—one congressional aide called it "the apple pie of the '80's"—the missing-children problem received widespread, bipartisan support. Leading congressional claims-makers included conservative Republican Senators Paula Hawkins and Mitchell McConnell and liberal Democratic Representative (after 1984, Senator) Paul Simon. In 1984, both McConnell and Simon campaigned on their record of work for missing children.

5. Twelve of these children (all abducted by noncustodial parents) were recovered in the weeks following the program's initial broadcast (U.S. House 1984, 52–53). Later broadcasts had similar results. Several media figures became claims-makers themselves. Television journalist Kenneth Wooden, who founded the National Coalition for Children's Justice, was especially prominent.

6. I have renamed another of Toulmin's original concepts. To avoid confusion, I have substituted "conclusion" when referring to his concept C, restricting the use of "claim" to the constructionists' sense of the term.

7. Obviously, this scheme of classifying statements is an analytic device. Claims-makers do not consciously sort their statements into grounds, warrants, and conclusions. Selection and classification of statements are the analyst's—not the member's—work.

8. The discussion in this chapter treats the empirical truth of claims as problematic. As will be seen, some claims made about the missing-children problem came under attack, and there were counterclaims. Examining the rhetoric of claims-making does not require establishing the validity of any particular claim.

The use of grounds statements in claims-making resembles the process of belief amplification in recruiting members for social movements (Snow et al. 1986), or scientists' cognitive claims (Aronson 1984).

9. Obviously, criteria for legitimate grounds vary over time and space. Where claims grounded in divine revelation once carried considerable rhetorical power, today's policymakers more often view official statistics or scientific results as the means of establishing facts (see Gusfield 1981).

10. From 1981 to 1986, the *Reader's Guide to Periodical Literature* listed fourteen articles longer than one page about the missing-children problem generally (rather than about specific cases). Eight began with one or more horrific examples. Journalists relied on this device when the issue was fresh; only one of the five articles published in 1986 opened with an example.

11. In contrast, Kristin C. Brown of Child Find testified before the same hearing: "Our Executive Director is Gloria Yerkovich. Her daughter, Joanna, has been missing since December 20, 1974" (U.S. Senate 1981, 73). Brown did not explain that this was a child snatching.

This sort of reticence serves to keep attention focused on atrocity tales that should enlist everyone's sympathy. Even accounts of stranger-kidnappings sometimes glossed over details that might strike some as discrediting. Thus a fund-raising mailing from the National Child Safety Council contained a letter from a mother describing her son's disappearance: "My husband was at work and I was in the kitchen." This neglects to mention that the couple was divorced and living in different states (Kurczewski and Lewis 1986).

12. This confusion extended to private-sector campaigns to distribute pictures of missing children. Jay Howell, executive director of the National Center for Missing and Exploited Children, noted that some organizations limited their displays to children taken by strangers (U.S. House 1985b, 31).

13. In response, missing-children claimants countered with new statistics of their own, arguing that their critics undercounted abductions by strangers (National Center 1986a) and even suggesting that the total number of missing children might be "well over the 1.8 million estimated by various national groups" (U.S. Senate 1985b, 30). For a summary of the conflicting claims and counterclaims, see N. Spitzer (1986). I discuss this debate in detail in chapter 3.

14. Occasional claims did identify particular segments of the population as being most at risk, e.g., rural children (Smith 1986), children of single mothers (U.S. House 1984, 108), or upper- and middle-class children (Jordan 1985).

Claims that a problem has an extensive range also keep attention focused on particular aspects of the problem. Pelton (1981) suggests that claims that child abuse occurred throughout the social structure promoted a "myth of classlessness," in spite of evidence that child abuse was concentrated among the poor. While this circumvented potential critics who might have refused to support further social programs for the poor, it also implied that the causes of child abuse lay in individual pathology, rather than the social structure. As a consequence, programs aimed at combating child abuse focused on individual treatment, rather than on the social conditions within which abuse occurred (Nelson 1984).

15. There are, of course, other possibilities. A person might be persuaded, not by the warrant explicitly offered, but by some other warrant—perhaps one that the person making the argument would not find valid. Similarly, constructionist interpretations often feature actors who act out of self-interest, although their public warrants are more principled.

The acceptability of warrants varies across time and space. Legal history, for instance, can be viewed in terms of shifts in the readiness with which particular warrants are validated.

16. In describing recruitment to social movements, Snow et al. (1986) speak of value amplification. For a broader discussion of values and claims-making, see Spector and Kitsuse (1977).

17. The following year, Wooden reappeared before the same House subcommittee, declaring: "Because all missing children are grouped in the same Federal solution package, national paranoia is on the rise, and an army of child-saving charlatans is marching over the newly-turned soil of parental fears" (U.S. House 1985a, 58).

18. There were occasional hints that some children were more priceless than others. The Dee Scofield Awareness Program charged: "The children being taken by the criminals in this country are usually the stable, conscientious, highminded and intelligent ones who would one day become leaders of our society" (U.S. Senate 1981, 195).

19. Compared to most other claims, a 1984 statement by then-judge Mitchell McConnell offered a sophisticated analysis, listing several factors that "influenced this serious system disfunction [sic]." The list began with two relatively general factors—"child liberation, which is a product of societal change" and "increasing openness regarding homosexual activities"—before addressing more specific items (U.S. Senate 1984, 42–44).

20. Although most claimants referred to limited resources and avoided attacking the police, the Dee Scofield Awareness Program argued that corruption was a major cause of officials' failure to deal with missing children (U.S. Senate 1981, 194–95).

21. In exploring the missing-children problem, Congress and the press rarely sought out representatives of existing runaway institutions. When given a chance to speak, these people—who had a stake in current policies—carefully distanced themselves from the missing-children movement. William Treanor, of the National Youth Work Alliance, noted

> the importance of distinguishing between runaways and missing children. . . . Missing children are, of course, the innocent targets

of criminal activity. Much thought must be given to properly implementing the Missing Children's Assistance Act so that runaway centers don't become targets for either law enforcement or missing children's advocates (U.S. Senate 1984, 229).

Similarly, June Bucy of the National Network of Runaway and Youth Services argued: "The system of youth shelters in place . . . has a ten year track record of success" (U.S. Senate 1985a, 68).

22. According to Crewdson (1988, 113), "the monumental effort to track down missing children has yet to recover a single child abducted by a stranger." As the search for missing children became more public, problems emerged. Child-search organizations began to compete for contributions and media coverage, and some private groups began criticizing the most visible missing-children crusaders (N. Spitzer 1986; U.S. House 1986b, 1986c). For instance, Charles A. Sutherland (quoted at the beginning of this chapter) was a trustee of Search Reports, Inc. Some organizations also came under attack for deceptive practices (see Blumenthal 1984; Chollet and Sorkin 1988; Kilzer 1985; McNair 1985).

23. In one of the few sociological analyses of rhetoric, Heritage and Greatbatch (1986) examine reactions to speeches at British political party conferences—a setting in which the audience is likely to share the speaker's values.

Students of rhetoric have examined various recent social movements (see P. Burgess 1968; Lake 1986). But these analyses pay relatively little attention to sociological issues, e.g., how rhetoric varies according to the movement's objectives and audiences.

CHAPTER THREE

1. Apparently the references to Health and Human Services figures were to a study that estimated the number of runaways in 1975 (Office of Juvenile Justice 1985).

2. Claims-making in the 1970s and 1980s often reflects the labeling theorists' critique of official statistics (see Kitsuse and Cicourel 1963). Crusaders warn that organizational practices cause the phenomenon in question to be undercounted or overlooked altogether. They are then in a position to offer their own estimates of what fraction of all cases appear in the official counts.

3. However, other missing-children statistics survived. Gelles and Straus (1988, 18) acknowledge that stranger-abduction statistics were exaggerated, then continue, "hundreds of thousands of children are snatched by parents embroiled in custody disputes."

4. In spite of the study's severe methodological limitations, its results received wide circulation and continue to be cited by NCMEC representatives, federal officials, and the press (Andrews 1986, 140; U.S. House 1986a: 45–46; 1986b, 37).

193

5. Here, and in much of what follows, we will be examining statistics collected by criminal justice agencies. Sociologists know that official statistics are imperfect measures of crime. Any agency's statistics reflect its organizational practices. How do cases come to the agency's attention? What criteria do agency members use in deciding to record a case? What classification scheme do members use? Official statistics are a product of officials' activities: "Rates can be viewed as indices of organizational processes rather than as indices of certain forms of behavior" (Kitsuse and Cicourel 1963, 137). As we will see, different agencies have their own reasons for being concerned with missing children and their own criteria for deciding when to count a child as missing.

6. In fact, the police classified only 15 percent of these cases as kidnappings, attempted kidnappings, or abductions. This probably reflects the gap between the officers' sense that the category kidnapping should be limited to relatively serious offenses, and the broad definition of kidnapping found in most states' laws. On the difficulties of restricting the legal definition of kidnapping to relatively serious crimes, see Diamond (1985). NCMEC officials emphasized that they derived their definition of kidnapping from the statutes (U.S. House 1986b, 38–40).

7. These figures include a small proportion of cases from Canada, Puerto Rico, the Virgin Islands, and assorted U.S. territories.

8. Missing-children crusaders long believed that the NCIC's figures were far too low, that they failed to list as many as 90 percent of all missing children. Since most states now require law enforcement agencies to notify the NCIC, it seems likely that reporting has become reasonably complete. The total number of missing persons reported to NCIC rose 156 percent from 1981 to 1985, when 386,144 cases were entered.

9. Probably most of the cases classified as unknown were runaways; the two categories have similar age, sex, and race distributions. New York's relatively thorough reporting apparatus registered 25,318 missing children during 1988, including 124 classified as "Lost/Wandered Away" (New York State Division 1989: 17). Extrapolating from New York's proportion of the nation's children, we arrive at a national estimate of 366,400 missing children of all sorts—a large figure, but well below the often-cited 1.8 million.

10. Comparisons of state and federal SHR data require some care. California's 1984 figure seems unusually high; the state's 28 cases include 5 children who died in a single incident—a mass murder in a San Diego fast-food restaurant. Applying the same criteria to the 1985 California SHR results in a total of only 21 cases. On the other hand, the federal total may be too low. Whereas California lists a precipitating event for every homicide, the federal data include 251 cases where the circumstances surrounding the killing were classified as unknown. (It seems likely, however, that few of these deaths

194

were felony-related; in both state and federal SHRs, cases identified as felony-related accounted for 21 percent of the total.)

After reviewing evidence from several sources, Hotaling and Finkelhor (1988; see also Office of Juvenile Justice and Delinquency Prevention 1989) offer a "best guess," a range for the number of children murdered after being abducted by strangers—52 to 158 per year. In short, homicide statistics—which show fewer than 1,500 juvenile victims per year and are generally regarded as among the most complete criminal records—are hard to reconcile with some missing-children claims: "2,000 kids . . . fall to the sexual battle in America per year" (U.S. House 1984, 56); "four to eight thousand [stranger-abducted children] a year are murdered" (ABC, 24 May 1982).

11. "A 1984 survey of members of the College of American Pathologists found evidence that there are fewer than 100 bodies or skeletons of young persons remaining unidentified at the end of 1983" (Hotaling and Finkelhor 1988, 14).

12. The following year, when New York did classify missing children, the records revealed that runaways accounted for the great majority of the state's cases (New York State Division 1988).

13. Originally scheduled for late 1988, the announcement of this study's results was delayed more than a year.

14. Once a debate over measuring a social problem's extent is resolved by adopting official, standardized record keeping, new difficulties can emerge. Officials may be reluctant to update the measure as conditions change, or people may use the measure in new, inappropriate ways (Block and Burns 1986).

CHAPTER FOUR

1. The attention this article received marked the culmination of efforts, particularly by the U.S. Children's Bureau, to identify child abuse as a social problem. However, these earlier efforts received little notice outside the child-saving establishment (Nelson 1984, 32–50).

2. The emphasis on very young (and therefore very vulnerable) children had rhetorical power, but it served another purpose, too. Kempe et al. (1962) framed their discovery of the battered-child syndrome as a sort of medical detective story, in which pediatric radiologists identified abuse as the cause of fractures. These experts diagnosed a problem in patients who were too young to explain their injuries. Older children, who were presumably able to speak for themselves, seemed to need this expertise less (Pfohl 1977).

3. The image of the battered child continues to typify child abuse. I found eight recent (1982–88) social problems textbooks that used photographs to illustrate their discussions of child abuse. While these books de-

195

fined child abuse broadly, seven of the pictures showed infants or toddlers with visible injuries.

4. The new laws were designed to elicit widespread reports of suspected abuse. The organization of social control agencies always affects the incidence of deviance discovered. Thus Currie (1968, 16) identifies the organizational conditions that supported "an enormously effective machine for the systematic and massive production of confessed deviants"—European witchcraft prosecutions: (1) "invulnerability to restraint from other social institutions"; (2) "systematic establishment of extraordinary powers for suppressing deviance, with a concomitant lack of internal restraints"; and (3) "a high degree of structured interest in the apprehension and processing of deviants."

5. By 1988, there were signs that the missing-children movement's domain was expanding. While the first two National Conferences on Missing and Exploited Children maintained a narrow focus, the announcement for the third (1988) conference listed "contributing areas": drug, alcohol, and substance abuse, teen pregnancy, child pornography, teen suicide, child abuse, children of domestic violence, and AIDS.

6. Even organizations of pedophiles, such as the Rene Guyon Society, the Childhood Sensuality Circle, and the North American Man/Boy Love Association, offered prochild ideologies that advocated child-abuse prevention and treatment, while denouncing corporal punishment in schools and circumcision (de Young 1984). Claims about missing children and sexual abuse often pointed to these groups—their small memberships notwithstanding—as evidence that there were organized threats to children.

7. Spector and Kitsuse (1977, 130–58) review several attempts to develop natural histories of social problems and offer one of their own. In general, these theories present social problems development as a single trajectory (e.g., from discovery of the problem to its solution). I suspect it will prove more useful to imagine several simultaneous, interacting processes. Thus, here I focus on a rhetorical issue—how a problem's definition changes. This limited natural history is intended to complement—rather than contradict—natural histories that focus on policy formation and other processes.

8. This survey is described in more detail in chapter 8.

CHAPTER FIVE

1. Not everyone subscribes to these arguments. Some critics warn that the impact of television news has been exaggerated (see Robinson and Levy 1986).

Sociological studies of the media's role in claims-making routinely focus on newspapers and popular magazines, rather than television. The print media are more accessible for analysis: they are available in library collections, and there are established techniques for measuring coverage (e.g., counting articles indexed in the *Reader's Guide to Periodical Literature*). However, it is possible to study television news coverage. In particular, Vanderbilt University's Television News Archive offers a data base—a nearly complete collection of network news broadcasts since 1968. The archive publishes the *Television News Index and Abstracts* and makes available videotapes of broadcasts in its collection.

2. *Television News Index and Abstracts* is a useful, but imperfect, resource for researchers. Some early years do not include weekend broadcasts. Moreover, the *Index*'s scheme for classifying stories is not always clear, and it has shifted over time. While the *Index* listed many stories under the general heading "Children," I found it necessary to review several other headings, including "Crime," "Murder," and "Sex," to identify other relevant stories. Still, I failed to find some stories by this approach. A 1979 piece on the disappearance of Etan Patz, for instance, was not listed under any of the headings I routinely checked. While I made an effort to identify the population of network news stories about threats to children, I undoubtedly missed some relevant pieces.

3. Throughout this chapter, I refer to "film." This is traditional, if outdated, usage. Technically, most network news stories are now recorded on videotape.

4. Hallin (1988) notes that network news sound bites (i.e., uninterrupted statements by individuals) grew shorter from 1965 to 1985. A typical sound bite is now about ten seconds, so that interviews ordinarily are condensed to one or two sentences.

5. The relationship between these authorities and the networks is symbiotic. By interviewing these sources, the networks turn them into authorities; being selected for an interview designates these individuals as qualified to speak on the issue and thereby validates their expertise. In return, the individuals cooperate with their interviewers, lending the weight of authority to the broadcast.

Because feature stories on a given topic are infrequent, few of these authorities became regular sources. This contrasts with hard news beats, where reporters often come to rely on particular sources (Gans 1979).

6. I began this research assuming that there would be few important differences among the networks in the way they covered stories about threats to children. However, some differences did emerge, and I will note those that seem interesting.

While many critics imply that the networks are all alike, Nimmo and Combs (1985) found differences in the networks' coverage of six major crises. Unfortunately, their portraits are hard to recognize in table 5.1. For instance, they suggest that "it is the interpretive reports from official settings (often using interviews with 'experts') that are the backbone of CBS nar-

197

ratives" (Nimmo and Combs 1985, 181), while on ABC "the leading actors are the common folk, members of the populace with nothing to gain and everything to lose" (182). Yet my data show that ABC relied most heavily on authorities, while CBS used the largest proportion of ordinary citizens as sources.

7. The media's tendency to let officials, rather than activists, frame issues has been noted in studies of feminist (Tuchman 1978), antiwar (Gitlin 1980), and environmental (Molotch and Lester 1974; Schoenfeld et al. 1979) movements.

8. Hughes (1940) gives the history of the human-interest story as a form of news. However, research by Iyengar and Kinder (1987) suggests that network news stories using vivid personal examples to typify social problems are actually less persuasive than less dramatic stories.

9. A former runaway, Treanor became a spokesperson for the runaway shelters, voicing their suspicions of the missing-children movement. All three networks used him as a source critical of NCMEC policies.

10. During the same period, CBS broadcast other stories expressing reservations about threats-to-children claims-making. A piece shown on 5 June 1985 interviewed preschool teachers who said they worried they might be charged with molestation, a psychiatrist who spoke of a "witchhunt kind of hysteria," and a father who, during divorce proceedings, had been accused of molestation (the charge was dropped), while a story on 13 March 1986 about child-molestation cases involving Chicago teachers also referred to unfounded accusations and concerns about a witchhunt. A piece on 23 February 1987 concerned false accusations of child abuse. And, while all three networks carried stories about the Finders—variously described as a Satanic cult or "an international child-abuse ring" (CBS, 6 February 1987)—only CBS broadcast a follow-up, noting that police had "backed off" earlier accusations of sexual abuse and relabeling the Finders "a mysterious, nontraditional life-style group" (CBS, 11 February 1987).

NBC's coverage resembled that on CBS. A 6 December 1985 story began with Tom Brokaw announcing, "NBC's John Hart now has discovered the [missing-children] problem may be greatly overstated." The story itself contrasted NCMEC claims with FBI statistics and included interviews with Treanor and another critic. NBC also broadcast a story on false accusations of child molestation and abuse (23 April 1985).

11. CBS and NBC did not broadcast stories on this hearing (U.S. House 1986b), nor was it covered in the *New York Times*, the *Washington Post*, or the *Los Angeles Times*.

12. Barkin and Gurevitch (1987) argue that network news stories about unemployment frequently offered simple explanations, but that these explanations were not guided by a consistent theoretical framework.

13. Here the network news seems to share the underlying assumptions of

entertainment programming. Gitlin (1983) argues that an ideology of individualism frames television dramas, so that the focus is on individuals rather than institutions: villains cause problems, forcing victims to suffer, until heroes solve the problems. Similarly, news stories describe threats to children in terms of individual victims and individual villains.

14. As the McMartin and Jordan investigations proceeded, the charges against most of the defendants were dropped. The network news reports left the question of the conspiracies' existence unresolved. Introducing a report on the dismissal of all remaining charges in the Jordan case, Peter Jennings stated the story's theme: "There is still no complete information on what really happened" (ABC, 22 October 1984).

15. Chapter 8 offers evidence that television's typification of the missing-children problem helped shape public opinion.

CHAPTER SIX

1. There is no master list of recent genre fiction, let alone a classification of books by theme. Therefore it is impossible to identify the population of relevant novels or draw a random sample of those books. I selected and read more than fifty novels for this chapter (see appendix A for a list). Some were books I came across during my own leisure reading, some were recommended by friends, and I found others while browsing in bookstores. They range from major best sellers to works published by small lesbian/feminist presses, from prizewinners to banal examples of hack writing. While I cannot argue that they offer a statistically representative sample, I believe they reflect much of the range of recent writing about threats to children in the two genres.

2. While these books began a period of new popularity for horror novels, horror films had long been a Hollywood staple, and film versions of all three novels appeared by 1973. Other big-budget horror movies centered on children followed (e.g., *The Omen* [1976]).

3. Stephen King offers a similar interpretation (Underwood and Miller 1988, 8–9). Regarding horror films from this period, Ryan and Kellner (1988, 172) state:

> Polls at the time suggested that parenting was becoming a less and less desirable occupation in a postindustrial culture of increased leisure and an expanding singles life. . . . The children of the rebellious subcultures of the sixties and early seventies, who rejected parental authority, must have seemed fairly monstrous to an older generation of more conservative Americans.

4. During the same period, horror films began concentrating on child-victims. Beginning with *Halloween* (1979), dozens of mad-slasher pictures showed assailants stalking and murdering a series of young people. The

popular *Friday the 13th* series featured Jason, a child-monster, slaughtering child-victims.

5. Popular culture producers also resurrected old titles that seemed to fit the new mood. Mary Higgins Clark's 1975 novel *Where are the Children?* was filmed in 1986, at the height of the interest in missing children. And the cover illustration for the 1988 paperback edition of Robert Bloch's *The Kidnapper* (1954) featured a terrified boy looking out a car window—a scene that does not appear in the book.

6. Vachss has given interviews that emphasize both his expertise and his commitment to children's causes (see Pooley 1987).

7. Only the child-victims are new; hard-boiled heroes regularly uncover conspiracies. The detective's "investigation comes up against a web of conspiracy that reflects the presence of a hidden criminal organization; finally, the track leads back to the rich and respectable levels of society and exposes the corrupt relationship between the pillars of the community and the criminal underground" (Cawelti 1976, 148–49).

8. Here again, the theme is consistent with the hard-boiled formula: "evil has become endemic and pervasive; it has begun to crumble the very pillars of middle-class society" (Cawelti 1976, 156).

9. Such revelations also provide dramatic moments in recent films, e.g., *Nuts*. In William Kienzle's novel *The Rosary Murders* (1979), a serial murderer's motivation springs from incest (he was abusing his daughter, confessed to a priest but received no help, and begins killing Catholic clergy after his daughter commits suicide). This motive is revealed midway through the book and plays no important role in the plot. In contrast, the movie version (1987) stages the revelation of incest in a much more dramatic fashion (a nun breaks a vow of silence to reveal the awful truth), and the killer confesses at the film's climax.

Similarly, popular nonfiction found drama in sexual abuse, with dozens of titles ranging from autobiographies of incest survivors to book-length treatments by reporters (Crewdson 1988; Hechler 1988). And, of course, there was the lively debate among intellectuals over Freud's interpretation of his patients' incest reports (Malcolm 1984; Masson 1984).

10. Missing children who are not recovered have been the subject of more serious fiction, e.g., Ian McEwan, *The Child in Time* (1987), Susan Beth Pfeffer, *The Year Without Michael* (a 1987 novel for young adults), and Charles Dickinson, "1-800-YOUR BOY" (1988). These works focus on parents' fears of losing children and the family's sense of loss when a child disappears. Other nongenre fiction, e.g., Walker Percy, *The Thanatos Syndrome* (1987), concerns other threats to children.

11. Because most comic books present fantastic plots and characters, realistic treatments of social problems are relatively uncommon. The issues that I used for my analysis include *Lois Lane* 1–2 (Aug.–Sept. 1986);

Peter Parker, the Spectacular Spider-Man 64 (March 1982); *New Teen Titans* 26–27 (Dec. 1982–Jan. 1983); *Spider-Man and Power Pack* 1 (1984); *Power Pack* 23 (June 1986); *Elementals Special* 1 (March 1986); *Elementals* 27 (July 1988); and Max Allan Collins and Terry Beatty, *Ms. Tree* (New York: PaperJacks, 1988).

Other forms of popular culture aimed at children and adolescents may make greater use of plots concerning threats to children. Engelhardt (1987) notes that kidnappings are common in children's television programs. And young adult fiction increasingly addresses realistic problems, including incest (Hadley Irwin's *Abby, My Love* [1985]) and molestation (John MacLean's *Mac* [1987]).

12. This is not to say that women never appear as victims. The great majority of the victims in mad-slasher movies are female, and young women are usually the targets in thrillers about serial murderers (Caputi 1987). Just as claims about threats to children are reflected in popular culture, there are films and novels that seem influenced by claims-making about rape and serial murder. These works portray women-victims as somehow modern, unlike the traditional, vulnerable innocent; they are often independent, sexually liberated, or strong enough to take revenge.

CHAPTER SEVEN

1. On the reliability of this index, see Troyer and Markle (1983, 41–42).

2. In addition, I checked all entries under "Halloween" in the *Reader's Guide to Periodical Literature, Television News Index and Abstracts,* and the computerized medical data base MEDLINE. I found a single additional case of "Halloween appendicitis" reported in a medical journal (Conforti, Smego, and Kazarian 1987). This report, which noted that Halloween sadism is "a disturbing reality," involved a boy who had swallowed a pin a week *before* Halloween, although the authors state that "the patient had eaten Halloween treats and sweets from several sources outside his home." The analysis that follows is restricted to the seventy-eight cases reported in the newspapers and includes every case that the news report treated as an instance of Halloween sadism. As noted below, some of the cases included were of questionable authenticity.

3. A survey distributed in several Kansas and Oklahoma communities found that a quarter of those who had distributed treats in 1981 did not do so in 1982, and that a fifth of the 1981 trick-or-treaters were not allowed out in 1982 (Wemhamer and Dodder 1984).

4. In 1985, I published a short piece in *Psychology Today,* arguing that Halloween sadism was an urban legend (Best 1985). My article received considerable press attention and may have contributed to the limited coverage of Halloween sadism reports in the years that followed (Best 1986).

5. Sometimes the particulars of these cases are forgotten, so that the

deaths continue to be used as proof that Halloween sadists pose a real threat. Trubo (1974, 28) describes Toston as "the victim of a sadistic prankster" (see also Degh and Vazsonyi 1983, 12).

6. Certainly other elements of everyday life, while not receiving as much attention, are far more hazardous. In 1980–81, according to the U.S. Consumer Product Safety Commission (1982), sixty children under age five died in "product associated deaths' involving nursery equipment and supplies; another thirteen deaths involved toys.

7. In one apparent hoax,

> a youth claimed to have ingested an insecticide-saturated candy bar. . . . Testing showed no traces of any chemicals in the youth's blood. . . . Although there was insecticide on one end of the bar, the side of the candy bar that had been bitten into was insecticide-free (National Confectioners Association et al., n.d.).

Similarly, over 80 percent of the reports of so-called copycat poisonings that followed the Tylenol deaths apparently were fabricated (Church 1982). Some were anonymous pranks, but others involved publicity seekers or schemes to collect insurance settlements from manufacturers. As in the case of Halloween sadism, the threat was exaggerated: congressional hearings denounced "a new kind of thug that is stalking the American communities" (U.S. House 1982, 2), while psychiatrists speculated that "copycat criminals may have weak ego structures and 'have difficulty running their lives'" (Webster 1982).

8. The term "urban legend" is generally used by folklorists to distinguish modern folk tales from those told in traditional societies; it ignores the differences between contemporary urban and rural communities. Brunvand's (1981, 1984, 1986, 1989a) books present several dozen such tales.

9. See Grider (1984). Degh and Vazsonyi also view Halloween sadism as an urban legend—one grounded in fact: "Murderous assaults against children on All Hallows Eve seem to have become customary, pardonable, justifiable, and, so to say, fashionable to some people" (1983, 13); they attribute these acts to "an unorganized, nameless vigilance group" (1983, 15).

10. Gelles and Straus begin their book *Intimate Violence* (1988, 17) by repeating a version of "The Attempted Abduction," noting: "The mere telling of this story is enough to send a shiver down the back of a parent." However, they do not mention that this tale has been well documented as an urban legend.

11. Bromley (1988) distinguishes between urban legends and subversion myths about powerful, organized conspiracies that threaten the entire society. He argues that the many contemporary stories about Satanists belong to the latter category.

12. This case involved giving children pennies heated on a skillet. Apparently this was an early image of Halloween sadism; Grider (1984) recalls a

heated-pennies legend circulating among Texas children in the 1940s. Of course, the fear of Halloween sadism also seems linked to traditional warnings about accepting candy from strangers.

13. The possibility that their children might adopt disapproved values may have suggested betrayal to some parents, creating another source of strain—ambivalence toward one's children. In chapter 6, I suggested that such ambivalence found expression in the child-monsters and evil innocents of early 1970s horror fiction—a genre traditionally associated with Halloween.

The concern with growing drug use may have been especially important in fostering the initial fear of Halloween sadism. Although only one of the seventy-eight newspaper reports involved "hippies" giving drugs to children, early oral versions of contaminated-treat tales often took this form. Years passed before the razor blade in the apple became the standard image for Halloween sadism. Six of the twelve incidents reported before 1967 involved over-the-counter or prescription drugs; only one involved a sharp object. In contrast, fifty-one of the sixty-six reports after 1966 involved razors or other sharp objects, while only four involved drugs. (The most common dead baby joke involves razor blades [Dundes 1979].) Of course, razor blades, pins, and so on are readily available equipment, which would make it easy to carry out hoaxes.

14. Similarly, the Tylenol poisonings raised the prospect of attacks via product contamination. Like the Atlanta murders, these real crimes by an anonymous sadist led to warnings about Halloween sadists (Nimmo and Combs 1985).

15. This fear also found expression in mad-slasher films. Interestingly, the first of these films was *Halloween* (1979).

16. Grider (1984, 132) agrees: "The Razor Blades Syndrome expresses a deep-rooted fear of strangers, a distrust of old customs and traditions, an acknowledgement of child abuse and infanticide, and an ambivalence toward random, wanton violence."

17. Presumably incidents continued to be reported during this period. The decline in press coverage may have reflected journalists' doubts about the authenticity of the reports (*Editor and Publisher* 1973), as well as their recognition that the reported incidents were minor and, given the well-established nature of the legend, no longer newsworthy.

18. While the press routinely interpreted these actions as responses to Halloween sadism, many attempts to restrict trick-or-treating were, in fact, prompted by more traditional Halloween problems, e.g., vandalism or children struck by cars (see Trubo 1974). Recently radiologists have begun questioning whether hospitals ought to x-ray children's treats. These critics do not doubt that Halloween sadism poses a real threat, but they warn that the programs may leave hospitals liable if they fail to detect poison and other contaminants (Calvanese 1986; Malott 1987).

19. Social constructionists usually avoid asking whether social conditions can explain the emergence of claims-making; they prefer to focus on the process once claims begin being made (Spector and Kitsuse 1977). However, Troyer and Markle (1983) suggest that strain usually, if not always, precedes claims-making.

20. Similarly, one common legend about Satanists warns that they plan to abduct children for human sacrifices on Friday the thirteenth.

21. When they are inconsistent with modern practices, earlier forms of celebrating may be forgotten. On the drunken, riotous Christmas customs of the nineteenth-century working class, see Davis (1982).

22. The intense reaction to the Tylenol murders reflected consumers' dependence on mass-produced food and medications. "The revolt of the product is the ultimate nightmare for a society like ours" (Spiro 1982, 11). However, new standards for tamper-resistant packaging apparently reestablished confidence in product safety.

CHAPTER EIGHT

1. The data in this chapter come from six surveys. The *Los Angeles Times* Poll on child sexual abuse was a national telephone survey of 2,627 adults, conducted in late July 1985 (see Crewsdon 1988; Timnick 1985a, 1985b). The California Poll involved a statewide telephone survey of 1,023 adults during late September and early October 1986 (Field Institute 1987). The ABC News/*Washington Post* Poll was a national telephone survey of 1,506 adults during late October 1985 (ABC News Polling Unit 1985). The American Chicle Youth Poll conducted face-to-face interviews with a national sample of 1,000 respondents, eight to seventeen, during mid-November 1986 (Roper Organization 1987). Price and Desmond (1987) distributed a questionnaire to 315 fifth-grade students in a large Midwestern city. Data from the sixth study, a July 1986 telephone survey of 503 Illinois parents of children under age eighteen, come from an unpublished paper (Lavrakas and Rosenbaum 1987).

Most of this chapter presents a secondary analysis of data from the *Los Angeles Times* Poll (hereafter abbreviated LATP), the California Poll (hereafter CP), and the American Chicle Youth Poll (hereafter ACYP).

2. Throughout this chapter, unless noted otherwise, chi-square is used as a test of statistical significance and Cramer's v as a measure of association.

3. All of the intercorrelations among these eight items were positive and statistically significant (Pearson's r shown in the table below). Each item had three or four possible responses. The Index of Concern adds the responses to the eight items to measure the respondent's overall level of concern about threats to children. The combined index has a strong reliability coefficient (alpha = .81). In the analysis that follows, index respondents are grouped into four quartiles.

204

INTERCORRELATIONS AMONG INDEX OF CONCERN ITEMS

Items	Kid-napping	Molest-ing	Pornog-raphy	Missing Serious	Kidnap Danger	Risk to Respon-dent's Child	Stranger-abduction Crisis
More Child Abuse	.43	.59	.37	.30	.31	.22	.32
More Kidnapping		.44	.30	.32	.36	.25	.40
More Molesting			.46	.29	.34	.28	.37
More Child Porn				.24	.29	.20	.29
Missing Serious					.50	.27	.50
Kidnap Danger						.47	.58
Risk to Respon-dent's Child							.37

4. In personal communication, Gary Alan Fine has argued for the baby-boomer—or "symbolic demography"—explanation. He suggests that the higher incidence of concern for threatened children among those over sixty-five may simply reflect a general tendency for older people to be fearful.

The *Los Angeles Times* Poll data offer a rough test of this argument. Respondents were asked to assess the seriousness of the crime problem in their community—a question which resembles standard fear-of-crime questions. When we reexamine the relationship between age and concern about sexual abuse, while controlling for the respondents' assessments of local crime, we find:

ASSESSMENT OF COMMUNITY'S CRIME PROBLEM

Age Group	Very Serious (%)	Fairly Serious (%)	Not Very Serious (%)	Hardly Any Crime (%)
18−29	32	23	23	36
	($n = 44$)	(135)	(217)	(213)
30−39	33	21	16	22
	(39)	(108)	(229)	(231)
40−64	19	29	16	28
	(47)	(193)	(297)	(363)
65+	40	33	36	41
	(15)	(55)	(101)	(152)

Percent responding that there are more news stories about child abuse because "there is more child abuse going on today then there used to be

Regardless of their assessment of the local crime problem, older respondents had the highest incidence of concern about child abuse, while the older baby-boomers (aged thirty to thirty-nine, born from 1946 to 1955) generally displayed low levels of concern. While the LATP questions are imperfect measures, the pattern predicted by the baby-boomer-parent hypothesis simply does not emerge.

5. In contrast, those in the most concerned quartile were least likely to mention magazines as a source of information ($p < .05$—$v = .11$). Items

asking about newspapers, radio, and word of mouth as influences showed no significant differences.

6. Seven of the thirteen vignettes were presented in independent items, but there were two items featuring three related vignettes. Thus, respondents were first asked whether a fourteen-year-old seduced by a fourteen-year-old girl was a case of sexual abuse. If the respondent replied no, then the interviewer asked about a fourteen-year-old boy seduced by an eighteen-year-old girl (and, if the answer was again no, about a twenty-two-year-old woman seducing a fourteen-year-old boy). However, if the respondent labelled either of the first two vignettes abusive, the interviewer moved on to the next item (about a fourteen-year-old girl seduced by a fourteen-year-old boy). In other words, the questionnaire design assumed that anyone who viewed the first vignette as abusive would find the next two abusive. In computing the index, anyone responding positively to the first vignette received three points, while those who responded positively to the second vignette received two points, and so on.

7. Respondents first were asked: "When you were a child, can you remember having any experience you would now consider sexual abuse—like someone trying or succeeding in having any kind of sexual intercourse with you, or anything like that?" Twelve percent of the sample (318 respondents) said they had. Those who denied being victimized were asked up to three more questions about other experiences they would now consider abuse: "someone touching you, or grabbing you, or kissing you, or rubbing up against your body" (210 additional respondents said yes); "someone taking nude photographs of you, or someone exhibiting parts of their body to you, or someone performing some sex act in your presence" (52 respondents); and "oral sex or sodomy" (5 respondents). The analysis that follows treats all respondents who answered yes to one of these questions as former victims.

8. Respondents were read a list of eight reasons and could give up to two reasons.

9. Correlations with the Index of Concern were highly significant ($p <$ .001) for all four items rated on the ten-point scale: teach to report sexual abuse (Pearson's $r = .25$); teach to avoid strangers ($r = .40$); inspect Halloween treats ($r = .38$); and review lyrics ($r = .40$). Grouping Index of Concern scores into quartiles, we find that 96 percent of those in the most concerned quartile strongly agreed that children should be taught to avoid kidnapping; the percentage fell to 71 percent in the least concerned quartile (chi-square—$p < .001$—$v = .16$).

10. The Gallup Poll also asked a parallel question about satisfaction "with the way things are going in your personal life." In polls from 1979 to 1987, substantial majorities (73 to 84 percent) declared themselves satisfied with their personal lives (*Gallup Report* 1987).

CHAPTER NINE

1. "The central problem for a theory of social problems is to account for the *emergence,* nature, and maintenance of claims-making and responding activities" (Spector and Kitsuse 1977, 76—emphasis added). However, Spector and Kitsuse go on to warn against approaching claims-making's emergence from some angles. Studying "participants to find individual and social characteristics that predict participation in [claims-making] activities deflects attention away from the organization of claims-making itself" (1977, 82). Similarly, values should be seen as a resource for claims-makers, not a cause of their behavior. Spector and Kitsuse (1977, 96) conclude: "Premature consideration of the causes of any phenomenon turns attention to the supposed antecedents of the activity, rather than to the activity itself."

2. Obviously, it is difficult to measure the incidence of claims-making over time. However, Goldstone (1980) suggests that social movements tend to have greater success during periods of national crisis.

3. Such analyses sometimes challenged basic cultural assumptions. For instance, Kitzinger (1987: 79–80) argues the movement against sexual abuse should not emphasize children's innocence because "the notion of childhood innocence is itself a source of titillation for abusers"; "it stigmatizes the 'knowing' child"; and "it is an ideology used to deny children access to knowledge and power."

APPENDIX
Recent Fiction about
Threats to Children

HORROR FICTION
Andrews, V. C. 1979. *Flowers in the Attic*. New York: Pocket Books.
———. 1980. *Petals on the Wind*. New York: Pocket Books.
———. 1981. *If There Be Thorns*. New York: Pocket Books.
———. 1984. *Seeds of Yesterday*. New York: Pocket Books.
Blatty, William Peter. 1971. *The Exorcist*. New York: Harper and Row.
Devon, Gary. 1986. *Lost*. New York: Warner.
Greenburg, Dan. 1987. *The Nanny*. New York: Macmillan.
Gresham, Stephen. 1987. *Midnight Boy*. New York: Zebra.
Keene, Joseph E., and William W. Johnstone. 1987. *Baby Grand*. New York: Zebra.
King, Stephen. 1974. *Carrie*. New York: Doubleday.
———. 1975. *'Salem's Lot*. New York: Doubleday.
———. 1977. *The Shining*. New York: Doubleday.
———. 1979. *The Dead Zone*. New York: Viking.
———. 1980. *Firestarter*. New York: Viking.
———. 1981. *Cujo*. New York: Viking.
———. 1983. *Pet Sematary*. New York: Doubleday.
———. 1986. *It*. New York: Viking.
Levin, Ira. 1967. *Rosemary's Baby*. New York: Random House.
Saul, John. 1977. *Suffer the Children*. New York: Dell.
Stewart, Michael. 1984. *Far Cry*. New York: PaperJacks.
Straub, Peter. 1975. *Julia*. New York: Pocket Books.
———. 1979. *Ghost Story*. New York: Pocket Books.
Tryon, Thomas. 1971. *The Other*. New York: Knopf.
Wood, Bari. 1987. *Amy Girl*. New York: New American Library.

CRIME AND DETECTIVE FICTION
Bloch, Robert. 1988 (1954). *The Kidnapper*. New York: Tom Doherty.
Campbell, Robert. 1986. *In La-La Land We Trust*. New York: Mysterious Press.

Dean, S. F. X. 1987. *Nantucket Soap Opera*. New York: Atheneum.

Forrest, Katherine V. 1987. *Murder at the Nightwood Bar*. Tallahassee: Naiad.

Frey, James N. 1987. *The Long Way to Die*. New York: Bantam.

Kellerman, Faye. 1987. *Sacred and Profane*. New York: Arbor House.

Kellerman, Jonathan. 1985. *When the Bough Breaks*. New York: Atheneum.

———. 1986. *Blood Test*. New York: Atheneum.

———. 1987. *Over the Edge*. New York: Atheneum.

Kienzle, William. 1979. *The Rosary Murders*. Mission, KS: Andrews & McMeel.

Lundy, Mike. 1987. *Baby Farm*. New York: Lyle Stuart.

Parker, Robert B. 1974. *God Save the Child*. Boston: Houghton Mifflin.

———. 1975. *Mortal Stakes*. Boston: Houghton Mifflin.

———. 1981. *Early Autumn*. New York: Delacorte.

———. 1982. *Ceremony*. New York: Delacorte.

———. 1986. *Taming a Sea-Horse*. New York: Delacorte.

———. 1988. *Crimson Joy*. New York: Delacorte.

Reynolds, William J. 1986. *Moving Targets*. New York: St. Martin's.

Schutz, Benjamin M. 1986. *Embrace the Wolf*. New York: Bantam.

———. 1987. *All the Old Bargains*. New York: Bantam.

Vachss, Andrew H. 1985. *Flood*. New York: Donald I. Fine.

———. 1987. *Strega*. New York: Knopf.

Valin, Jonathan. 1980. *The Lime Pit*. New York: Dodd, Mead.

Wilson, Barbara. 1986. *Sisters of the Road*. Seattle: Seal Press.

OTHER FICTION

Chase, Samantha. 1988. *Postmark*. New York: Tudor.

Clark, Mary Higgins. 1975. *Where Are the Children?* New York: Dell.

Dickinson, Charles. 1988. "1-800-YOUR BOY." Atlantic 261 (March): 62–68.

Dorner, Marjorie. 1987. *Nightmare*. New York: Warner.

Gutcheon, Beth. 1981. *Still Missing*. New York: G. P. Putnam's Sons.

Irwin, Hadley. 1985. *Abby, My Love*. New York: Macmillan.

MacLean, John. 1987. *Mac*. Boston: Houghton Mifflin.

McEwan, Ian. 1987. *The Child in Time*. Boston: Houghton Mifflin.

Murphy, Gloria. 1986. *Nightshade*. New York: Donald I. Fine.

———. 1987a. *Bloodties*. New York: Donald I. Fine.

———. 1987b. *Nightmare*. New York: Popular Library.

Percy, Walker. 1987. *The Thanatos Syndrome*. New York: Farrar, Straus & Giroux.

Pfeffer, Susan Beth. 1987. *The Year Without Michael*. New York: Bantam.

REFERENCES

ABC News Polling Unit. 1985. ABC News/*Washington Post* Poll 206 (October).

Abrahms, Sally. 1985. "The Villain in Child Snatching is Usually . . . a Parent." *Wall Street Journal,* 19 March: 28.

Adams, W. C. 1986. "Whose Lives Count?" *Journal of Communication* 36 (Spring): 113–22.

Adler, Patricia A., and Peter Adler. 1978. "Tinydopers." *Symbolic Interaction* 1:90–105.

Altheide, David L. 1976. *Creating Reality.* Beverly Hills: Sage.

Andrews, Lori B. 1986. "Are We Raising a Terrified Generation?" *Parents* 61 (December): 139–42, 228–32.

Anonymous. 1976. *What Everyone Should Know about Child Abuse.* South Deerfield, MA: Channing L. Bete.

———. 1979. "I Kidnapped My Own Son." *Good Housekeeping* 189 (October): 26–36.

———. 1981. *What Everyone Should Know about the Sexual Abuse of Children.* South Deerfield, MA: Channing L. Bete.

———. 1987. *Abortion Is Not a Sin.* Costa Mesa, CA: Pandit Press.

Arax, Mark, and Bill Billiter. 1987. "Flyers Stir Fears About LSD-Laced Rub-on Tattoos." *Los Angeles Times,* 9 December: 2-1, 4.

Arena, Jay M., and Miriam Bahar Settle. 1987. *Child Safety Is No Accident.* Rev. ed. New York: Berkley.

Aronson, Naomi. 1984. "Science as a Claims-Making Activity." In Joseph W. Schneider and John I. Kitsuse, eds., *Studies in the Sociology of Social Problems,* 1–30. Norwood, NJ: Ablex.

Barker, Martin. 1984. *A Haunt of Fears: The Strange History of the British Horror Comics Campaign.* London: Pluto Press.

Barkin, Steve M., and Michael Gurevitch. 1987. "Out of Work and On the Air." *Critical Studies in Mass Communication* 4:1–20.

Berenstain, Stan, and Jan Berenstain. 1985. *The Berenstain Bears Learn about Strangers.* New York: Random House.

211

Berry, Joy. 1984. *Alerting Kids to the Danger of Kidnapping.* Waco, TX: Word.

Besharov, Douglas J. 1985. "'Doing Something' about Child Abuse." *Harvard Journal of Law and Public Policy* 8:539–89.

———. 1986. "Unfounded Allegations—A New Child Abuse Problem." *The Public Interest* 83:18–33.

Best, Joel. 1985. "The Myth of the Halloween Sadist." *Psychology Today* 19 (November): 14, 16.

———. 1986. "Famous for Fifteen Minutes." *Qualitative Sociology* 9: 372–82.

———, ed. 1989. *Images of Issues: Typifying Contemporary Social Problems.* New York: Aldine de Gruyter.

Block, Fred, and Gene A. Burns. 1986. "Productivity as a Social Problem: The Uses and Misuses of Social Indicators." *American Sociological Review* 51:767–80.

Blumenthal, Ralph. 1984. "Registry of Missing Children Faces State Inquiry." *New York Times,* 21 May: B2.

Blumer, Herbert. 1971. "Social Problems as Collective Behavior." *Social Problems* 18:298–306.

Boegehold, Betty. 1985. *You Can Say "No."* New York: Golden Books.

Boles, Jacqueline, and Phillip Davis. 1988. "Defending Atlanta: Press Reactions to a Movie on the Missing and Murdered Children." *Journal of American Culture* 11 (Fall): 61–66.

Boorstin, Daniel J. 1964. *The Image.* New York: Harper & Row.

Brigman, William E. 1984. "Circumcision as Child Abuse," *Journal of Family Law* 23:337–57.

Bromley, David G. 1988. "Folk Narratives and Deviance Construction." Unpublished paper.

Brown, Edward J., Timothy J. Flanagan, and Maureen McLeod, eds. 1984. *Sourcebook of Criminal Justice Statistics.* Washington, DC: U.S. Department of Justice, Bureau of Justice Statistics.

Brown, Harold O. J. 1977. *Death before Birth.* Nashville, TN: Thomas Nelson.

Brunvand, Jan Harold. 1981. *The Vanishing Hitchhiker.* New York: Norton.

———. 1984. *The Choking Doberman.* New York: Norton.

———. 1985. "Urban Legends in the Making." *Whole Earth Review* 48 (Fall): 124–29.

———. 1986. *The Mexican Pet.* New York: Norton.

———. 1989a. *Curses! Broiled Again!* New York: Norton.

———. 1989b. Personal communication.

Burgess, Ann Wolbert, ed. 1984. *Child Pornography and Sex Rings.* Lexington, MA: Lexington.

Burgess, Parke G. 1968. "The Rhetoric of Black Power." *Quarterly Journal of Speech* 54:122–33.

212

Bussing, Sabine. 1987. *Aliens in the Home: The Child in Horror Fiction.* Westport, CT: Greenwood.

Cahan, William G. 1985. "Abusing Children by Smoking." *New York Times,* 9 March: 23.

Calvanese, Jerry. 1986. "Should We X-Ray Halloween Candy?" *American Journal of Roentgenology* 147: 854–55.

California Attorney General. 1984. *Opinions of the Attorney General of California* 67: 235–41. Sacramento: California Department of Justice.

Campbell, Richard. 1987. "Securing the Middle Ground: Reporter Formulas in *60 Minutes.*" *Critical Studies in Mass Communication* 4: 325–50.

Cantor, Muriel G., and Suzanne Pingree. 1983. *The Soap Opera.* Beverly Hills: Sage.

Caplow, Theodore. 1982. "Christmas Gifts and Kin Networks." *American Sociological Review* 47: 383–92.

Caplow, Theodore, and Margaret Holmes Williamson. 1980. "Decoding Middletown's Easter Bunny." *Semiotica* 32: 221–32.

Caputi, Jane. 1987. *The Age of Sex Crime.* Bowling Green, OH: Bowling Green University Popular Press.

Carroll, Michael P. 1987. "'The Castrated Boy.'" *Folklore* 98: 216–25.

Cawelti, John G. 1976. *Adventure, Mystery, and Romance.* Chicago: University of Chicago Press.

Cerra, Frances. 1986. "Missing Children." *Ms.* 14 (January): 14–16.

Charlier, Tom, and Shirley Downing. 1988. "Justice Abused: A 1980s Witch-Hunt" (series). *Memphis Commercial Appeal,* January.

Chollet, Mary E., and Michael D. Sorkin. 1988. "'Child Find' Group Criticized by Police and Others." *St. Louis Post-Dispatch,* 18 May: 1, 8.

Christie, Nils. 1986. "The Ideal Victim." In Ezzat A. Fattah, ed., *From Crime Policy to Victim Policy,* 17–30. London: Macmillan.

Church, George J. 1982. "Copycats on the Prowl." *Time* 120 (8 November): 27.

Cocks, Jay. 1985. "Rock Is a Four-Letter Word." *Time* 126 (30 September): 70–71.

Cohen, Ronald D. 1985. "Child-Saving and Progressivism, 1885–1915." In Joseph M. Hawes and N. Ray Hiner, eds., *American Childhood,* 273–309. Westport, CT: Greenwood.

Collins, John. 1987. "Cult Rumors Rattle South Carolina." *The State* (Columbia, SC), 14 March: 1-A, 8-A.

Conforti, Frederick P., Douglas R. Smego, and Kirk K. Kazarian. 1987. "Halloween Appendicitis." *Connecticut Medicine* 5: 507.

Connelly, Mark Thomas. 1980. *The Response to Prostitution in the Progressive Era.* Chapel Hill: University of North Carolina Press.

Conrad, Peter, and Joseph W. Schneider. 1980. *Deviance and Medicalization.* St. Louis: Mosby.

Conte, John R. 1977. "Child Sexual Abuse." In Philip Houda, ed., *Encyclopedia of Social Work*, 255–60. 17th ed. Washington: National Association of Social Workers.

Converse, Philip E., et al. 1980. *American Social Attitudes Data Sourcebook*. Cambridge: Harvard University Press.

Corrigan, Dean. 1989. "Strike Corporal Punishment from Schools—Its Use Is Abuse." *Houston Chronicle*, 2 April: 4H.

Cravens, Hamilton. 1985. "Child-Saving in the Age of Professionalism, 1915–1930." In Joseph M. Hawes and N. Ray Hiner, eds., *American Childhood*, 415–88. Westport, CT: Greenwood.

Crewdson, John. 1988. *By Silence Betrayed: Sexual Abuse of Children in America*. Boston: Little, Brown.

Crystal, Stephen. 1987. "Elder Abuse: The Latest 'Crisis.'" *The Public Interest* 88:56–66.

Currie, Elliott P. 1968. "Crimes Without Criminals: Witchcraft and its Control in Renaissance Europe." *Law and Society Review* 3:7–32.

Daniels, Les. 1975. *Living in Fear: A History of Horror in the Mass Media*. New York: Scribner's.

Davis, Susan G. 1982. "'Making the Night Hideous.'" *American Quarterly* 34:185–99.

Degh, Linda, and Andrew Vazsonyi. 1983. "Does the Word 'Dog' Bite? Obstensive Action: A Means of Legend Telling." *Journal of Folklore Research* 20:5–34.

deMause, Lloyd. 1974. "The Evolution of Childhood." In Lloyd deMause, ed., *The History of Childhood*, 1–73. New York: Psychohistory Press.

Denver Post. 1985. "Missing Children" editorial. 19 May: 6H.

de Young, Mary. 1984. "Ethics and the 'Lunatic Fringe': The Case of Pedophile Organizations." *Human Organization* 43:72–74.

Diamond, John L. 1985. "Kidnapping." *American Journal of Criminal Law* 13:1–36.

Downs, Anthony. 1972. "Up and Down with Ecology—The 'Issue-Attention Cycle.'" *The Public Interest* 28:38–50.

Dundes, Alan. 1979. "The Dead Baby Joke Cycle." *Western Folklore* 38:145–57.

Eberle, Paul, and Shirley Eberle. 1986. *The Politics of Child Abuse*. Secaucus, NJ: Lyle Stuart.

Editor and Publisher. 1973. "Press Finds Halloween Sadism Rare But Warns of Danger." 106 (3 March): 22.

Eliasoph, Nina. 1986. "Drive-In Morality, Child Abuse, and the Media." *Socialist Review* 90:7–31.

Elliott, Susan Newhart, and Dianna L. Pendleton. 1986. "S. 321: The Missing Children Act—Legislation by Hysteria." *University of Dayton Law Review* 11:671–708.

214

Ellis, Bill. 1989. "Mickey Mouse LSD Tattoos." *FOAFtale News* 14:3–4.

Elshtain, Jean Bethke. 1985. "How We Succumb to Hype and Hysteria." *Progressive* 49 (September): 23–26.

Engelhardt, Tom. 1987. "The Shortcake Strategy." In Todd Gitlin, ed., *Watching Television,* 68–110. New York: Pantheon.

Epstein, Edward Jay. 1973. *News from Nowhere.* New York: Random House.

Erskine, Hazel. 1974. "The Polls: Fear of Crime and Violence." *Public Opinion Quarterly* 38:131–45.

Federal Bureau of Investigation. 1985. *Crime in the United States—1984.* Washington, DC: U.S. Government Printing Office.

Field Institute. 1987. "Threats to Children." *California Opinion Index* 2 (March): 1–4.

Fine, Gary Alan. 1979. "Cokelore and Coke Law." *Journal of American Folklore* 92:477–82.

———. 1980. "The Kentucky Fried Rat." *Journal of the Folklore Institute* 17:222–43.

———. 1985. "The Goliath Effect." *Journal of American Folklore* 98:63–84.

Fischer, Claude S. 1982. *To Dwell Among Friends.* Chicago: University of Chicago Press.

Fishman, Mark. 1978. "Crime Waves as Ideology." *Social Problems* 25: 531–43.

Flato, Charles. 1962. "Parents Who Beat Children." *Saturday Evening Post* 235 (6 October): 30, 32, 34–35.

Fontana, Vincent J., Denis Donovan, and Raymond J. Wong. 1963. "The 'Maltreatment Syndrome' in Children." *New England Journal of Medicine* 269:1389–94.

Freedman, Estelle B. 1987. "'Uncontrolled Desires.'" *Journal of American History* 74:83–106.

Friedrich, Otto. 1964. "There Are 00 Trees in Russia: The Function of Facts in Newsmagazines." *Harper's* 229 (October): 59–65.

Fritz, Noah J., and David L. Altheide. 1987. "The Mass Media and the Social Construction of the Missing Children Problem." *Sociological Quarterly* 28:473–92.

Gallup Report. 1982. "One in Seven Americans Reports Knowing of Instance of Child Abuse in Own Neighborhood." 197:28–29.

———. 1986. "Americans More Fearful of World War Than Are People of Other Nations." 255:6–7.

———. 1987. "Public Mood Shows No Sign of Brightening." 266:25–26.

Gamson, William A. 1988. "A Constructionist Approach to Mass Media and Public Opinion." *Symbolic Interaction* 11:161–74.

Gans, Herbert J. 1979. *Deciding What's News.* New York: Pantheon.

Garrett, Karen Ann, and Peter H. Rossi. 1978. "Judging the Seriousness of Child Abuse." *Medical Anthropology* 2:1–48.

Gelles, Richard J., and Murray A. Straus. 1988. *Intimate Violence.* New York: Simon and Schuster.

Gentry, Cynthia. 1988. "The Social Construction of Abducted Children as a Social Problem." *Sociological Inquiry* 58:413–25.

Gilbert, Neil. 1988. "Teaching Children to Prevent Sexual Abuse." *The Public Interest* 93:3–15.

Gillespie, Dair L., and Ann Leffler. 1987. "The Politics of Research Methodology in Claims-Making Activities: Social Science and Sexual Harassment." *Social Problems* 34:490–501.

Ginsburg, Marsha. 1988. "Collins Foundation Presence Still Felt." *San Francisco Examiner,* 4 December: B1, 3.

Giovannoni, Jeanne M., and Rosina M. Becerra. 1979. *Defining Child Abuse.* New York: Free Press.

Gitlin, Todd. 1980. *The Whole World Is Watching.* Berkeley: University of California Press.

———. 1983. *Inside Prime Time.* New York: Pantheon.

Goldstone, Jack A. 1980. "The Weakness of Organization." *American Journal of Sociology* 85:1017–42.

Goodwin, Joseph P. 1989. "Unprintable Reactions to All the News That's Fit to Print." *Southern Folklore* 46:15–39.

Gore, Tipper. 1987. *Raising PG Kids in an X-Rated World.* Nashville: Abingdon.

Gorney, Cynthia. 1988. "The Baffling Case of the McMartin Preschool." *This World (San Francisco Chronicle),* 26 June: 10–14.

Gray, Herman S. 1989. "Popular Music as a Social Problem." In Joel Best, ed., *Images of Issues,* 143–58. New York: Aldine de Gruyter.

Grider, Sylvia. 1984. "The Razor Blades in the Apples Syndrome." In Paul Smith, ed., *Perspectives on Contemporary Legend,* 128–40. Sheffield, England: Centre for English Cultural Tradition and Language.

Griego, Diana, and Louis Kilzer. 1985. "Truth about Missing Kids: Exaggerated Statistics Stir National Paranoia." *Denver Post,* 12 May: 1A, 12A.

Gusfield, Joseph R. 1981. *The Culture of Public Problems: Drinking-Driving and the Symbolic Order.* Chicago: University of Chicago Press.

———. 1985. "Theories and Hobgoblins." *Society for the Study of Social Problems Newsletter* 17 (Fall): 16–18.

Hallin, Daniel C. 1986. *The "Uncensored War."* New York: Oxford University Press.

———. 1987. "We Keep America on Top of the World." In Todd Gitlin, ed., *Watching Television,* 9–41. New York: Pantheon.

———. 1988. "The Coming of the Ten-Second Sound Bite." Unpublished paper.

Hallin, Daniel C., and Palolo Mancini. 1984. "Speaking of the President." *Theory and Society* 13:829–50.

216

Harris, Paul. 1988. "Reagan Vetoes Kids Programming Bill." *Variety* 333 (9 November): 35.

Hart, Roderick P., Patrick Jerome, and Karen McComb. 1984. "Rhetorical Features of Newscasts About the President." *Critical Studies in Mass Communication* 1:260–86.

Hatch, Jane M., ed. 1978. *The American Book of Days*. 3d edition. New York: Wilson.

Hawkins, Paula. 1986. *Children at Risk*. Bethesda, MD: Adler & Adler.

Hazelrigg, Lawrence E. 1986. "Is There a Choice Between 'Constructionism' and 'Objectivism'?" *Social Problems* 33:S1–S13.

Headley, Bernard D. 1986. "Ideological Constructions of Race and the 'Atlanta Tragedy.'" *Contemporary Crises* 10:181–200.

Hechler, David. 1988. *The Battle and the Backlash: The Child Sexual Abuse War*. Lexington, MA: Lexington.

Heritage, John, and David Greatbatch. 1986. "Generating Applause: A Study of Rhetoric and Response at Party Political Conferences." *American Journal of Sociology* 92:110–57.

Hilgartner, Stephen, and Charles L. Bosk. 1988. "The Rise and Fall of Social Problems: A Public Arenas Model." *American Journal of Sociology* 94:53–78.

Hirschel, J. David, and Steven P. Lab. 1988. "Who Is Missing?: The Realities of the Missing Persons Problem." *Journal of Criminal Justice* 16:35–45.

Hotaling, Gerald T., and David Finkelhor. 1988. "Estimating the Number of Stranger Abduction Homicides of Children." Unpublished paper.

Huffman, James R., and Julie L. Huffman. 1987. "Sexism and Cultural Lag: The Rise of the Jailbait Song, 1955–1985." *Journal of Popular Culture* 21 (Fall): 65–83.

Hughes, Helen MacGill. 1940. *News and the Human Interest Story*. Chicago: University of Chicago Press.

Hull, Karla. 1986. *Safe Passages*. Berkeley: Dawn Sign Press.

Illinois State Police. 1987. "Children Reported Missing During 1986." Unpublished.

Investigative News Group. 1988. "Satanic Cults and Children." "Geraldo" transcript 206.

Isaacs, Susan and Robert Royeton. 1982. "Witches, Goblins, Ghosts." *Parents* 57 (October): 66–69.

Iyengar, Shanto, and Donald R. Kinder. 1987. *News That Matters*. Chicago: University of Chicago Press.

Jacobs, Norman. 1965. "The Phantom Slasher of Taipei." *Social Problems* 12:318–28.

James, Jennifer, et al. 1977. *The Politics of Prostitution*. Seattle: Social Research Associates.

Jares, Sue Ellen. 1981. "A Victim and a Childnapper Describe the Agonizing Problem of the 'Stolen' Kids of Divorce." *People* 15 (9 February): 40, 42.

Joe, Karen A. 1988. "Milk Carton Madness." Paper presented before the Pacific Sociological Association.

Johnson, Donald M. 1945. "The 'Phantom Anesthetist' of Mattoon." *Journal of Abnormal and Social Psychology* 40: 175–86.

Johnson, John M. 1985. "Symbolic Salvation: The Changing Meanings of the Child Maltreatment Movement." *Studies in Symbolic Interaction* 6: 289–305.

———. 1989. "Horror Stories and the Construction of Child Abuse." In Joel Best, ed., *Images of Issues,* 5–19. New York: Aldine de Gruyter.

Jordan, Mary. 1985. "The Search for Missing Children." *Washington Post,* 25 May: A1, A10.

Kantrowitz, Barbara. 1986. "Anatomy of a Drug Scare." *Newsweek* 108 (November 24): 85.

Kantrowitz, Barbara, and Connie Leslie. 1986. "Teaching Fear." *Newsweek* 107 (10 March): 62–63.

Karlen, Neal. 1985. "How Many Missing Kids?" *Newsweek* 106 (7 October): 30, 35.

Kell, Gretchen. 1989. "Campaign Against Child Kidnapping Begins." *Fresno Bee,* 11 February: A2.

Kelly, Liz. 1988. "What's in a Name? Defining Child Sexual Abuse." *Feminist Review* 28: 65–73.

Kelly, Mike (California Missing/Unidentified Persons Program). 1986. Personal communication.

Kempe, C. Henry, et al. 1962. "The Battered-Child Syndrome." *Journal of the American Medical Association* 181: 17–24.

Kendrick, Walter. 1987. *The Secret Museum.* New York: Penguin.

Kerckhoff, Alan C., and Kurt W. Back. 1968. *The June Bug.* New York: Appleton-Century-Crofts.

Kevin Collins Foundation for Missing Children. 1987. "Editorial: Is There a Problem of Stranger Abduction?" *Newsletter* 3 (Spring).

Kilzer, Louis. 1985. "Public Often Not Told the Facts in Missing-Children Cases." *Denver Post,* 22 September: 1A, 14A.

Kitsuse, John I., and Aaron Cicourel. 1963. "A Note on the Use of Official Statistics." *Social Problems* 11: 131–39.

Kitzinger, Jenny. 1988. "Defending Innocence: Ideologies of Childhood." *Feminist Review* 28: 77–87.

Klapp, Orrin E. 1964. *Symbolic Leaders.* Chicago: Aldine.

Klemesrud, Judy. 1970. "Those Treats may be Tricks." *New York Times,* 28 October: 56.

————. 1972. "Trick-or-Treating Till Stroke of 7." *New York Times,* 1 November: 30.

Kolata, Gina. 1988. "Rumor of LSD-Tainted Tattoos Called Hoax." *New York Times,* 9 December: B1, B5.

Kraizer, Sherryll Kerns. 1985. *The Safe Child Book.* New York: Dell.

Kraybill, Eugene. 1986. "Scaring our Kids." *U.S. News and World Report* 100 (10 February): 81.

Kurczewski, Norbert A., and Glenn R. Lewis. 1986. *Someone Took Him.* Kent, WA: Profiles Mini-books.

Lake, Randall A. 1986. "The Metaethical Framework of Anti-Abortion Rhetoric." *Signs* 11:478–99.

Lanning, Kenneth V. 1987. *Child Molesters: A Behavioral Analysis.* 2d ed. Washington, DC: National Center for Missing and Exploited Children.

Lavrakas, Paul J., and Susan M. Rosenbaum. 1987. "Attitudes towards the Missing Children Issue." Paper presented before the American Society of Criminology.

Leerhsen, Charles. 1982. "Parents of Slain Children." *Newsweek* 99 (12 April): 84.

Lenett, Robin. 1985. *It's O.K. to Say No!* New York: TOR.

Lenett, Robin, and Dana Barthelme. 1986. *Sometimes It's O.K. to Tell Secrets!* New York: TOR.

Lewis, Harold. 1986. "The Community as Child Abuser." *Hastings Center Report* (December): 17–18.

Lippis, John. 1982. *The Challenge to Be "Pro-Life."* Santa Barbara, CA: Pro Life Education.

Lofland, John. 1981. "Collective Behavior." In Morris Rosenberg and Ralph H. Turner, eds., *Social Psychology,* 411–46. New York: Basic Books.

————. 1988. "Consensus Movements." *Research in Social Movements, Conflicts and Change* 11: in press.

Luckenbill, David F. 1985. "Entering Male Prostitution." *Urban Life* 14: 131–53.

Lyons, Arthur. 1988. *Satan Wants You.* New York: Mysterious Press.

Magistrale, Tony. 1985. "Inherited Haunts: Stephen King's Terrible Children." *Extrapolation* 26:43–49.

Malcolm, Janet. 1984. *In the Freud Archives.* New York: Knopf.

Malott, Jack C. "X-Ray Halloween Candy: A Public Service?" *Radiology Management* 9 (Fall): 78–79.

Manson, Rebecca, and Judy Marlot. 1988. "A New Crime, Fetal Neglect." *California Western Law Review* 24:161–82.

Masson, Jeffrey M. 1984. *The Assault on the Truth.* New York: Farrar, Straus & Giroux.

Mawyer, Martin. 1987. *Silent Shame: The Alarming Rise of Child Sexual Abuse and How to Protect Your Children from It.* Westchester, IL: Crossway.

Maxson, Cheryl L., Margaret A. Little, and Malcolm W. Klein. 1988. "Police Response to Runaway and Missing Children." *Crime and Delinquency* 34:84–102.

McAdam, Doug. 1983. "Tactical Innovation and the Pace of Insurgency." *American Sociological Review* 48:735–53.

McCarthy, John D., and Mayer N. Zald. 1977. "Resource Mobilization and Social Movements." *American Journal of Sociology* 82:1212–41.

McNair, Jean. 1985. "Va. Probing Advertising Tactics of Publication on Missing Children." *Washington Post,* 20 August: B3.

Medalia, Nahum Z., and Otto N. Larsen. 1958. "Diffusion and Belief in a Collective Delusion." *American Sociological Review* 23:180–86.

Mehan, Hugh, and John Wills. 1988. "MEND: A Nurturing Voice in the Nuclear Arms Debate." *Social Problems* 35:363–83.

Meriwether, Margaret H. 1986. "Child Abuse Reporting Laws." *Family Law Quarterly* 20:141–71.

Merry, Sally Engle. 1981. *Urban Danger.* Philadelphia: Temple University Press.

Meyer, Linda D. 1984. *Safety Zone.* Edmonds, WA: Chas. Franklin Press.

Miller, Carl. 1985. "Child-Abduction Worries Excessive, Area Poll Finds." *Denver Post,* 13 May: 1A.

Molotch, Harvey, and Marilyn Lester. 1974. "News as Purposive Behavior." *American Sociological Review* 39:101–12.

———. 1975. "Accidental News." *American Journal of Sociology* 81:235–60.

Nathan, Debbie. 1987. "The Making of a Modern Witch Trial." *Village Voice* 32 (29 September): 19–32.

———. 1988. "Victimizer or Victim?" *Village Voice* 33 (2 August): 31–39.

National Center for Missing and Exploited Children. 1986a. "An Evaluation of the Crime of Kidnapping as It Is Committed against Children by Nonfamily Members." Washington, DC: NCMEC.

———. 1986b. "State Legislation to Protect Children." Washington, DC: NCMEC.

National Child Safety Council. 1986. *Abducted Children Directory.* Jackson, MI: NCSC.

National Confectioners Association, Chocolate Manufacturers Association, and National Candy Wholesalers Association. n.d. "Halloween/1982: An Overview." Unpublished paper.

Nelson, Barbara J. 1984. *Making an Issue of Child Abuse.* Chicago: University of Chicago Press.

Nemecek, David F. (National Crime Information Center). 1986. Personal communication.

New York State Division of Criminal Justice Services. 1986. "Children Reported Missing in New York State, 1985." Albany: NYSDCJS.

———. 1988. "Reported Missing Children in New York State, 1987." Unpublished.

———. 1989. *Reported Missing Children in New York State, 1988.* Albany: NYSDCJS.

New York Times. 1950. "Punish Halloween 'Witch,' Angry Parents Demand." 3 November, 52.

———. 1982. "Child Abductions a Rising Concern." 5 December, 77.

Newman, Susan. 1985. *Never Say Yes to a Stranger.* New York: Perigee.

Newsweek. 1975. "The Goblins Will Getcha. . . ." 86 (3 November): 28.

Nimmo, Dan, and James E. Combs. 1985. *Nightly Horrors.* Knoxville: University of Tennessee Press.

Odean, Kathleen. 1985. "White Slavers in Minnesota." *Midwestern Journal of Language and Folklore* 11:20–30.

Office of Juvenile Justice and Delinquency Prevention. 1985. "Statistics on Missing Children: The Need for a Measured Approach." Unpublished.

———. 1987. "National Studies of the Incidence of Missing Children." Unpublished.

———. 1989. "Stranger Abduction Homicides of Children." *Juvenile Justice Bulletin* (January): 1–7.

Parachini, Allan. 1984. "Some Parents May Shake Their Children to Death." *Los Angeles Times,* 10 February, V-1.

Parenting Adviser. 1988. "Street-Smart Safety." Knoxville, TN: Whittle.

Parents League of the U.S. 1986. "An Open Letter to Parents from Parents" (advertisement). *New Republic* 3743 (13 October): 29.

Parness, Jeffrey A. 1986. "The Abuse and Neglect of the Human Unborn." *Family Law Quarterly* 20 (Summer): 197–212.

Pelton, Leroy H. 1981. "Child Abuse and Neglect: The Myth of Classlessness." In Leroy H. Pelton, ed., *The Social Context of Child Abuse,* 23–38. New York: Human Sciences Press.

Pfohl, Stephen J. 1977. "The 'Discovery' of Child Abuse." *Social Problems* 24:310–23.

Pivar, David J. 1973. *Purity Crusade.* Westport, CT: Greenwood.

Playboy. 1986. "The Playboy Forum." 33 (November): 41.

Podesta, Jane Sims, and David Van Biema. 1989. "Running for Their Lives." *People* 31 (23 January): 71–88.

Pooley, Eric. 1987. "The Last Angry Man." *New York* 20 (25 May): 42–46.

Pogue, Gregory. 1987. "Human Resources Bulletin #6." Unpublished.

President's Child Safety Partnership. 1987. *Final Report.* Washington, DC: U.S. Government Printing Office.

Price, James H., and Sharon M. Desmond. 1987. "The Missing Children Issue." *American Journal of Diseases of Children* 141:811–15.

Pride, Mary. 1986. *The Child Abuse Industry*. Westchester, IL: Crossway.

Reinarman, Craig. 1988. "The Social Construction of an Alcohol Problem: The Case of Mothers Against Drunk Drivers and Social Control in the 1980s." *Theory and Society* 17:91–120.

Reino, Joseph. 1988. *Stephen King: The First Decade, Carrie to Pet Sematary*. Boston: Twayne.

Ridley, Florence H. 1967. "A Tale Told Too Often." *Journal of American Folklore* 26:153–56.

Riesman, David. 1950. *The Lonely Crowd*. New Haven: Yale University Press.

Robinson, John P., and Mark R. Levy. 1986. *The Main Source*. Beverly Hills: Sage.

Robrahn, Steve. 1988. "Rumors of Devil Worship Spread in E. Ky." *Lexington (KY) Herald-Leader*, 12 September: B1.

Rodgers, Daniel T. 1980. "Socializing Middle-Class Children: Institutions, Fables, and Work Values in Nineteenth-Century America." *Journal of Social History* 13:354–67.

Roper Organization. 1987. *The American Chicle Youth Poll*. Morris Plains, NJ: Warner-Lambert.

Rose, Vicki McNickle. 1977. "Rape as a Social Problem: A Byproduct of the Feminist Movement." *Social Problems* 25:75–89.

Rossi, Peter H. 1987. "No Good Applied Social Research Goes Unpunished." *Society* 25 (November): 74–79.

Rudy, David R. 1988. "The Adult Children of Alcoholics Movement." Paper presented before the Society for the Study of Social Problems.

Rush, Florence. 1980. "Child Pornography." In Laura Lederer, ed., *Take Back the Night*, 71–81. New York: William Morrow.

Russell, Diana E. H. 1986. *The Secret Trauma: Incest in the Lives of Girls and Women*. New York: Basic Books.

Ryan, Michael, and Douglas Kellner. 1988. *Camera Politica*. Bloomington: Indiana University Press.

Salter, Stephanie. 1988. "A Child of God or Hell?" *Fresno Bee*, 2 October: G1.

San Francisco Chronicle. 1970. "Capsule Caused Halloween Death." 10 November: 3.

Sanger, William W. 1972 (1858). *The History of Prostitution*. New York: Arno.

Sanoff, Alvin P. 1982. "Our Neglected Kids." *U.S. News and World Report* 93 (9 August): 54–58.

Santino, Jack. 1983. "Halloween in America." *Western Folklore* 42:1–20.

Saratogian (Saratoga, NY). 1988. "Judge Rules Mom's Smoking is a Form of Child Abuse." 5 May: 3A.

Schechter, Harold. 1988. *The Bosom Serpent*. Iowa City: University of Iowa Press.

Schneider, Joseph W. 1985. "Social Problems Theory: The Constructionist View." *Annual Review of Sociology* 11: 209–29.

Schneider, Peter. 1987. "Lost Innocents: The Myth of Missing Children." *Harper's* (February): 47–53.

Schoenfeld, A. Clay, Robert F. Meier, and Robert J. Griffin. 1979. "Constructing a Social Problem." *Social Problems* 27: 38–61.

Schur, Edwin M. 1980. *The Politics of Deviance.* Englewood Cliffs, NJ: Prentice-Hall.

Scritchfield, Shirley A. 1989. "The Social Construction of Infertility." In Joel Best, ed., *Images of Issues,* 99–114. New York: Aldine de Gruyter.

Seligmann, Jean. 1988. "Emotional Child Abuse." *Newsweek* (3 October): 48, 50.

Sharper Image. 1986. Catalog (April).

Sheppard, Nathaniel, Jr. 1980. "Atlanta and Miami Curbing Halloween." *New York Times,* 31 October: A14.

Shorter, Edward. 1977. *The Making of the Modern Family.* New York: Basic Books.

Silver, Jessica Dunsay. 1986. "Baby Doe." *Family Law Quarterly* 20 (Summer): 173–95.

Simpson, Jacqueline. 1983. "Urban Legends in *The Pickwick Papers." Journal of American Folklore* 96: 462–70.

Smelser, Neil J. 1962. *Theory of Collective Behavior.* New York: Free Press.

Smith, Preston. 1986. "Rural Abductions." *Successful Farming* 84 (February): 10.

Snow, David A., et al. 1986. "Frame Alignment Processes, Micromobilization, and Movement Participation." *American Sociological Review* 51: 464–81.

Sonenschein, David. 1984. "Breaking the Taboo of Sex and Adolescence: Children, Sex and the Media." In Ray B. Browne, ed., *Forbidden Fruits,* 111–32. Bowling Green, OH: Bowling Green University Popular Press.

Spangler, Susan E. 1982. "Snatching Legislative Power: The Justice Department's Refusal to Enforce the Parental Kidnapping Prevention Act." *Journal of Criminal Law and Criminology* 73: 1176–1203.

Spector, Malcolm, and John I. Kitsuse. 1977. *Constructing Social Problems.* Menlo Park, CA: Cummings.

Spiro, Peter. 1982. "Chaos by the Capsule." *New Republic* 187 (6 December): 10–11.

Spitzer, Brian C. 1987. "A Response to 'Cocaine Babies'—Amendment to Florida's Child Abuse and Neglect Laws to Encompass Infants Born Drug Dependent." *Florida State University Law Review* 15: 865–84.

Spitzer, Neil. 1986. "The Children's Crusade." *Atlantic* 257 (June): 18–22.

223

Stanley, Lawrence A. 1988. "The Child-Pornography Myth." *Playboy* 35 (September): 41–44.

Stinchcombe, Arthur L., et al. 1980. *Crime and Punishment*. San Francisco: Jossey-Bass.

Stone, Gregory P. 1959. "Halloween and the Mass Child." *American Quarterly* 11:372–9.

Suttles, Gerald D. 1972. *The Social Construction of Communities*. Chicago: University of Chicago Press.

Tatar, Maria. 1987. *The Hard Facts of the Grimms' Fairy Tales*. Princeton, NJ: Princeton University Press.

Thackrey, Ted, Jr. 1982. "Trick or Treat Subdued Amid Poisoning Scares." *Los Angeles Times*, 1 November: 1, 28.

Thompson, Hunter S. 1983. *The Curse of Lono*. New York: Bantam.

Thornton, Jeannye. 1983. "The Tragedy of America's Missing Children." *U.S. News and World Report* 95 (24 October): 63–64.

Time. 1977. "Child's Garden of Perversity." 109 (4 April): 55–56.

Timnick, Lois. 1985a. "22% in Survey Were Child Abuse Victims." *Los Angeles Times*, 25 August: 1, 34.

———. 1985b. "Children's Abuse Reports Reliable, Most Believe." *Los Angeles Times*, 26 August: 5, 12.

Toulmin, Stephen Edelston. 1958. *The Uses of Argument*. Cambridge: Cambridge University Press.

Toulmin, Stephen Edelston, Richard Rieke, and Alan Janik. 1979. *An Introduction to Reasoning*. New York: Macmillan.

Troyer, Ronald J., and Gerald E. Markle. 1983. *Cigarettes*. New Brunswick, NJ: Rutgers University Press.

———. 1984. "Coffee Drinking." *Social Problems* 31:403–16.

Trubo, Richard. 1974. "Holiday for Sadists." *PTA Magazine* 69:28–29.

Tuchman, Gaye. 1978. *Making News*. New York: Free Press.

Turbak, Gary. 1982. "Missing: 100,000 Children a Year." *Reader's Digest* 121 (July): 60–64.

Turner, Patricia A. 1987. "Church's Fried Chicken and the Klan." *Western Folklore* 46:294–306.

Twitchell, James B. 1985. *Dreadful Pleasures: An Anatomy of Modern Horror*. New York: Oxford University Press.

Uhlenbrock, Tom. 1988a. "Level of Abductions Called Exaggerated." *St. Louis Post-Dispatch*, 9 October: 1, 8.

———. 1988b. "Missing-Child Movement Has Lost Its 'Glamour.'" *St. Louis Post-Dispatch*, 10 October: 1, 6.

Underwood, Tim, and Chuck Miller, eds. 1988. *Bare Bones: Conversations on Terror with Stephen King*. New York: Warner.

U.S. Attorney General's Advisory Board on Missing Children. 1986. *Amer-*

ica's Missing and Exploited Children. Washington, DC: Office of Juvenile Justice and Delinquency Prevention.

U.S. Consumer Product Safety Commission. 1982. *Annual Report.* Washington, DC: Government Printing Office.

U.S. House of Representatives. 1977. *Sexual Exploitation of Children.* Hearings held by the Subcommittee on Crime, Committee on the Judiciary. 95th Cong., 1st sess., 23, 25 May, 10 June, 20 September.

————. 1980. *Parental Kidnaping.* Hearings held by the Subcommittee on Crime, Committee on the Judiciary. 96th Cong., 2d sess., 24 June.

————. 1981a. *Implementation of the Parental Kidnaping Prevention Act of 1980.* Hearings held by the Subcommittee on Crime, Committee on the Judiciary. 97th Cong., 1st sess., 24 September.

————. 1981b. *Missing Children's Act.* Hearings held by the Subcommittee on Civil and Constitutional Rights, Committee on the Judiciary. 97th Cong., 1st sess., 18, 30 November.

————. 1982. *Hearing on Tamper-Resistant Packaging for Over-the-Counter Drugs.* Hearings held by the Subcommittee on Health and the Environment, Committee on Energy and Commerce. 97th Cong., 2d sess., 15 October.

————. 1983a. *To Amend the Child Abuse Prevention and Treatment and Adoption Reform Act of 1978.* Hearings held by the Subcommittee on Select Education, Committee on Education and Labor. 98th Cong., 1st sess., 9 March.

————. 1983b. *Health and the Environment, Miscellaneous—Part 1: Unintended Pregnancy and the Public Health Aspects of Abortion.* Hearings held by the Subcommittee on Health and the Environment, Committee on Energy and Commerce. 98th Cong., 1st sess., 28 June.

————. 1983c. *Oversight Hearing on Child Support Enforcement.* Hearings held by the Subcommittee on Select Education, Committee on Education and Labor. 98th Cong., 1st sess., 12 September.

————. 1984. *Title IV, Missing Children's Assistance Act.* Hearings held by the Subcommittee on Human Resources, Committee on Education and Labor. 98th Cong., 2d sess., 9 April.

————. 1985a. *Oversight Hearing on the Missing Children's Assistance Act.* Hearings held by the Subcommittee on Human Resources, Committee on Education and Labor. 99th Cong., 1st sess., 21 May.

————. 1985b. *Photograph and Biography of Missing Child.* Hearings held by the Subcommittee on Postal Personnel and Modernization, Committee on Post Office and Civil Service. 99th Cong., 1st sess., 25 June.

————. 1986a. *The Federal Role in Investigation of Serial Violent Crime.* Hearings held by the Subcommittee on Government Information, Justice, and Agriculture, Committee on Government Operations. 99th Cong., 2d sess., 9 April, 21 May.

————. 1986b. *Oversight Hearing on the Missing Children's Assistance Act.* Hearings held by the Subcommittee on Human Resources, Committee on Education and Labor. 99th Cong., 2d sess., 4 August.

————. 1986c. *To Authorize Federal Assistance for the Establishment and Expansion of State Missing Children Clearinghouses.* Hearings held by the Subcommittee on Human Resources, Committee on Education and Labor. 99th Cong., 2d sess., 11 September.

U.S. Senate. 1973. *Child Abuse Prevention Act, 1973.* Hearings held by the Subcommittee on Children and Youth, Committee on Labor and Public Welfare. 93d Cong., 1st sess., 26, 27, 31 March; 24 April.

————. 1979. *Parental Kidnaping, 1979.* Hearings held by the Subcommittee on Child and Human Development, Committee on Labor and Human Resources. 96th Cong., 1st sess., 17 April.

————. 1981. *Missing Children.* Hearings held by the Subcommittee on Investigations and General Oversight, Committee on Labor and Human Resources. 97th Cong., 1st sess., 6 October.

————. 1982. *Exploited and Missing Children.* Hearings held by the Subcommittee on Juvenile Justice, Committee on the Judiciary. 97th Cong., 2d sess., 1 April.

————. 1983a. *Child Kidnaping.* Hearings held by the Subcommittee on Juvenile Justice, Committee on the Judiciary. 98th Cong., 1st sess., 2 February.

————. 1983b. *Serial Murders.* Hearings held by the Subcommittee on Juvenile Justice, Committee on the Judiciary. 98th Cong., 1st sess., 12 July.

————. 1984. *Missing Children's Assistance Act.* Hearings held by the Subcommittee on Juvenile Justice, Committee on the Judiciary. 98th Cong., 2d sess., 7, 21 February; 8, 13, 21 March.

————. 1985a. *Private Sector Initiatives Regarding Missing Children.* Hearings held by the Subcommittee on Juvenile Justice, Committee on the Judiciary. 99th Cong., 1st sess., 22 May.

————. 1985b. *Missing and Exploited Children.* Hearings held by the Subcommittee on Juvenile Justice, Committee on the Judiciary. 99th Cong., 1st sess., 21 August.

————. 1986. *Abolishing the Office of Juvenile Justice and Delinquency Prevention.* Hearings held by the Subcommittee on Juvenile Justice, Committee on the Judiciary. 99th Cong., 2d sess., 5 March.

USA Today. 1988. "Preventing Halloween Tricks" (chart). 28 October: D1.

Useem, Bert, and Mayer N. Zald. 1982. "From Pressure Group to Social Movement." *Social Problems* 30:144–56.

Van Buren, Abigail. 1983. "Dear Abby." *Fresno Bee,* 31 October: D2.

————. 1987. "Dear Abby." *Los Angeles Times,* 1 July: V-3.

Victor, Jeffrey S. 1989. "A Rumor-Panic About a Dangerous Satanic Cult in Western New York." *New York Folklore* 15:23–49.

Vobedja, Barbara. 1985. "Abduction Publicity Could Scare Children." *Washington Post,* 25 November: A1, A6.

von Hoffman, Nicholas. 1985. "Pack of Fools." *New Republic* 193 (5 August): 9–11.

Wachter, Oralee. 1986. *Close to Home.* New York: Scholastic.

Wattleton, Faye. 1986. "Teen Pregnancy." Address at Fresno, CA (29 October).

Webster, Bayard. 1982. "Experts Theorize about 'Copycat Syndrome.'" *New York Times,* 30 October: 6.

Weinstein, Steve. 1988. "No Place to Hide." *Los Angeles Times,* 13 April: VI-6, 12.

Weisberg, D. Kelly. 1984. "The 'Discovery' of Sexual Abuse." *U.C. Davis Law Review* 18:1–57.

———. 1985. *Children of the Night.* Lexington, MA: Lexington.

Wemhaner, J. D., and Richard Dodder. 1984. "A New Halloween Goblin." *Journal of Popular Culture* 18:21–24.

Westin, Av. 1982. *Newswatch.* New York: Simon and Schuster.

Wexler, R. 1985. "No One Is Safe in the War Against Abuse." *Progressive* 49 (September): 19–22.

Willard, Charles Arthur. 1982. "Argument Fields." In J. Robert Cox and Charles Arthur Willard, eds., *Advances in Argumentation Theory and Research,* 24–77. Carbondale: Southern Illinois University Press.

———. 1983. *Argumentation and the Social Grounds of Knowledge.* University: University of Alabama Press.

Wishy, Bernard. 1968. *The Child and the Republic.* Philadelphia: University of Pennsylvania Press.

Wood, Robin. 1978. "Return of the Repressed." *Film Comment* 14 (July): 24–32.

Woolgar, Steve, and Dorothy Pawluch. 1985. "Ontological Gerrymandering: the Anatomy of Social Problems Explanations." *Social Problems* 32:214–27.

Zelizer, Viviana A. 1985. *Pricing the Priceless Child.* New York: Basic Books.

Ziegelmueller, George, and Jack Rhodes, eds. 1981. *Dimensions of Argument.* Annadale, VA: Speech Communication Association.

INDEX

229